1999

Merry Christmas
Bryant

Have a Blessed
New Year

Cnaie N. Brown

PURPLE REIGN

PURPLE REIGN

The Artist Formerly Known as Prince

Liz Jones

A CITADEL PRESS BOOK
Published by Carol Publishing Group

Carol Publishing Group edition, 1999

Published by arrangement with Little, Brown, & Co., U.K.

A Citadel Press Book
Published by Carol Publishing Group
Citadel Press is a registered trademark of Carol Communications, Inc.

Editorial, sales and distribution, rights and permissions inquiries
should be addressed to Carol Publishing Group, 120 Enterprise Avenue,
Secaucus, N.J. 07094

Carol Publishing Group books may be purchased in bulk at special
discounts for sales promotions, fund-raising, or educational purposes.
Special editions can be created to specifications. For details, contact
Special Sales Department, Carol Publishing Group, 120 Enterprise Avenue,
Secaucus, N.J. 07094

Manufactured in the United States of America
10 9 8 7 6 5 4 3 2 1

Library of Congress Cataloging-in-Publication Data

Jones, Liz.
Purple Reign : The Artist Formerly Known as Prince / Liz Jones.
p. cm.
Originally published: London : Little, Brown, 1997.
"A Citadel Press book."
Includes discography (p,), bibliographical references
(p.), and index.
ISBN 0-8065-2065-5
1. Prince. 2. Rock musicians—United States—Biography.
I. Title.
ML420.P974J66 1998
781.66'092—dc21

[B]   97-51915
CIP
MN

For T.
He knows

Contents

Acknowledgments

Many thanks to , Eileen Murton for research, Andrew Gordon, Tony Barrell, Barry Burchell, Jo Spreadborough and Laurent Fintoni. Thanks also to Robin Morgan, editor of the *Sunday Times Magazine*, Alan Light, Chiedo Nkwocha and *Vibe*, David Fricke and *Rolling Stone*, Charles Aaron and *Spin*, Greg Tate, Lee Leschasin at EMI, WEA, J. R. Reynolds and *Billboard*'s research department, *Melody Maker*, Tony Mitchell, Rickey Vincent, bell hooks, Vernon Reid, the staff at Paisley Park and the NPG, the Minneapolis Public Library, Cheryl Johnson, the *Minneapolis Star Tribune* and its library, City Pages, Jim Walsh and the *St Paul Pioneer Press*, the National Sound Archive, and all the staff at News International Library.

The author and publisher are grateful to the following for permission to quote from or reproduce copyright material:

ALBUM REVIEWS
For You © 1978 by Bob Protzman/*St Paul Dispatch*; *Prince* © 1980 by the *Los Angeles Times*; *Dirty Mind* © 1980 by the *Minneapolis Tribune*; *Controversy* © 1981 by City Pages, Inc.; *1999* © 1982 by Steve Sutherland/ *Melody Maker*; *Purple Rain* © 1984 by the *Los Angeles Times*; *Around the*

Prologue

Abbey Road Studios, London, 24 October 1996

A handful of journalists have been invited to Studio Three in the building where the Beatles recorded over thirty years before. We have been summoned to listen to seven tracks from Capitol-EMI's new signing, Prince. The man who does, of course, no longer go by that name had struck a deal only days before with the company to release what is rumoured to be three CDs of amazing new music. Outside the studios, girls huddle in groups, oblivious to the rain, buttonholing journalists who are being allowed into the building. Are they waiting in the cold in the hope they might get to hear the album, to garner gossip about the former Prince? 'Nah. Liam and Noel are in there, aren't they.' Indeed, the Gallagher brothers are holed up inside, working on tracks for the next Oasis album.

Those of us who are here to listen to the new tracks from the upcoming Prince opus, *Emancipation*, piped direct from America by Integrated Services Digital Network, are first relieved of our coats, jackets, bags, mobile phones. No preview cassettes would be released to the press prior to the album's release on 19 November. Instead we are offered exotic fruit. A similar event is being held in New York. Here in London, EMI's dashing young president, J. F. Cecillon, makes a short speech about how proud EMI are to be working with such a great artist, and that the new album is the best music he has heard in years. The head of marketing would later instruct all the retail staff that they were required to shift half a million copies by Christmas. As the music blasts out of the state-of-the-art studio console, most people continue chatting and eating and drinking. Those who listen hear the unexpected: cover versions, a first for Prince, and very soon the outstanding. By track three most people are listening. By track seven J. F. Cecillon is beaming.

Prince's new set of shackles – for he had long complained that he was a slave as far as Warner, his old record company, was concerned – had been crafted by his dapper New York attorney, L. Londell McMillan, who had helped The Artist, as he now wanted to be called, set up a new label, NPG Records. McMillan was spotted lurking at the edge of the stage during Prince's cursory TV appearances to promote *Chaos and Disorder*, his swansong album for Warner Records after almost twenty years. McMillan looks like a young and handsome Malcolm X. Clearly, he is not a man to be messed with. 'My goal was to wipe "slave" off his face,' he says. 'The new arrangement with Capitol-EMI will benefit both parties greatly.'

The deal is this. It will be for one album only. Prince will deliver the completed work to EMI, who will market and promote it, probably taking 25 per cent. It will go on sale in Britain at £19.99 (often less), and Prince will earn $3 or $4 a copy. He *could* make a great deal of money. But it is a gamble to release such a huge body of work so soon after his last album stiffed, especially in the competitive pre-Christmas marketplace. 'All the stakes are higher,' The Artist would tell me later.

Prince likened EMI's role to that of 'a florist – they just have to deliver the flowers'. But they were going to have a job convincing press, TV, radio and the general public that Prince really was worth another shot.

'I actually like the new album a whole lot,' says Jimmy Jam from his home in Minneapolis. The former member of Prince's rivals The Time is now one half, with Terry Lewis, of the hugely successful partnership that launched Janet Jackson's career into the stratosphere, and most recently collaborated with the queen of hip-hop soul, Mary J. Blige and Boyz II Men. 'But I think he is someone whose talents will not fully be recognised, unfortunately, until he goes away. One of the problems is the fact that he is so prolific you never get a chance to miss him, you never get a chance to go like, wow. He's constantly in your face.'

I drive home from Abbey Road elated, full of fresh enthusiasm for writing this book. That's what happens with Prince. Start forgetting how brilliant and innovative and entertaining he is, and all you have to do is stick 'When Doves Cry' or 'Anna Stesia' or 'Adore' on the turntable. His music doesn't date. But fans change; they just keep getting younger. Will the Gallagher brothers still be making music in ten, twenty years' time? Maybe.

But this would be Prince's third album in the space of a year. Perhaps the most telling thing he said to me later was that he was a slave to his music; it was an immense gift and a terrible curse. That statement would become, sadly, very true. Those EMI marketing and press and retail people in the studio that day would have to do a whole lot more than just deliver the flowers. And Prince and his wife, Mayte, were about to discover that their personal life – and, more specifically, the way Prince handled what was going on in his personal life – was about to jeopardise everything.

PURPLE REIGN

1

Let's fall in love get married have a baby

November 1996. Two days before I am due to fly out to interview The Artist Formerly Known as Prince, I get a call on my mobile phone. His new baby has been born premature, dreadfully deformed and dangerously ill. At the start of the week when Prince is set to launch the most important album of his career, a week that will mark his divorce from Warner and what could very well be his last chance at convincing the world he wasn't a has-been, tragedy has struck. At the end of almost a year of faxing, phoning and pleading for a chance to hear his side of his life story, I go home, assuming the interview is out of the question and understanding that, for once, unlike all the other times he had cancelled journalists and TV appearances and concerts – hell, even albums – he has a very good reason. My guess is that he doesn't want to talk or even think about business. But no. The next day I am informed my presence is still expected. I begin to doubt whether Prince really has any control over any aspect of his life.

While being driven out to Chanhassen, the nondescript Minneapolis suburb that is home to his Paisley Park recording complex, past interminable fast-food joints and petrol stations, I am reading a clipping from that morning's London *Times* that has been faxed to my hotel. It explains the condition of Prince and Mayte's afflicted child, saying that 'craniosynostosis' is the premature closure of the sutures of the skull. In sufferers the skull is distorted into bizarre shapes, hence the condition's more familiar name: 'clover-leaf syndrome'. The clipping says that, in this baby's case, the orbits of the eyes are very flat and the eyes prominent. But it also says the condition is hereditary, 'hence the interest in the pop singer's abnormally short stature'. It says that Prince is 'little taller than Napoleon. In addition, the pop star's head is slightly out of proportion to his body, although neither his height nor his unusually shaped head would excite comment were it not that his newborn son suffers from craniosynostosis.' Oh dear. Who needs the *National Enquirer*?

Inside Paisley Park, still being vacuumed after the launch party two nights before (no smoking or drinking was allowed, which explained the music industry executives who had been huddled outside, preferring to freeze at ten below than not smoke; the debris is scattered Cap'n Crunch, Prince's favourite cereal), everything is calm. Expectant. Gone is the rather risqué decoration of a few years back (although plastic lilies, rather like the one on the notorious *Lovesexy* album cover, are everywhere), and the interior has obviously had a face-lift. There are two women in an office answering fan mail; Prince's new personal assistant, Erlene Mojica (she was hired as a nanny; her twin sister, Arlene, was hired as Mayte's bodyguard), is in the kitchen fixing lunch; Kirk Johnson, one-time dancer with Prince, drummer in the new line-up and best man at his wedding, is making small talk, happy to show me round. In the wardrobe department, Bonnie Flesland and her two assistants are preparing clothes for the upcoming world tour: 'They have to be strong enough to stand up to The Artist's antics on stage, and to being washed every day.' It was Bonnie who designed and handmade the gown for Mayte's Valentine's Day wedding to Prince. She also made the outfits for the groom and the best man. A pair of Prince's black lace trousers are on a hanger by the door. They don't look substantial enough to withstand sitting down, let alone a couple of funky chickens and James Brown splits. In

Mayte's office, a big smiley face hangs on the wall. In Prince's VCR is a video of the movie *Clueless*. A copy of *The Seat of the Soul* by Gary Zukav is on the floor; Jimi Hendrix is on the hi-fi.

This interview is going to be difficult. Prince is still insisting that the baby, who weighed 7lb 12oz at birth, is still alive, although he admitted 'there is a problem, but it's for the best' on *The Today Show*. I have already heard, though, that the baby has not survived. Prince and Mayte didn't even get the chance to take him home. They had a service in the hospital chapel and had his body cremated the day he died.

You already know Prince is in the building before you spot him: the atmosphere changes, vacuums are turned off, people are a bit nervous. These are staff, remember, who see him practically every day. He has driven up to the building in his BMW and here he is, with that purposeful, slightly pigeon-toed gait, his body tilted forward. Bit of a swagger.

His assistant, Adam Levin, is on edge. Prince has refused to do a photo session for *The Face* magazine, despite the fact that the photographer, Steven Klein, and his two assistants have already flown in from New York, and despite the fact that it was Klein who took the stunning pictures of him that appeared in British *Vogue* in 1990, sporting a demonic grin in one, his hair in a bun in another. He would cancel another shoot a few months later, after only one roll of film had been shot, because he didn't 'dig the vibe'. He insists on owning as many photographs of himself as possible, particularly portraits. Interestingly, the cheque he sent *Harper's Bazaar* for their May 1997 pictures of him and Mayte, by Patrick Demarchelier, was stamped 'P. R. Nelson'. The man who throws a fit if he sees his name in print as anything other than a squiggle does, it seems, have to compromise sometimes.

'Whatever you do, don't call him Prince,' Adam instructs me. Even the woman from EMI who is handling his international press affairs, and who looks as if she could eat the Gallagher brothers for breakfast, is unsure how to handle the star. Seated in a booth in

Prince's little dining-room, she tells Adam that she needs Prince to approve some photographs so that she can give them to the press. 'Someone has to take me to him, I can't just go up to his office,' she insists again and again. Eventually, and much to everyone's surprise, Prince flounces in and asks her what it is she needs. 'Oh, so now you're eating my cheesecake,' he says to me, deadpan, as he walks past my table and catches me eating the contents of his (very clean) fridge.

David Sinclair once wrote in *The Times* that shaking hands with Prince is like trying to shake hands with a ghost. Today he feels more like a friendly ghost – mischievous, courteous, flirtatious and coy. He never used to like to shake hands, but not because he thought it was beneath him. 'Brothers always feel like they got to give you that real firm handshake. Then you can't play the piano the next day.' He laughs easily – a big, throaty, dirty sound. When he's listening to you, he looks away and down, so that when it's his turn to speak you get the full effect of that dramatic sweep as the eyes bat up towards you. He has a habit of placing the fingers of his left hand in front of his mouth, something he learned as a teenager to hide those little pointy teeth at the side. He's disconcertingly quick to take the measure of someone: he immediately mimics my nervous stuttering, corrects my mistakes, but is genuinely pleased when you can quote one of his lyrics to him or recall a particular moment on stage. He's glad you've been paying attention. Through the window we can clearly see the playground he had built for his child so that he could watch him play while he worked. By his desk are pictures of Miles Davis and Charlie Parker. Miles is fondly recalled. Prince points out that Miles recorded seventeen album sides of music for Columbia between August 1969 and August 1970. John Coltrane is also someone he identifies with, although 'Coltrane's wife said that he played twelve hours a day. I could never do that, play one instrument for that long.'

He is obviously tired of talking about the situation with Warner – it soon becomes obvious he is under some sort of contractual obligation, part of the severance deal, that means he must stop badmouthing them. At the album launch, he was saying of certain

Warner executives 'I love you, man', and he swears he invited them all to the party. Now, though, he wants to put it all behind him, and is bursting with enthusiasm about the new record: 'Did you like it? It's the best work I've done. It took about a year to make. There was no cutting, no editing, no guest stars I didn't want. The second disc is my favourite. I think my favourite track is "The Holy River": eight minutes long – now, I would never have been able to do that with Warner looking over my shoulder. We as black people can do the same thing white people have always done. We can buy and sell for our own people.'

This time around he feels he is in complete control, that black people should have seized control decades ago. 'What record companies do ain't brain surgery.' He insists that part of the proceeds of *Emancipation* will go to charity; he has long supported work with disabled or disadvantaged children. 'The entertainer Prince gave us $300,000,' says Marva Collins, who has run two schools in the poorest neighbourhoods of Washington, DC, for twenty-one years. 'He's the only one who has ever done benefit concerts for us. He comes to visit us when he can, talks to the kids. He says he wishes he had been able to go to a school like mine.' He even cast the redoubtable Ms Collins in his 'Most Beautiful Girl In The World' video – she is surrounded by smiling children of all races.

'What would I do with the money?' he says now. 'I live in Minneapolis, for chrissakes!'

He seems angry at the bad press he has been getting all these years. He feels misunderstood, seems desperate to dispel the consensus that he is out of his mind and irrelevant. 'Let's see: I'm broke and I'm crazy. I get more props for being crazy than I do for being normal. Look at me, there's no insanity whatsoever. Lots of times, I'm told I'm too cosmic-headed, but it keeps me grounded to have my head in the clouds. It helps me to cope with what's going on down here.'

The venom and scorn poured upon him at the time of the name change surprised even Prince. Cheryl Johnson, who writes a gossip column in the local *Minneapolis Star Tribune*, refers to him as

'Symbolina'. He became 'The Artist People Formerly Cared About' in the words of Howard Stern, New York talk-radio host.

'Changing my name made perfect sense to me. A lot of people call me "sir" now. They never did *that* before. What should you call me? My wife just says, "Hey". If she said, "Prince, get me a cup of tea," I'd probably drop the cup.'

Black people, he says, still call him Prince: 'They say, "Because you are a Prince to us."' But even he does not know what sound the symbol should represent. 'One day I'll hear a sound that will give me a feeling of what my name will sound like.' Anything, it seems, is better than Skipper, the name he had all through school.

'I was ridiculed for writing "slave" on my face, and I don't mean to take away from the suffering of slaves in the American South, but America is a slave to money. I don't own the masters to my records, and if you don't own your masters, your master owns you. I don't own "Purple Rain". I know how to play it, though.' (The machines in recording studios that make copies are known in the business as 'slaves'.)

But isn't it scary being without the protection of the vice-presidents and marketing men and press officers and accountants and managers and lawyers who have surrounded you since you signed your first record deal?

'Do I look scared? I have people around me, you just can't see 'em. When I signed that deal, I didn't have a choice. Own your masters. There, it's a real simple statement, but nobody bothered to tell me that. Your songs are your children. You seen all them gold records downstairs? They mean nothing to me. They ain't why I make music every day. I could care less how I'm doing on *Billboard*.'

The only thing he seems to care about is Mayte. 'I've never been this much in love before,' he says, and he should know. He has written almost 1,000 songs on the subject. He says he doesn't speak to any of his ex-girlfriends. After he got married, he says, 'the phone just stopped ringing'.

When Mayte arrives, she is wearing a beige knee-length dress with matching long jacket – more Armani than Arabian Nights. Prince is quick to wrap his arms around her legs. 'Mayte has me in studio rehab right now,' he says. 'She's trying to stop me recording so much.' What does she want you to do instead? 'The lawn.' She would say later that Prince is a romantic, not because he sends her flowers, but because he writes beautiful songs for her. She also says he is very funny, always making jokes. 'I'm not funny, I'm serious,' he replies, feigning a straight face.

His longtime friend Alan Leeds agrees with Mayte. Leeds was Prince's tour manager and sometime label vice-president for ten years, from the *1999* album in 1982 until May 1992. He still lives in Minneapolis; he is currently handling the career of new soul star Maxwell, a big Prince fan. 'It's nice that Prince has started to open up,' says Leeds. 'It's good people find out he's a brilliant, articulate guy. He's a fun guy. People would always say to me, "Oh, it must be strange to be around him, he's so weird, so uncommunicative," but once you get to know him he's anything but that: he's glib, he's the life of the party.'

'I work through the night all the time,' says Prince. 'It's hard to sleep when you can do this. I get noisy, rambunctious sometimes. Mayte keeps me mellow. She always knew we were going to be together. I've known her since she was sixteen; she was like my kid sister, my best friend.' She is Puerto Rican but was brought up in Germany, where her father was serving in the American armed forces. Prince says he first met her in 1990. She had been 'dragged' to his concert in Barcelona by her mother and sister. Two weeks later, he spotted her outside a concert in Frankfurt: 'I said to Rosie Gaines, who was with me, "There's my future wife."' After the meeting, Mayte's mother sent Kirk Johnson a tape of her daughter's speciality: belly-dancing. (Her party trick is to lie on the floor, place 75 cents on her bare midriff, and flip the coins with her stomach muscles.) He passed the tape on to Prince. 'It had a photo of her on the front and I fell in love,' Prince says. He invited her to America to join his new band. 'She cried when she saw the baby's crib in my house. I said, "Why are you crying?" She said it was because she had never imagined my house with a crib in it before. I've always been close to God, but I took things for granted.'

'I believe in reincarnation,' says Mayte of what brought them together. 'I think there's a connection in Egypt, through my music and dancing. When I met him he was still called Prince [he shudders].'

He is reluctant to talk about his son, but says they plan to have 'lots more children, at least ten. Mayte is hoping to get some twins in there, get two over at once.' When he was questioned on *The Today Show*, he tried to explain his obliqueness on the subject: 'We both believe words can breathe reality. How we look at the situation is very important. What we say is very important. If you leave things in God's hands you'll find out everything, anything that happens we accept. It happened for a reason.' Mayte would only say: 'We'll never forget our little boy who died, but we're now trying to have another baby.' A month later, in January, American newspapers ran the story that the couple were planning to adopt – possibly in Europe, to avoid the parents being able to claim parentage later. The reports stated that they didn't care how much it cost, or what race the child was, as long as he was healthy.

Prince's face is heavily made up, his huge brown eyes framed by mascara'd lashes. He has bony hands – 'musician's hands' – mani-cured nails, a huge diamond-encrusted wedding ring. He is very slight, weighing only about 120 pounds, and he admits to having a 27-inch waist. He has always had a sweet tooth: cookies, ice-cream, Betty Crocker Supermoist cake. Now, though, he says he has com-pletely changed his diet: he hasn't eaten red meat for almost ten years and has recently given up chicken and fish. As he says on the *Emancipation* track 'Joint 2 Joint', he now eats his cereal with soya milk, because 'cows are for calves'. His new band are all vegetarian. Prince is keen to stress that his people, i.e. African-Americans, have the worst diet in the US.

Oprah Winfrey had embarrassed him on her TV show by remark-ing on how glamorous he is. 'Are you always this pretty?' she asked, meaning, was he always dressed up to the nines, with colour-coordinated clothes and with his hair, which hasn't had a kink in it for twenty years, sprinkled with gold dust? Even at 4 A.M., on a sortie to his local Dairy Queen to buy a chocolate malt for his then pregnant wife, he was sporting full make-up, a matching red jumper and trousers and red high heels. When we meet he is wearing a purple silk outfit under a camel mohair overcoat, and matching purple high heels. He can do anything in those shoes: make love, take a bath, leap backwards on to a grand piano.

'He is kind of an odd dresser,' remarks Cheryl Johnson. 'But he could have a more normal life than the one he chooses to live here in Minnesota. Mayte seems quite lonely, stuck out in that mansion. I'm told by people who see her that she breaks down sometimes, seems kind of weepy. You do see her around occasionally, though. She goes to dance classes in town. He chooses to come out with bodyguards, in the full works, even to the movies. He could just turn up late and sit in back. I don't think he ever goes out without make-up. He and I are a lot alike in that regard.'

The house where Prince, Mayte and their two dogs and two cats live is only a few minutes' drive from Paisley Park. It is shielded from the main road by a dense wall of high trees, and a security gate prevents fans ringing on his doorbell, singing his songs to him while standing on his lawn, or driving by with his music blaring from their car stereos – the reasons he moved from his purple house down the road. Although the house is impossible to see from the road, from the fields at the back it is completely open. His next-door neighbour will even let you photograph it from her garden ('Come in, you'll get a better view through the fence in the yard'). The most striking thing about the wooden house is that all three storeys are baby blue, with the window frames painted bright pink – even the garden shed is blue and pink. The house has wooden decks and balconies. Despite the fact that this is Minnesota, in the frozen north, there is a hard tennis court and an outdoor pool. He has several acres of grounds – enough room for a small lake and the windmill he has transported from Holland at great expense (yes, that story is, strangely but very obviously, true). During a convention held in town by his fan club, Controversy, half a dozen members hired a biplane to fly over the house; a local pilot was offering half-hour trips for $80. Prince's stepbrother, Duane, couldn't believe what he was seeing. 'God almighty,' he laughed, 'I might be head of security, but I never dreamed we'd need camouflage netting.'

On *The Today Show*, the popular host Bryant Gumbel described Prince as 'semi-normal; you go to NBA games'. Prince, wearing an orange ribbed polo-neck, black lace trousers and orange striped high heels, was asked if he owned a blazer. He said no. Does he own a pair of khakis? He shook his head and covered his face with his hands. Gumbel asked him if he would ever wear normal, more manly shoes like the ones *he* was wearing. Prince looked askance: '*Hell* no.' It was a great TV moment.

Prince returned in January 1997, as a surprise on Gumbel's last *Today Show* after fifteen years on the air. Viewers couldn't believe what they saw. Prince was dressed in a formal black suit, a tie, and ordinary shoes. He then performed a version of 'Raspberry Beret' with the new lyric, 'If the competition goes tacky / Keep on wearing those khakis.'

He even dared to make an appearance on the Rosie O'Donnell show, performing 'Somebody's Somebody' and 'The Holy River'. O'Donnell got on his nerves by calling him 'Tafkap' and 'Taffy'. 'You know what Taffy rhymes with, don't you,' Prince said. 'It rhymes with good night.' She then called him Prince. 'Actually, that's better than Taffy,' Prince said. 'Lord have mercy.'

He also appeared on VH1, talking affably to comedian Chris Rock about his supposed rivalry with Michael Jackson, his early religious experiences, and about his plans for the money he had raised for charity over the years from concerts and the sales of *Emancipation*. He said he wanted to build a school, and maybe a hospital.

The smiling, self-deprecating side of Prince wasn't the only one on show, though. At the end of January he went to the South Beach nightclub, where a longtime fan went up to him and said, 'I just wanted to tell you, I really like your new CD.' Prince's reply was, 'And your point would be what?' His bodyguard also evicted a young woman from a love seat so that Prince could sit down. When she tired of standing, she asked if she could sit in the spare seat. 'I'll be leaving in five minutes. Then you can sit down,' was his reply.

'I asked Prince what his friends would say about him,' says the journalist Ekow Eshun, who interviewed him for *The Face*. 'He looked confused. He said that all his friends were in that building, inside Paisley Park.' But what would friends who are on the payroll say about him? Does he have any friends who don't work for him? For a man who has always surrounded himself with women who were close friends, being a newly married man, with no woman daring to ring him, must be difficult. Even those closest to him have found his huge fame to be an obstacle. Back in 1985, *Rolling Stone* reporter Neal Karlen came to interview him in his purple house, and asked if he was lonely. 'To be perfectly honest, I wish more of my friends would come by . . . A lot of the time they think I don't want to be bothered. When I told Susannah [Melvoin, then Prince's girlfriend] that you were coming over, she said, "Is there something I can do? Do you want me to come by to make it seem like you have friends coming by?" I said no, that would be lying. And she just put her head down, because she knew she doesn't come by to see me as much as she wants to, or as much as she thinks I want her to.'

Even today the band members who were with him the longest find it hard to get past the fame barrier. Eric Leeds, saxophonist and younger brother of Alan, was a fully-fledged member of Prince's band until 1989, and has collaborated on stage and on record ever since, releasing a solo record, *Times Squared*, on Prince's label in 1991. He even played on *Emancipation*. 'I'm not associated with Prince in any way,' he says now. When I spoke to Leeds he was working on putting a jazz band together with trumpet-player Brian Lynch, who also worked on *Emancipation*. He was also finally thinking of forsaking the Twin Cities of Minneapolis and St Paul, and the cold, for New York. 'Paisley Park is closed for everyone except Prince, but even when it was open it wasn't really economical for recording jazz. Why have I lasted with Prince this long? I play an instrument that he never played.'

'Eric was back in the band for *Emancipation*, then he had a row with Prince over not being paid for rehearsal time,' says Matt Fink, who was with Prince's band as keyboard-player for twelve years. 'I tried to make contact with Prince again recently, but he's not returning my calls. When I heard he had lost his child, I knew how he was feeling because my wife and I lost our first child nine months into the pregnancy. We have a little boy now, and I was in the area with my wife and son and on a whim we dropped in at Paisley. His security people said he wasn't in but that I could leave him a message. I wrote something, but maybe they never passed it on. I said, "Can I look around the building?" because it had been completely redone, and they said, "No, we want to keep our jobs, we're not allowed to let anybody in here, including ex-band members." I said, "Do you know who I am?" But they didn't even care. I said, "I helped build this place." I was really offended by that.'

'There's not a soul working at Paisley now that I know,' says Karen Krattinger, Prince's personal assistant and general manager of production for five years after the *Purple Rain* tour. 'I did protect Prince but I didn't shelter him. I never withheld anything. If I said so-and-so from your past has contacted me, and if he said, "I never want to hear that name again" – and that happened on a few occasions – I had to be honest with that person. I told them, "I'm sorry, this is the way it is." I would never say Prince and I were friends. We didn't party – I was too busy being the adult on duty. He didn't have any friends unless they were on the payroll. It's so sad. Dez Dickerson, who lives near me in Nashville; Jimmy Jam and Terry Lewis, Jerome Benton – these are the people who should be his friends, but after they left him he never spoke to them again. It's sad that someone so brilliant spent his whole life in the studio. He was missing so much more. Maybe he didn't realise people loved him for the person he is. He thought it was because they wanted something from him. If I could ever get a message to him, I would just tell him, thank you. We were like family.'

'Ordinary people in Minneapolis think he's mad,' says Jim Walsh of the *St Paul Pioneer Press*. 'But among local musicians he is universally respected. I said to him recently that he has nowhere else left to play here except at Paisley, that he seemed a little like a caged rat. But he got defensive, said he goes to the movies, goes to the ballet, rents videos and goes out to dinner. He said, well, if I'm a prisoner in Paisley Park then so is everyone else who goes to work at a desk every day.'

Local people were pleased when Prince decided to get married at the Park Avenue United Methodist Church, where he used to take part in youth activities as a teenager. The rumours about the wedding being held in Paris were merely to get the world's press on the wrong foot; an American citizen wanting to get married in France would be required to reside there for forty-five days before the ceremony. But on the Monday before the big day, Prince was spotted visiting his dermatologist and the Blue Ridge Dental Center in Minnetonka. During the rehearsal for the ceremony, Mayte was reportedly reduced to tears. But the crowd of two hundred or so outside the church on the day didn't get much of a glimpse of the happy couple: a canopy covered the distance from limousine – or, in the groom's case, from the inside of a white van marked 'Mark's Carpets' – to the church door.

Inside, the guests included Prince's mother, Mattie; his stepfather, Hayward Baker; and the woman who was like a second mother to him, Bernadette Anderson. Mayte's parents and her sister, who was a bridesmaid, were there. The ceremony was performed by the best man's brother, the Reverend Keith Johnson. Notably absent from the guest-list was Prince's father, John L. Nelson. Prince says now they are 'estranged'. He says his most enduring memory of his mother is of her crying, and of him trying to comfort her. When asked if his father had ever abused him physically – a charge his father has always denied – he says, 'He had his moments.'

The interior of the church was overrun with white flowers with touches of gold – orchids, lilies, roses – and lit by hundreds of white candles. Six flower-girls scattered petals. Twenty homing pigeons were set free. The music was Mozart, Handel and Prince – a wedding suite, 'Kamasutra'. Prince wore white bell-bottoms; Mayte wore a white dress, cut short in front and scooped low at the back. When she had to say the words, 'I, Mayte Garcia, take thee . . . to be my lawful, wedded husband,' she pointed to the symbol she was wearing as a necklace. After the Reverend had read a poem about how the bride and groom were destined to be together for ever, there was a lingering kiss. Mayte signed the register 'Mayte Garcia Nelson'.

The couple stepped into a waiting white limousine and headed for the reception at Paisley Park (less generous reports stated that guests were charged $27 a head). The honeymoon was spent in Honolulu, but poor old Mayte wasn't getting her new husband all to herself. He couldn't resist giving concerts to 8,000 people on the Saturday, Sunday and Monday nights.

He says now that, for the first time in his life, he is taking a break, thinking of going on holiday. It is the first time, he says, that he has been reading reviews of his latest release and not already been in the studio putting the finishing touches to the next one. On the sleeve notes to *Emancipation*, though, he was already plugging his next release, a collection of bootlegged material called *Crystal Ball*, and rumoured to comprise five CDs. His phone line, 1-800-NEW-FUNK, was selling a cassette of two official bootleg tracks for $25. Come June, his next album, *The Truth*, rumoured to be acoustic, was also on the cards. His site on the Internet, 'The Dawn', was an elaborate ad for *Emancipation*: 'What if someone told you that this 36-song, three-CD set was the definitive work that ⚥ spent his whole career in preparation for? When you visit a museum you are asked to make a donation to view the relics of the past. We're asking that you make a donation to hear the future . . .' His lyrics are usually printed on the sleeves; those for *Emancipation*, perhaps because of the number of songs, were not, but could be purchased separately from 1-800-NEW-FUNK or read on his new Web site, 'Love 4 One Another'.

Incidentally, the excellent Web site for Prince fans run by Steve Hammer, music editor of *Nuovo* magazine in Indianapolis, closed down in April 1997. It had provided accurate and exhaustive information on Prince, but Hammer got fed up with being plagued by 'mutant idiots' and, like the many fans he was in contact with, was disillusioned with Prince's behaviour around the release of *Emancipation*. 'The stuff about the baby left a bad taste in the mouth,' he says. In its two and a half years, the site was accessed more than half a million times. (Hammer now runs, among others, a page for the singer and sometime Prince collaborator Rosie Gaines.)

Prince is, at last, taking stock of his life, because the control freak who inscribes 'produced, composed, arranged and performed by Prince' on every album has made a recent discovery about himself. In therapy, he has found out that he has another person inside him, although 'I haven't figured out what sex it is yet'. He says that Prince was a character he created to get him through his parents' rows and the taunts at school, where they would call him names – 'anything small' – and he decided to change his name because he no longer was that person or needed that person. He is used to making jokes about his height. When asked by Oprah Winfrey if he felt he had grown since he left Warner, he replied, 'No, I'm pretty much the same size.'

I tell him that bell hooks, the African-American feminist and cultural critic, has told me he is the only man she would ever go out on a date with. 'I'm in touch with my feminine side, yeah,' he replies. hooks even uses his lyrics in her poetry classes. She says that all her college undergraduates are puzzling over 'If I Was Your Girlfriend', trying to work out whether Prince is a man or a woman.

He bangs both hands on his chair and shakes his head. His eyes fill with tears. 'I can't tell you what it means to me when you tell me something like that. No one tells me stuff like that. No one writes that. No one told me "Purple Rain" is Eric Clapton's favourite song. I only just found that out. I always felt I didn't get respect for being a good guitarist. That's success to me, that college kids are reading my lyrics like they're poems. Or when the Fugees perform "The Cross". That means my music is reaching a whole new generation.'

But has he really got anything left to say to young people – particularly young black people – pushing forty and never lived in a ghetto? In the week *Emancipation* entered the charts, firmly positioned at numbers one and two were new releases from Snoop Doggy Dogg and Tupac Shakur. Prince expresses his sorrow at Tupac's death in a drive-by shooting in September 1996; he felt he was a great talent, a great loss. 'I'm a big supporter of hip-hop, but not the negative stuff. When hip-hop artists sample my music, they must say something positive.' Black music is now selling better than ever before, with artists like D'Angelo and the aforementioned Fugees, whose *The Score* sold eleven million copies worldwide in 1996, and here is a musician who crossed firmly into the white mainstream with the fourteen-million-selling *Purple Rain* in 1984. Is it too late for him to cross back? On the new album, he has been accused of playing the race card (he can't win, can he, really?) with lyrics such as 'Style is when all black men are free' ('Style'). He even apes former NWA member and now legendary producer Dr Dre in 'Emale'. But why would kids listen to him when they have Snoopy and Tupac?

'I offer an alternative, a future. I never wanted race to be an issue, I wanted people to respect me for my music, not whether I was black or white.'

I tell him Tricky says exactly that. Tricky says he could be the British Prince. He wears dresses. He has girls on guitar. He says there's no black or white to his music, and there's nothing like it.

'Yeah, I've heard the name. What's his music like?' His new album is psychedelic, trip-hop, not really jungle but experimental, a bit too London, I say, doubtful that he would really be into it.

'Can you send it to me? Is it out yet?' asks the multi-Grammy-winner who lives in Minneapolis, for chrissakes, with its Mall of America, the largest mall in the world but where you can't buy the new Tricky album (I tried). If Minneapolis hadn't been out in the middle of nowhere, it couldn't have produced a one-off like Prince. There's nothing like him.

'What's the album called?' he asks, opening the door to his office, shaking hands.

'*Pre-Millennium Tension.*'

'Ah,' he says, smiling. 'But isn't that just a longer way of saying 1999?'

2

I wasn't born like my brother handsome and tall

Prince and his stepbrother Duane grew up together. Prince's father had married Duane's mother and they were in the same grade, on the same basketball team, went after the same girls. They would make faces in photo booths together, Duane's Afro twice the size of Prince's, Prince never quite managing a smile. Duane was better at basketball than Prince, and he always had girls around him. Prince was fed up just sitting on the benches and not starting on the team – he was fast and agile, just not tall enough – so he packed it in. He was tired of all the girls wanting to go out with the jocks. 'My older brother was the basketball star,' he told Robert Hilburn of the *Los Angeles Times* in 1981. 'He always had girls around him. I think I must have been on a jealous trip, because I got out of sports.' So he decided he was going to concentrate on what he was good at.

Duane was supposed to keep Prince out of trouble, but it was Duane who would later keep getting himself in the headlines and the courts. When Prince started making money, he put Duane on the payroll, first as a bodyguard, then as head of security. Soon he was more or less running things at Paisley Park. But he would perform his duties a little too enthusiastically – his evictions from Prince's parties and concerts became legendary. The force with which he threw his girlfriend Jean Ladwig out of the studio and into the car park landed him with a lawsuit for assault. He has spent time under house arrest. When it came to running Prince's affairs, he was a little out of his depth. But that was something Prince has always done – put his friends and relatives and friends *of* relatives on the payroll, then have to fire them when it all went haywire.

Duane says that since leaving Prince's employ he has become an evangelist. 'I'm into ministry and stuff,' he told Cheryl Johnson. He also says that he is writing four or five songs a night, and 'that's not normal'. He mentions that he has a new business venture in the pipeline – 'a Bill Gates thing'. When asked about Prince, he says, 'I don't know anything about him. I don't talk to him any more.' Duane faxed the *Minneapolis Star Tribune* a portion of his life story, which seemed to centre around chemical dependency, and an invitation to a concert he was giving at a local club. He feels his talents have been overlooked for far too long. At the top of the fax was the name and telephone number of the sender: Paisley Park Retail. 'I'd better get that off there,' he says. 'This is my fax machine now.'

'I'm going to leave you with a question,' says Prince's half-sister Sharon Nelson Blakley. 'Why is it that Prince's family is not out and noticed and seen and making money? You can't guess, 'cause you gonna be wrong. People stand at my desk and go, "How come you're not with him? How come you're not making a million dollars?"'

Sharon Nelson tells me she won't talk to me about her little brother without being paid. (She gave a TV interview in 1992 to pay a medical bill. Prince had given her money for the bill, but it was bigger than she had expected.) She says that she is about to be made redundant from her job at a bank. I tell her that I do not pay for interviews, but her desire to talk about her grievances gets the better of her anyway.

She is in her forties (she'll admit to twenty-nine), is separated and lives in Manhattan. As well as the job at the bank, she has her own record label, Vive, named after her late mother, Vivienne, John L. Nelson's first wife. 'I have a partner, she's the lyricist, and we have enough lyrics for hundreds of musicians, should they call us. We're waiting to deal with anyone, regardless of race, colour or creed. We have gospel, we have R&B, we have hip-hop, we have country and western, we do house, we do classical, we do all the music.'

She tells me she persuaded her father to fly to New York to make a record. 'Now, nowhere is there recorded my father playing piano, and he is now eighty-one. It's called "Father's Song". I did the rap. This was the first time he was able to do this. He's still talking about it.'

John and Vivienne's marriage produced three children – Sharon, Lorna and Johnny. 'Prince's only full sister is Tyka,' says Sharon. 'But she doesn't look the most like Prince. I look more like him.'

Prince stayed with Sharon while he was touting his early demo tapes around the record companies. 'That's me. He stayed with me. I'm the one,' she says. Her other claim to fame is that she inspired the fictional incestuous relationship Prince describes in 'Sister' on *Dirty Mind*. Lorna took Prince to court, claiming that she wrote 'U Got The Look'. It took three appeal court judges to tell her that she didn't. Sharon says that Johnny is now homeless, living on the streets of Minneapolis. 'You know how cold it is,' Sharon says. 'I had a dream that I changed the sound of music for the next three years. Maybe that will happen and then I will be able to help my other brothers and sisters.' She says that all the family still live in Minneapolis, 'Except me. I can't understand why they stayed there. Tyka is back there too. We won't go over to hers, 'cause that's another book.'

Sharon says that her record label can also 'do the Minneapolis music. The Minneapolis sound came from my father. He played that sound with the Prince Rogers combo, long before Prince ever did.'

She also claims that Prince's songs don't amount to much any more because her father wrote all the good ones. 'My children are all 6ft 4in,' she says. 'They call him Uncle Prince. I don't know what they would call him now if they saw him. We're estranged right now but maybe one day the family will get together. We're gonna need some outside help to do that. We could be bigger than the Wayans or the Jacksons. Bigger. Big. Big. Big.'

Prince's father, John L. Nelson, sold his story to the *Sun* in 1994. He said that he and his son had fallen out over the credits to the *Batman* album. Prince only gave him a credit for 'Scandalous', and that was scandalous. He told the tabloid that he needed to supplement his pension by returning to his pop career. 'I manage to live on a pension from a factory where I worked for thirty-five years. As the composer of the songs I made chump change. Our family is too proud to ask for any money.' He admits he earned $250,000 for *Purple Rain,* but he made a mistake on his tax returns and lost it.

'Once I made it,' says Prince, 'got my first record contract, I was able to forgive.' What Prince had to forgive is hard to know for sure, but songs such as 'Papa' on the *Come* album ('Don't abuse children or they turn out like me') and 'Da, Da, Da' on *Emancipation* ('U could see a man who beats his child as a good father or U could see this man as a father beating on himself') do not show fatherhood in a very good light. The portrayal of his screen father in *Purple Rain*, as a wife-beating washed-up jazz pianist, was, says Prince, the work of the screenwriter, and therefore fictional.

During *Purple Rain* and *Around the World in a Day*, right up until *Batman*, in fact, Prince and his father got along. They did indeed write songs together: 'Computer Blue', 'The Ladder', 'Christopher Tracy's Parade'. After the money came in for *Purple Rain*, and as soon as Prince's custom-built new mansion was ready, he gave his father his old two-storey purple house down the road from Paisley Park (John Nelson claims he paid for it) and a purple BMW. Prince could be seen driving around town in the 1966 white T-Bird his dad gave him. His father would drive gingerly behind in his purple car, waving at Prince every time his son looked round to check how he was doing. That John Nelson was very different from the gun-toting character in the movie. He says he's never even owned a gun. Prince thought his father was cool then. He was a little afraid of him.

Prince and his father dress a lot alike. John wears stack heels, a huge crucifix around his neck. He looks young for his age. 'I named my son Prince because I wanted him to do everything I wanted to do. He's done all of it. Nobody else has ever listened to what I do and did anything about it. I played in a lot of places, they said go home and practise. They couldn't follow – he listened,' he said on *A Current Affair* in 1991, a television tabloid show Prince had forbidden him from appearing on (they let John play a piano solo). John Nelson had played piano for strip joints downtown. As a little boy, Prince would stand backstage and watch the girls, see the garish costumes. As his father says, Prince's stage shows aren't so far from old-fashioned burlesque.

'There was a time when we didn't live together,' says Prince of his father now. 'When I met him again he was a jewel. He was the most beautiful person I knew. And we are again estranged, but hopefully we can hook up again. If not, that's his experience, you know? And he is living his experience and what he wants. I'm living mine the way I want. You know, it would be cool if we hooked up, but, hey, you can only hope.'

The history of black people in Minnesota goes back to 1802 and the birth of George Bonga, the son of a black frontiersman and a Chippewa woman. Minnesota is on the upper reaches of the Mississippi and was one of the last states carved out of the northern territory. It was always a free state, always a very liberal state because of the number of immigrants, not just African-Americans but settlers from Eastern Europe who went there and wrestled their livelihood off the plains. Minnesota always had a greater degree of tolerance. During the 1850s, free black people and fugitive slaves migrated there. Some had been turned back from the Canadian border. Others, used to eking a living off the land down south, came here rather than to the huge metropolises of Chicago, New York City and Washington, DC.

Minnesota was in the record books long before Prince came along. On 6 March 1868, the legislature amended the state constitution by granting a franchise to male blacks, 'civilised' Indians and mixed-bloods over the age of twenty-one. It was one of the few states to enfranchise its black citizens voluntarily, two years before the adoption of the Fifteenth Amendment. Schools were also desegregated at that time. The racial unrest that swept the nation after the First World War did not affect the Twin Cities that bestride the Mississippi. But the vast majority of local black people were still restricted to employment in menial jobs – the men to jobs as porters, waiters, cooks, janitors or on the railroad, and the women to domestic service.

Between 1950 and 1970, the number of black people in Minneapolis increased by 436 per cent, owing to the struggle for civil rights intensifying in the South, which meant that for most black folk, life just got worse. There were still regular lynchings in Louisiana in the 1950s. There were riots in the Twin Cities in 1968 as well as in Watts, Detroit, Cleveland and New York.

Today only about 1 per cent of Minnesotans are black, and over half of them live in Minneapolis. It has one of the safest downtown areas in the country: there are professional baseball and basketball teams, concert halls, theatres and cinemas, as well as the Mall of America – just as well, since for half the year the state is under several feet of snow. The high schools are relatively safe, but there are gangs in the city, and crack cocaine came here in the early 1980s, as it did to every other urban centre in America. The police department introduced a Zero Tolerance campaign in November 1996 – similar to New York City's successful policy for cracking down on petty crime. There were ninety-seven murders in Minneapolis in 1995, mostly gang- or drug-related – a remarkably small number for an American city.

'For the most part, neighbourhoods and schools are mixed, but are divided on economic lines,' says David Taylor, dean of the University of Minnesota and professor of history. 'Minneapolis is an area highly concentrated with educated folk. More than 10 per cent of the student body at the University of Minnesota are of colour.

'Minneapolis is looked on by the rest of America as a place where blacks and whites have mixed over a long period of time. One of the reasons for that is historical. When people migrate, the males go forward and try to find a place to settle down. There were a lot of single black men looking for spouses, so there were a lot of marriages between immigrant whites and blacks, as well as with the Indian community. One of the myths is that because Minneapolis has a greater percentage of mixed-race children, it therefore has greater tolerance for inter-racial couples. All the experiences I have had, it has been difficult if you are in a mixed-race relationship. People still look askance at you. But if Prince had been elsewhere, he probably wouldn't have had the opportunity for mixing with white people, and for the musical experimentation he had. My own brother is a musician and most of the bands have been racially mixed and he never thought anything of it. It's not a bad place to live.'

'Oh, so I'm the Brian Epstein of Minneapolis,' laughs Owen Husney, who would become Prince's first manager and secure his teenage client's deal with Warner Brothers. 'Minneapolis had been a musical Mecca for a long time prior to Prince. The town had a label called Soma Records in the 1950s and 1960s, and it had a lot of hits. It was all due to one man, Amos Heilicher, who started the Sam Goody chain of record stores.'

Heilicher is credited with starting modern music distribution, and Soma (Amos spelt backwards) became one of the top distributors in the US. The label had several top-five *Billboard* hits in the early 1960s and was only eclipsed by the arrival of the Beatles, who made its brand of anodyne, squeaky-clean pop rather dated. 'When I left high school I went to Amos, who's a relative, and cut a record,' says Husney. 'I had a hit in the summer of '65 called 'Turn On Your Love Light', spent four or five years on the road. I was making a bloody fortune. It was just like *That Thing You Do!*, the Tom Hanks movie.'

When Husney's gigs changed from shows in front of 2,000 screaming kids to a week at the Holiday Inn, he went to work for radio stations, promoted concerts and formed The Ad Company, making commercials. He also had a management company called American Artists.

There was a flourishing jazz and blues scene downtown in the 1950s, with black and white musicians playing in the same bands, sitting at the same tables – unheard of in Chicago or Detroit or even New York. And in the 1960s, Minnesotan kids like Bob Dylan were evidence of a flourishing folk scene that was an antidote to the cheerful pop of the Amos label.

'Amos was signing local kids and letting them know that you could make music in your basement and you could have a hit, even a national hit,' says Husney, 'even if you were from Minneapolis.'

John L. Nelson arrived in Minneapolis in the mid-1950s. He had left the racism of Louisiana to look for work in the north. His father's family had been sharecroppers; his grandparents had been slaves. He doesn't know how his family came by the name of Nelson; Louisiana was not as progressive as the rest of the nation when it came to record-keeping. Parish court-houses were burnt to the ground, even if someone had bothered to write your name down.

'My grandfather, John's grandfather, it was a racially mixed family,' Prince's mother, Mattie Shaw, said in the first biography of Prince, *Inside the Purple Reign*, by local journalist Jon Bream. 'I never did a family tree.' John has some Italian in him. Mattie was part African-American, part Native American, part white. Prince would later play on the confusion when dealing with journalists who wouldn't just listen to his music. 'His mother is Italian, his father half black' – *Rolling Stone*. 'His father is black and Italian' – *Los Angeles Times*. 'His father is black, his mother Italian' – *New York Daily News*.

I meet Maurice, a fine-looking man in his late fifties, on the way back to my hotel from an abortive trip to the Mall of America. Maurice is driving the cab. He is married to Marge, who is John Nelson's cousin. 'I came here in 1956,' he says. 'Me and John came from the Deep South. Came here like everyone, looking for jobs. John was a jazz piano player, but he wasn't top rate, you know. I got to play with John Coltrane. Now little Prince is like him – off stage, Coltrane was real quiet, but you knew you were standing next to greatness the moment he got out on that stage. John never played with Coltrane. I have dinner over at John's house, at the purple house. I went to the premiere of *Batman*.'

John Nelson formed a little band, the Prince Rogers Trio, with a black saxophone player and a white drummer. He already knew of Mattie Shaw from when he played at community dances at the Phyllis Wheatley settlement on the north side, the poor part of town where all the black people lived. Mattie was a singer, sixteen years his junior, and she was already the mother of a child. John was married, to Vivienne, with three small children. Mattie looked a little like Billie Holiday, and sang like her, too. John was short, 5ft 4in or so, but handsome, suave, a real ladies' man. Mattie joined the trio as a singer, and they played at the jazz and supper clubs around the area known as Seven Corners. When they married, in 1956, she gave all that up. Prince was born at the Mount Sinai Hospital in Minneapolis on 7 June 1958. Tyka was born two years later. Mattie put her career on hold, but after their divorce in 1965, when Prince was seven, she started studying for a master's degree in social work. John worked at the Honeywell Electronics factory – music didn't really bring in enough money. Prince says he takes after his mother's wild side; his father was more serene.

The name on Prince's birth certificate reads 'Prince Roger Nelson' (he later added a temporary 's' to Roger to make it sound better). But he was always known as Skipper, an affectionate nickname given to him by his mother. He didn't like to be called Prince: that was one hell of a weird name. Like most of the black population in Minneapolis, he went to church every Sunday, scrubbed and polished and dressed in his best clothes. He enjoyed the gospel singing, and went to choir practice. He had a sweet voice that would pipe up above the others. He went to youth club meetings in the church where, thirty years later, he would get married. He played football on the streets, shot hoops in the back yard.

'There is a lot of religion in your music. Where does that come from?' Prince doesn't like the word religion. 'Spirituality, yes. I never practised organised religion. I was made to go to church when I was young; the most I got out of that was the experience of the choir. As far as a message, most of that was based on fear. I don't think God is to be feared in that way. I think he's a loving God.

'A lot of my early songs were really about spirituality, except you couldn't say the word God on the radio. "Dearly Beloved", "Let's Go Crazy", were about God and Satan. God to me was to stay happy, stay focused.'

Prince says today that he first created another personality when he was five. He went through a lot of therapy to find that out, at the age of thirty-eight. 'I'm a typical Gemini,' he says, laughing. It was something he would do throughout his career, use alter egos – Camille, Joey Coco, Jamie Starr – not just to conceal his identity but to explore a different facet of his personality. He didn't ever want to be just plain old Prince. He says that he was ridiculed at school. Kids called him 'Butcher Dog', because they said he resembled a German shepherd. Or 'Princess'. How did he handle that? He didn't stand a chance in fights, although he was fit and wiry. 'That's probably when that other person got created. Somebody to love you and care about you and not ridicule you.'

Sharon says her father taught her to play the piano. 'And then, because he worked so much, he sent me for piano lessons and I played for sixteen years,' she says. 'I love Mozart.' Prince taught himself to play piano. When his father walked out, he left his piano behind. The first tunes Prince learned were the themes from his favourite TV shows, *Batman* and *The Man from U.N.C.L.E.* (he still comes out with the Bond theme on stage). He sat on cushions to reach the keys. Was music an escape, like creating that other person? 'Very much so, hours and hours and hours away. By the time I was eight, I had a pretty good idea what the piano was all about.'

Prince first ran away from home at the age of twelve. He didn't get on with his stepfather, Hayward Baker, whom his mother had married when Prince was nine. He went to stay with his Aunt Olivia, but she was old and couldn't stand his guitar-playing. He then went to live with his dad, who had also remarried, but his dad kicked him out. Prince recalled phoning him from a booth and begging him to let him come home. He wouldn't. 'Guess how many times I've changed addresses,' Prince asked Cynthia Horner, interviewing him in 1979 for *Right On!* magazine. 'Twenty-two times!'

Prince first met Andre Anderson when they were standing in line for punishment at school. The two boys discovered their fathers had played in the same band. Their mothers knew each other from Sundays at the Church of the Seventh-Day Adventists. They started hanging out together, because Andre was as crazy about music as Prince was. Andre's mother, Bernadette, was a divorcée raising six kids of her own on the north side. She had been a schools campaigner in the 1960s, worked at the local black radio station, looked out for the black kids, kept them out of trouble. She took Prince on when he had nowhere else to go. He would later say in interviews that he would have been homeless, that he often went hungry. But things weren't quite that bad. John Nelson paid a nominal amount towards his keep.

At first the two boys shared a bedroom, but Prince couldn't stand looking at Andre's mess. Prince's clothes were always folded, his shoes lined up, his bed so tight you could bounce a dime off it. To spare him the mess, Bernadette let him sleep in the basement. She was a little worried about how that would look, to foster a kid and then make him sleep in the basement, but soon Andre was down there as well, and they would play Hendrix and Sly Stone. Sometimes she'd shout to keep the music down; mostly she didn't bother.

'Prince never said much,' she said. 'But he was an emotional volcano that could erupt at any moment. The fury showed itself when friends teased him.'

When Andre, in his turn an employee of Prince, told his story about libidinous goings-on with girls in that basement, Bernadette took it with good humour. She knew that most of the time it was just the two of them, practising and rehearsing, writing the odd dirty lyric. Prince had a vivid imagination. He would get a crush on a girl in school, maybe not even talk to her, but dream about her and write songs about what he would do to her. He wrote a lot of lyrics back then about unrequited love.

'God knows how Prince learned what men do,' says Tyka. 'Maybe from Andre.' Andre claims it was his idea that Prince dress in bikini briefs on stage. Perhaps he should have kept quiet about that one.

'Once my mother remarried, she had to try to teach me about the birds and the bees,' Prince says. 'I think, though I never asked her about this, that there was some plan to initiate me heavy and quick, so I was given *Playboy* magazine, erotic literature. I think it really affected my sexuality. The androgyny? I wasn't searching for a sexual identity. I was just being me. There was a little acting going on too.' Is there still a little acting going on now? The last time he talked of finding pornographic magazines under his mother's bed, when he was embroidering his rather tame adolescence with stories of wild sex with older women, his mother was so upset he immediately admitted he had made it all up. Is he telling the truth this time around? He has concocted so many different versions of his life, perhaps he no longer knows what really happened and what was just his imagination.

The question Owen Husney was asked most often about Prince was, 'How come he's so talented when there's no black radio stations?' Husney worked at the one black station, KUXL, which was on the air from ten in the morning until two in the afternoon. Young black people and hip white people listened to it, but when it was off the air they were forced to tune in to the white pop stations. If you grew up young and black in Chicago, Washington, DC, Los Angeles or New York City, black music was all you would listen to. You didn't pay any attention to what Pat Boone or the Rolling Stones were singing about: you just knew vaguely who they were and that they got their ideas from people like Little Richard or Muddy Waters. 'Listening to white radio was a positive thing that gave not just Prince but also Jimmy Jam and Terry Lewis and Andre Cymone [Anderson] a real, rounded way of finding out what was going on in music because they were forced to listen to white pop. It gave them a real edge,' says Husney.

Everyone knew when Prince was in school because they would hear him playing 'Midnight At The Oasis', the hit by Maria Muldaur. His music teacher would lock the rehearsal room so that he could practise undisturbed every lunchtime. By the time he was thirteen, his chronic shyness was firmly in place. In class at Bryant Junior High, he was very quiet. In senior high, at Central High School, unless he was playing music you wouldn't have known he was there. He wasn't into books. He was always doodling in class, a habit he still has – he draws smiley faces on almost every note he sends. He was substituting symbols for letters even in school: 4 instead of 'for'; U for 'you'; a picture of an eye for 'I'. He experimented for years with the symbol that would become his name, and would sign autographs with it. He didn't fit in, so he refused even to try; he just decided to go his own way.

He was an odd figure around school, with huge hair – but then every single member of the basketball team had an Afro. He favoured enormous flares. Tank tops. A knitted hat like the one Sly Stone wore. Platforms. His taste in clothes hasn't really changed that much since, except that now he can afford to have them custom-made. Even small men's sweat pants drown him. Black lace leggings are pretty odd for a man, but, as Bryant Gumbel pointed out, you just can't see Prince wearing a blazer. Back then, he adapted what he could find. He would raid the local army surplus store. He still does that today – for the *Emancipation* launch concert, all his stage technicians wore white jumpsuits, the kind worn to avoid contamination, bought from the same store. He doesn't like his roadies to wear mismatching denims and grubby old T-shirts.

'I was at school with Prince,' says Audrey, who now works in the Minneapolis Public Library. 'We had the same music teacher, Mr Hamilton. It was a pretty mixed school – blacks, whites, some Indians. Even the teachers were mixed. No one knew Prince was talented until one lunchtime, when he and his friends put on a little show in the lunch room. The lyrics were clean. We couldn't believe it because he was so quiet. Prince didn't ever get in any trouble. The kids didn't realise he had all this in him. You only ever saw him hanging out with his brother, Duane. I would always say "Hi" to Prince, but he would only mumble. Duane was more popular with the girls. Prince had a huge Afro. All the other kids wore T-shirts and jeans, but he was always dressed real well, in slacks, a leather jacket – clean and pressed. I never saw him out on a date, or even eat his lunch with a girl. We girls would all talk about who we liked, yakkety-yak, but no one ever mentioned Prince.'

He did have some girlfriends – one was even a cheerleader, and he gave her a small role when he made his first movie, *Purple Rain*. Another wanted to be a model when she left school. At parties, he stayed on the sidelines. He wouldn't drink. He wouldn't smoke. Duane was voted best dancer in junior high, but no one ever saw his little brother shaking his stuff.

Jim Hamilton, who had played with BB King, was the music teacher. Hamilton got a lot of respect from Prince. Mostly, though, Prince said he would start playing his own stuff and the teachers would get a bit mad. He wasn't able to read music. When he released his first album, he said that this inability hadn't got in the way of what he was doing. 'Maybe it will later, but I doubt it.'

At thirteen he formed a band called Grand Central, with Andre, his cousin Charles Smith, Andre's sister Linda, Terry Jackson and William Daugherty. William's cousin, Morris Day, would take his place on drums. They changed their name to Champagne when they all went to Central High. Prince started to sing as well as play guitar, but because he was so shy he would mumble and not look up. They played Ohio Players, Grover Washington, Prince. When he tried out his own compositions, the audiences at local hotels and gyms and school dances would cover their faces with their hands. Grand Central would try to outplay their rivals on the scene, Cohesion and Flyte Tyme.

Prince even took classes in the music business and song copy-righting, and of course he did well. He spent every spare moment rehearsing in Andre's basement or in music class. The guys would all hang out at Chuck Orr's guitar shop in town. Chuck didn't mind when Prince played his guitars for hours after school. Years later Prince would put lots of business Chuck's way, and Chuck would hang signed photos on the walls.

His first taste of publicity was in the school paper, the *Central High Pioneer*, on 13 February 1973. The interview was accompanied by a photograph of him, unsmiling, with his hair tumbling around his face, and the headline 'Nelson finds it hard to become known'. He said he played guitar, bass, keyboards and drums, but had given up the saxophone. He said he liked the school, because his music teachers, Mr Bickham and Mrs Doepkes, let him work on his own. He was already moaning about studios and record companies. 'I think it's hard for a band to make it in this state. I really feel that if we'd have lived in Los Angeles or New York or some other big city, we would have gotten over by now.'

When he graduated, Prince signed his cousin Charles's yearbook: 'Keep it black, Carlos Santana.' He went back to Central High shortly before it closed down in 1982. He was supposed to put in an appearance in the assembly hall, but the children were so hysterical he was forced to hide in the principal's office. His old music teacher, Jim Hamilton, wasn't surprised his former pupil had become a star so quickly. Prince had written in his graduation programme: Employment – Music.

Madonna was right when she said that Prince, like her, 'has a chip on his shoulder, he's competitive, he's from the Midwest, from a screwed-up home, and he has something to prove'.

Karen Krattinger, who was Prince's personal assistant for five years in the 1980s, became close to John Nelson. 'I appreciated my relationship with Prince's father, because my dad passed away when I was six. John still sends me Christmas cards, and he sends cassettes of his music to my mom. She would come up to Minneapolis to see me, and John would take her out to lunch. He was a very quiet man, and he and Prince were close at that time, right after *Purple Rain*. Prince was always asking me to get his dad on the phone. I didn't find Prince as close to his mother – I think he tried to do right by her. He was closest to Bernadette; she was wonderful. Whenever Prince had a party he would invite her; whenever he made a new album he'd say, make sure Bernadette gets one. I think he appreciated her because she never demanded anything from him; he never felt he had to do things for her, he did them because he wanted to. Mattie and Hayward

Baker's little boy, Omar, is a sweet kid. Prince is very fond of him. After I left Prince, he fell out with his father. He fell out with his sister Sharon. He seemed more and more isolated.'

'If you've been hurt as a child, you may not let people get close to you,' says Owen Husney. Others who have got close to Prince, such as Denise Matthews, a.k.a. Vanity, and band members Wendy Melvoin and Lisa Coleman, say they saw how damaged Prince was by his childhood. He would fly off the handle one moment, be very distant and quiet the next, or very affectionate and loving. 'There are multiple personalities in there,' wrote Jon Bream, who has observed him at close quarters for twenty years. 'The nice personality we are seeing now, I've seen it before.'

'Prince told me there was abuse in his childhood,' says Susan Rogers, who would work with him for many years as his studio engineer. 'He had a weird name, he was small. He was also extremely intelligent, and sensitive.' It was a recipe for disaster, or for him turning inward and creating something that would transcend all those obstacles. An outgoing kid with lots of friends and dates wouldn't have spent the time he needed to become an accomplished musician by his early teens.

Prince's constant fear is that women will not find him attractive. Hence the seductive, sensuous songs that are beautiful and frighteningly obsessed at the same time. He is also afraid of treating women the way he saw his father treat his mother. Hence his femininity, his androgyny, his uncanny understanding of women. He wants them to adore him, and he has used every ounce of his ability to get that. His need to control, his paranoia, his inability to trust those around him, his ever-present bodyguards, all stem from the chaos and disorder that surrounded him as a child. He was shut in his room at home by one domineering man after another. He was teased at school, out-dunked on the sports field, and happiest when locked in the music room at lunchtime.

While he was in his last year at school, Prince was approached with the tentative offer of a recording deal by Isaac Hayes, the legendary soul man who had composed, among many other things, the soundtrack for *Shaft*. Prince had loved the movie when he saw it downtown with his friends. He loved *Car Wash* as well, and *Superfly*, directed by that other local boy made good, Gordon Parks, Jr. They all combined his two loves, music and film. But much as he idolised Hayes, he wanted to graduate first, which he did, on his eighteenth birthday. He didn't even have a tassel on his mortar-board when he went up to get his certificate. He was in a hurry, but then he always had finished his assignments early. He says the reason he often records all the instruments himself is because it is quicker than explaining how to do it to someone else. He didn't want to waste time going to college, either. 'He's a very impatient person,' says Alan Leeds. 'Still is.' Prince went straight from high school into the studio.

'The first person Prince worked with and who gave him access to a studio was this wacky white Englishman who at that time had an enormous Afro,' says Dave Hill, author of the 1989 biography *Prince: A Pop Life*. (Prince swears he didn't know of the book's existence, but he did send Hill a Christmas card after it was published.) 'And Chris Moon himself says that to see him, a tall white Englishman, and a pint-sized black American wandering around Minneapolis together must have been the zaniest sight you can imagine.'

Chris Moon was the proprietor of Moon Sound Inc., a recording studio in south Minneapolis, where he recorded commercials and demo tapes for local groups. He had just written some songs, recorded with an acoustic guitar. He decided that what he needed was a piano player. He had previously recorded a local group, a bunch of kids really, called Champagne, in an eight-track studio. Moon gave the band's pianist a call. He knew he wouldn't have to pay him much. Prince turned up, excited to be back in the studio. When he had finished playing on the track, he asked Moon if he wanted some bass on it. Moon said, sure, but he couldn't afford to hire a bass-player. Prince said he didn't have to, he'd do it. He added some drums and an electric guitar just for good measure. And some backing vocals. Moon couldn't believe what he had just seen. In exchange for writing and playing, Prince got free studio time. They agreed to pool their talents and split the proceeds 50/50. The other members of Champagne were pretty fed up with that, and the group disbanded.

Armed with a demo tape of their songs, Prince and Moon went to New York. Prince believed that he would be signed straight away. The strange pair did in fact receive two offers, but both would have meant Prince relinquishing publishing rights. He hadn't come top of that class for nothing. One 1976 song, 'Since We've Been Together', he registered with ASCAP (the American Society of Composers, Authors and Publishers), the first of many.

But the early demos weren't quite strong enough to get anything better. While in New York, Prince stayed with his half-sister Sharon, who became interested in managing him. Moon had to get back to Minneapolis, leaving Prince to explore New York. But, once home, Moon had the bright idea of taking the tape, containing 'Soft And Wet', 'Machine', 'Leaving New York' and 'My Love Is Forever', to a local producer and management firm. He contacted Owen Husney. He was taking it to exactly the right person.

'When I met Prince in '75 or '76, I saw that the guy was gifted,' says Husney, 'but my genius was marketing his genius. My marketing instincts went wild. Here was this black kid from a town with under 1 per cent black population, amazingly gifted – not that race has any-thing to do with it, but most of the music coming out of the town was by young white artists. I knew that when I got on a plane to Cali with him the labels were going to be amazed. Coming out of Minneapolis with Prince was like coming out of Siberia with a major rock star.'

Husney called Prince at his sister's apartment in New York and told him to come home; he had a proposition. 'When we got together, Prince didn't have a lot of equipment. I went to a local doctor and an attorney and raised about $50,000 and bought a couple of guitars, paid for studio time, flights, and wrote Prince a weekly cheque of fifty or seventy-five bucks' spending money. My ad agency was doing $8 million a year and I walked out of that to look after Prince.'

Husney spent time developing the music on that first tape at Sound 80 in Minneapolis with David Rivkin, a local engineer. The songs were all five, six, seven minutes long, and the hooks didn't come back in. Prince had a tendency to play a song for so long and then just jam.

'I think I helped, although I stress it was Prince's genius, not mine,' says Husney. 'I made suggestions, edited what they had been doing – don't bore us, get to the chorus.

'I thought, boy, if I change his age back a year, these people will go wild. The best thing I could do was support his genius, not try to change it. I could tell he was very shy, had a very high IQ. I also knew he had a side that was very aloof and hidden, there was a lot going on inside even he didn't understand. I knew not to put him in a three-piece suit and tie and turn him into Marvin Gaye.'

Husney designed and paid for the press kit that he hoped would impress the A&R men. The black cover had just the one word, Prince (it was Husney's idea to drop his surname), and a picture, taken by a local fashion photographer, of the artist lit from behind so his hair became a halo. He was (very rare, this) smiling, albeit nervously. He looked as if he would rather be having a tooth pulled. Only fifteen were printed, at a cost of $100 each.

'Rehearsals took place in Pepe Willie's basement. He was like a godfather to those kids,' says Husney. Many years later, Willie, who had married Prince's cousin (her mother is Mattie Shaw's twin), would be denied entry along with Charles Smith, Prince's cousin and band member in Grand Central, to a concert at Paisley Park in August 1995. 'My most gracious first cousin had me and Pepe Willie removed,' says Smith. Willie said, 'No, we ain't got no tickets an' stuff, but this is Prince's cousin and my name is Pepe. I'm one of his producers, years ago.' They still didn't let them in.

While Prince was waiting to go to LA in the last few months of 1977, he recorded with Pepe Willie. Andre and Prince performed as studio musicians for Willie's band, 94 East (later released as *Minneapolis Genius – The Historic 1977 Recordings*). Prince used the sessions to record 'I Feel For You' and 'Do Me, Baby'. He was getting impatient again.

Prince and Husney at last flew to LA. 'I didn't want people to know too much,' says Husney. 'I wanted people to listen to his music, look at the press kit and start asking questions. I knew, once they were intrigued, I had them – I think Colonel Parker did that a little bit with

Elvis. The idea was that Prince was in the hallway, so when I played the music and gave the guy a press kit that said nothing, the A&R guy would say, "What's he like? What's he like?" I would say, well, see for yourself, let's get him in here. And then of course Prince would come strolling in, and say nothing anyway.'

Husney says that getting Prince the perfect deal wasn't really that difficult. Everyone could see he had an incredible talent. 'I had developed a relationship with Russ Thyret, who's now chairman of the board at Warner. A&M offered homes in Beverly Hills but wouldn't agree to three albums, so I passed. Columbia offered three albums, but I didn't catch their vision that they would bring Prince home all the way. Warner had a family feel; many of the people who were employed then are still there. I was a big believer in Mo Ostin, Lenny Waronker and Russ. They nurtured their artists.'

When they were being romanced by every label in town, Russ Thyret would take the time to talk to them about the music business, explaining to Prince what he could expect from Warner. 'Russ would say, get in the back seat of my car, and he had one of those old two-seater Mercedes, so Prince fit right in the back perfectly, and we would ride around LA while he talked about the music business,' says Husney. 'He absolutely got Prince, he understood him. We would go back to his house and lay on the floor and talk music. We had to go with Warner.'

Warner wanted Maurice White from Earth, Wind & Fire to oversee the recording, but Prince didn't want that. He thought Earth, Wind & Fire would be over in a year. 'He didn't want that sound placed on him. He wanted to go forward,' says Husney. Warner were still insisting that Prince have an experienced producer in the studio with him. 'I said to Russ, let's concoct a scheme here. Let's fly Prince out, tell him that Warner is giving him free studio time to fool around, and as he's recording we'll have producers come down to watch. At the end of the day, if you believe me that he can produce his own album, I want you to give it to him.'

While Prince was having fun in the studio, like a kid in a candy store, he had no idea that some of the most famous names in the business were watching him. He thought they were janitors. 'This little kid was laying down a drum track, then adding bass guitar, putting on a keyboard, building and building these tracks, and it took people like Teddy Templeman and Lenny Waronker about one minute before they all cornered me in the hallway and said, "He can do whatever he wants."' Prince became the youngest producer of a Warner Brothers record – a title he still holds.

Husney still lives and works in Minneapolis. He is a consultant to the two biggest local labels, Sam Goody and K-Tel. He and Prince no longer talk.

'I was his mentor, like a father to him,' says Husney. 'As time went on, my role was lessened. My wife and I were his surrogate family: just as Bernadette Anderson had given him a home, we gave him a home. I walked out of my business to make the album and get the deal. Our relationship was not based on, okay, how much money are we going to make from him? Our intentions were very pure: that's why God put me there, to make sure he was nurtured. I had been a musician, I had managed a lot of other acts. He knew that no manager after me cared the way I cared, even though he may not admit it. He listened to everything I had to say in the early days. One of the reasons we parted was that you couldn't tell him anything any more. I was not afraid to say no to him, and he didn't like that. When we broke up I think it was more like the breaking-up of lovers or a father and son. It was a lot deeper and a lot more hurtful than just the breaking-up of a manager and his artist.'

Prince, too, has stayed in Minneapolis. He says the cold keeps the bad people out. 'He's a remarkably provincial man,' says Alan Leeds. 'He could be more worldly than he has chosen to be. He wants to stay in his little cocoon.'

'You don't feel prejudice here,' Prince says. 'I know it exists, but you don't feel it as much.'

3

Life it ain't 2 funky unless it's got that pop

'I went through a lot when I was a boy. They called me sissy, punk, freak and faggot. See, the girls loved you, but the boys hated you. They called me Princess.'

That was the torment of the first freaky black man to wear make-up and challenge the acceptable image of black sexuality, to cross racial boundaries. Those are the words of Little Richard, who asked the questions 'Am I black or white? Am I straight or gay?' long before Prince ever did.

Of course, Prince has never denied his cultural heritage. His main-stream movie *Purple Rain* was littered with references to Little Richard, Jimi Hendrix, James Brown and Louis Jordan. You just had to know where to look. Anyone who thought his bejewelled turban and frilly white shirt in *Purple Rain* were fresh ideas had never seen Sly and the Family Stone. 'He said he didn't have access to black radio or music,' wrote Nelson George in *The Death of Rhythm and Blues*, 'but he's done a lot of catching up.'

'Sly Stone broke such new ground,' says Rickey Vincent, the author of *Funk*, a history that took until 1996, and a resurgence of interest in that music through hip-hop, to get published. 'When those pioneering black artists do things that are innovative, those watershed events are not really recorded by the American white-dominated press. Nobody bothered to take those people seriously and it had a lot to do with the racism of the music establishment.'

'Paranoia about purity is the real enemy of black cultural expression,' wrote Michael Eric Dyson in his book *Between God and Gangsta Rap*. 'Creolisation, syncretism and hybridisation are black culture's hallmarks. It is precisely in stitching together various fabrics of human and artistic experience that black musical artists have expressed their genius.'

Look at jazz: born out of the clash of cultures that arrived in America in the nineteenth century, from African drum music to Scottish reels, even German opera. 'I listened to all kinds of music when I was young, and I always said one day I would play all kinds of music and not be judged for the colour of my skin but the quality of my work,' Prince would say after the release of *Purple Rain*. It's no coincidence that Sly Stone, Jimi Hendrix and Prince reached musical maturity in cities with only tenuous links to black America: Sly in San Francisco, Hendrix in London and Prince in Minneapolis.

Hendrix's love of the guitar meant he fell out of favour with black audiences – that instrument was too associated with the blues, which in the 1960s smacked too deeply of subservience, of acceptance of one's lot in life. You also couldn't dance to him. 'To the audiences of Stax and Motown and James Brown, "Purple Haze" and "Hey Joe" just didn't do the do,' wrote Nelson George.

'The one thing Hendrix wasn't was a black star with a black audience, which meant his white fans never had the problem of being outnumbered by black people at his shows,' wrote Charles Shaar Murray in his biography of Hendrix, *Crosstown Traffic*. 'Prince unleashes patently Hendrix-derived flourishes as theatrical device and sound effect.'

Tony Mitchell, former music critic of *Sounds*, and one of the first British journalists to interview Prince, says, 'With Hendrix, there was sexual chemistry there – you didn't have to be gay, you could be a bloke and be into the obvious sexuality of this guy – and I found the same reaction watching Prince for the first time on his *Dirty Mind* tour in Amsterdam. You were open-mouthed at his audacity. He wasn't a virtuoso guitarist, so he wasn't like Hendrix in that way, but he was like him in that he held the audience, you shared in a wonderful musical joke. It was an overtly sexual performance, not in a macho black way. A softer, more girlish approach. An irresistible package.'

Both Hendrix and Prince were from broken homes, both introverts whose only interests were music and girls. What sets Prince apart is that he became famous in a very different era. He knows every trick in the book, from drop-dead dance moves to bug-eyed, cutie-pie poses. 'Prince understands self-mythologisation in a way no one in Hendrix's era possibly could,' said Shaar Murray.

'Prince will never commit suicide, nor die a self-destructive death. No bloodstains on the bed linen of the Chelsea Hotel. His self-love and controlled understanding of rock history could never allow it,' wrote Stuart Cosgrove in the *NME* in 1986.

Prince, though, denies that Hendrix was a big influence, citing instead Carlos Santana. The only reason he believes he is compared with Hendrix is 'because he's black. Hendrix played more blues. Santana played prettier.' Prince and Hendrix are very different: the control-freak, non-smoking Prince couldn't be further from the hopelessly messed-up Hendrix. Indeed, Carlos Santana, post-Woodstock, began listening to John Coltrane and Miles Davis, both huge influences on Prince's music. Prince mentions Davis, and particularly the tireless way he worked, again and again. 'Miles used to tell his musicians that he paid them to practise on the bandstand, to go for something beyond what they knew,' says Greg Tate, co-founder of the Black Rock Coalition and a *Vibe* magazine columnist. 'You don't get music that inspired unless you're ready to do the wild thing again and again.'

Prince also feels he's closer to Stevie Wonder and Joni Mitchell than anyone else in terms of songwriting. 'I remember what happened when Stevie did *The Secret Life of Plants*: they said it was no good,' he says. 'It was the same with Joni Mitchell. They said she was off her rocker. She taught me about space, silence.'

'Joni Mitchell has more African-American fans than maybe even she realises,' says Greg Tate, 'and has been a major influence on Prince, Seal, Cassandra Wilson. She is also someone who has made a career of putting musical progress ahead of the ring of the cash register.'

Sly Stone was just as drug-crazed as Hendrix; he took funk from James Brown, far too black and proud for most white folks, and served it up to the masses. Black culture has always followed what was happening on the street: the Harlem Renaissance of the 1920s was preceded by a movement inspired by Marcus Garvey; there was a similar surge in jazz and black writing after the Second World War, with segregation crumbling in schools, sport and the military. Sly's music and multicultural band were ignited by the Newark riots in 1967. His band were bathed in the hippie love of the 1960s, but in the 1970s his 'There's A Riot Going On' signalled the demise of the civil rights movement (it effectively ended in 1978 – when Prince had just signed his first record deal – with the Bakke decision, which ruled positive discrimination unconstitutional).

'People are just starting to realise how brilliant Sly was,' says Greg Tate. 'He got more ahead of his time as he went on. I think Tricky today is on the same level – he not only acknowledges a debt to Prince, but to Sly as well. Okay, so Sly's early stuff wasn't as political as James Brown's, but he foresaw the Panthers coming apart at the seams, he became despondent in his music.'

Today Sly's music lives on, in 'People Everyday' by Arrested Development, 'Humpty Dance' by Digital Underground, 'Rhythm Nation' by Janet Jackson. In the mid-1980s, when Sly was down on his luck, having been arrested for possession of cocaine in 1981, Prince was interested in producing some tracks with him. Prince was also keen to sign George Clinton, godfather of funk, to his label when he was at a similar low point. Clinton had experienced many of the problems Prince would manage to overcome: 'We were too black for white folks, too white for black folks. Too loud to play the black clubs, and had on those costumes and things,' said the man responsible for the likes of Snoop Doggy Dogg in the early 1990s (but is anyone an original? The legendary jazz artist Sun Ra was already wearing freaky costumes and knocking about in a spaceship back in the 1950s).

Prince also kneels at the altar of that other great creator of conscious lyrics, Curtis Mayfield, as far as his falsetto, if not his politics, is concerned (Curtis, now fifty-four and a paraplegic, released his new album, featuring former Paisley Park artist Mavis Staples, in 1997 through Warner, 'who put up the money, win or lose'). But it was the music of James Brown and Clinton that helped to shape Prince's funkiness. And it was the multi-culti funk philosophy that Prince dragged screaming from its near death in the 1970s to its astonishing revival today.

'Funk represents a time when there was optimism, attempts to deal with an integrated society, to live and work and dance together,' says Rickey Vincent. 'It was a great experiment, but it didn't work out.' Reagan's election in 1980 sounded funk's final death knell. It was replaced by disco, the whole idea of which was to wipe out funk's politicisation and replace it with mindless monotony ('It got on your nerves,' says George Clinton). Reagan's legacy of social policies has now come of age in black America. 'Today all kids have going for them is funk: Paris's gorilla funk, Warren G's G-funk, Goldie in the land of funk,' continues Vincent. 'The Ohio Players, Earth, Wind & Fire, Kool and the Gang were all trained in jazz, played blues, gospel, you could tell they had listened to Hendrix, they were liberated enough to take the entire richness of their tradition and European music. Funk could show not only how intelligent you were, how worldly you were, but also how well you can party.'

For Prince, an irresistible package. He was about to pick it up and party with it for twenty years.

For You was released in April 1978. Recording took place at the Sausalito Record Plant near San Francisco, and Prince stayed nearby in a house rented by Warner, babysat by Owen Husney, Husney's wife, Britt, and Tommy Vicari, brought in by Warner to oversee their new signing. 'I made Prince scrambled eggs, my then wife made him breakfast and lunch, washed his clothes,' says Husney. Tommy Vicari, ten years older than Prince, became like a big brother to him. Prince was in the studio six days a week, working until five or six in the morning – playing all twenty-seven instruments yourself is time-consuming. 'Prince was eighteen or nineteen, but he was like a forty-year-old guy – work was all he wanted to do,' says Husney. 'There was no trying to wake him up and get him out of bed in the morning. There were no drugs, no alcohol, he was a driven man. All we could do was hang on.'

Sly Stone was working in an adjacent studio and popped in to see what this new kid was up to. Prince, though, was too overawed to do more than hide under his hair. He asked to go to the studio where Michael Jackson was recording, but once there he wouldn't say a word. His future biographer Jon Bream flew across the country to interview him for the local paper. Prince refused to speak to him. He was also taken over to Carlos Santana's house during recording, where he had a bit more to say for himself. Mostly, though, he didn't want anyone else's music to affect what he was doing in the studio, and even banned any Stevie Wonder from being put on the turntable back at the house.

When the time came to take the all-important picture for the album cover, Prince was already telling Husney how he wanted to look. But because the record was going to be pitched as straight black pop, he looked like any other young black teenager of the time, even Jackson: the large Afro was all. But he got his way and refused to smile. He would never look as black in a photograph again.

'The album opens with Prince singing against forty-five other vocal tapes of himself – a Niagara of voices cascading and intertwining over and around each other in a dreamy, romantic melody,' wrote Tim Carr in the *Minneapolis Tribune*, which would later merge with the *Star*. Prince's falsetto was immediately compared in the press to the Bee Gees, but there was no way this album could be conceived as disco. Its dirtiest track, 'Soft And Wet', was co-written by Chris Moon, the lyrics written down by Prince with a purple felt-tip. But other than that, Prince wanted all the kudos; he even removed Tommy Vicari's name from the engineering credits.

The reason Vicari didn't last long – that no one lasts very long with Prince – is not because he can't form lasting working relationships; he just outgrows them. 'Prince has the ability to absorb everything in your brain while he's standing next to you,' says Husney, who parted company with him at the end of 1978. 'You don't even know he's doing it. Very early on, he would absorb things in the studio. It's not so much that he drops people, but he is like a miraculous sponge.'

The album did well on the R&B charts, reaching the top ten, but Prince was already having other ideas. He would mention the Lionel Richie song 'Three Times A Lady', how it couldn't be stopped – black people bought it, white people bought it.

'I wanted to make a different-sounding record,' he said in an interview with the *Minneapolis Tribune* in April 1978. 'We originally planned to use horns, but it's really hard to sound different if you use the same instruments. So I created a different kind of horn section by multi-tracking a synthesizer and some guitar lines. I got hip to Polymoogs [polyphonic synthesizers, now commonplace, on which it is possible to play chords] when I was here working at Sound 80. I was trying to get away from using the conventional sound of pianos and clavinets as keyboards. I think the main reason artists fail when they try to play all of the instruments is because either they can't play all of the instruments really well – there is usually a flaw somewhere – or they don't play with the same intensity on each track.' What makes the album sound like Prince? 'I guess it's just the basic sound. It's hard to classify Earth, Wind & Fire, for instance, but you can always tell it's them. It's not a brand of music, it's a group sound, an identity of their own. Maybe my voice, or just my total sound, who knows?' He was asked if he would add horns or woodwinds to his live band. 'Well, I'm going to pick up a flute pretty soon.'

He headed home, admitting that he was a physical wreck by the time the album was finished. But Warner were eager for their young prodigy to tour, and he and Husney set about putting together a band. 'I put David Rivkin's brother Bobby, who was a runner for me, and Matt Fink in the band, but obviously nothing is going to get past Prince,' says Husney. Prince admits that he was under pressure from his musician friends to have an all-black band, but he wanted some white musicians in the mix, as well as some women. 'Half the black musicians I knew only listened to one type of music,' he says. 'I had white friends, black friends, I never grew up in a particular culture.' Along with Andre Anderson, soon to become Cymone, who had often popped down to hang out while he was recording, Prince agreed to take on board Bobby Rivkin, soon to become Bobby Z, as his drummer, although local musicians told him there were better, black players available ('Bobby watches me like no other drummer would,' said Prince). Prince also chose two local white keyboard-players, Gayle Chapman and Matt Fink, over Jimmy Jam Harris, his old rival from high school. Jimmy Jam recognised Prince's talent early on. 'You could tell if someone could play guitar if they could play "Make Me Smile" by Chicago,' he says. 'Prince could play it note for note.' Prince described Fink as 'a technician. He can read and write like a whiz, and is one of the fastest in the world.' Dez Dickerson was recruited after he answered an ad for a guitarist.

'I grew up watching my older brother David play around town in his band,' says Bobby Z. David Rivkin would go on to work with Prince for many years. 'I first met Prince at Moon Sound recording studios here in Minneapolis. I knew of Prince playing in local bands with Andre and Morris Day and Jimmy Jam. I was the gofer for the ad agency owned by Owen Husney, who was looking after Prince. It was destiny: Prince and I would clear the desks and jam until six in the morning. Originally the band was just Prince, Andre and me.'

'A year before Prince finished his first album, when his demos were just starting to be shopped around, I got to hear his tape from Bobby Z, who came to see the band I was in,' says Fink. 'Bobby said, you got to hear this, this is something new and different – he plays all the instruments. But he's going to be looking for a band. I said, "As soon as he's ready, let me know." So I auditioned. Prince decided to hire me.'

The band made their debut on 5 January 1979. As he would continue to do throughout his career, Prince chose a local venue, the Capri Theater, to try out his live performance. Tickets were $4. To publicise the event, which had been staged at short notice, he gave an interview to Jon Bream for his local paper. He was already witty, ironic. When asked what qualities he had to help make him successful, he replied, 'Being tall.' What are your strengths and weaknesses? 'I'm a sucker for good legs.' What are your goals? 'I want to be a janitor.' He said he didn't know if his band read music, he hadn't asked them. He said he didn't want to appear shy on stage, and was working on that. Giggling, he told Bream that he had never talked this much in his life.

The performance that cold winter night in Minneapolis was far from polished. Prince wore denim jeans (rarely seen again), with legwarmers over the top. He was far from the beaming, smirking showman he would become: he stood at the microphone with his eyes closed. He no longer had to play his cheap imitation Telecaster – he had commissioned Charles Orr to make him a guitar and a bass with ivy vines on the fretboard. Prince would later say that he had a different guitar for every emotion. His commissions would also become rather more elaborate: one of his favourite symbol-shaped guitars – he has close to two hundred, all custom-made – was built by the German company Auerswald Instruments, with a ninety-year-old curly maple neck, ebony fretboard, Sperzel pegs, EMG pick-ups and gold-plated brass hardware. During his final performance with his next band, The Revolution, he would smash all his guitars on stage. 'We had a sense it would be the last time we'd be on stage together. He broke all his guitars – he'd never smashed guitars before,' says Wendy Melvoin, Revolution guitarist. 'We never played with him again.'

The audience on that first night all knew Prince – former school friends, musicians, cousins. But the next night, executives from Warner stood on the sidelines and deemed their new signing not quite ready for a full tour. 'We played that show at the Capri, an old movie theatre in north Minneapolis. It was twenty below zero,' says

Matt Fink. 'It was really rough; we had technical problems. The Warner guys said, "Sounds good, but you need to rehearse more."'

'I knew how to write hits by my second album,' Prince says today. And indeed, although his first had sold a respectable 100,000 copies, his second, *Prince*, topped a million, and was recorded in only six weeks. *For You*, he says, was made entirely on his own; on *Prince*, Andre Cymone sang vocal harmony on 'Why You Wanna Treat Me So Bad?'. His failure to be credited began the rift between the two former best friends. The only reason for the omission, says Prince, was 'there was a typo on the record', but he also says that Andre only sang a small harmony part 'that you really couldn't hear'. One track included on the album was 'I Feel For You', which Prince had composed for Patrice Rushen, on whom he had a crush. She had turned the track down, but it was later recorded by Chaka Khan, who had a British number-one hit with it in 1984. Prince had spent most of his teenage years with a poster of Khan on his bedroom wall.

This time, for the cover shot, Prince took his shirt off. The Afro was gone; his hair was long, relaxed. The album produced his first gold record, 'I Wanna Be Your Lover' (he was talking to Patrice Rushen), which went to number one on the black charts, and also went down well with the critics, who likened the album to *Off the Wall*, the latest hit by Prince's equally hard-working *doppelgänger*, Michael Jackson. Rather worryingly, *Rolling Stone* wrote that, with a bit more sophistication, Prince could become 'a solo Bee Gees of the libido'

Prior to the live shows to promote the album in 1980, Prince explained his rather odd appearance: 'I wear what I wear because I don't like clothes. It's the most comfortable thing I can find. Everybody thinks I'm gay or a freak, but it doesn't bother me. In the 1960s, people would go to concerts with their mother's clothes on and paint all over their face and it didn't even matter. They were just as wild as the acts were, if not wilder.'

At his next outing in Minneapolis, at the Orpheum Theater in February, he really was determined not to come across as shy. He wore zebra-patterned bikini briefs. He french-kissed Gayle Chapman on stage. With his father sitting in the audience, he performed 'Head' (the song).

'I'd hug the bass-player – he's a man,' remembers Prince, 'and I'd go kiss the keyboard-player – she's a woman. We had some of that going on.'

'Head' would drive Chapman from the band; her replacement, Lisa Coleman, sang along with the lyrics as Prince's idea of an initiation test. The tour would also herald the start of Prince's feud with that other carefully coiffed funkster, Rick James. Keen to build on his black audience, Prince supported James at larger venues in the US, and James, who deemed himself to be the original punk-funker, wasn't impressed by the interloper.

'At that time we were all struggling for an image,' says Matt Fink. 'New wave was starting but glam rock was still in. I was more flashy when I joined Prince – satin and sparkles and platform shoes and long hair. At first I was wearing a paratrooper's jumpsuit that Prince gave me. Then I was in a jailbird outfit with black and white stripes – that's what I wore when we went on *American Bandstand* – and Prince liked that. On tour with Rick James I was still in the jail suit and Rick did a song when he came on stage in a jail suit that he would rip off. Prince said to me, "You know what, I don't think you can wear the jail suit, 'cause it's too weird. What was your next idea?" I said, "How about a guy in a surgeon's outfit?" He said, "Even better, let's go with that." We were in Chicago, he had the wardrobe people run out to a surgical supply house, grabbed authentic gowns and masks and I became Dr Fink that night. It stuck.'

'Prince is out to lunch,' James would say later. 'He sings about giving head and incest. Something else: he doesn't want to be black.' In 1984 he accused Prince of modelling his new group, Vanity 6, on James's Mary Jane Girls. Prince, in an early display of paranoia, was convinced Rick was out to kill him, but Rick was too preoccupied with chasing women to bother with murder.

'I co-wrote "Dirty Mind",' says Matt Fink. 'I came up with the music, jamming at rehearsal one day, and Prince said, "This is great, let's go over to my house and record it." We spent the evening recording, just Prince and I, and we finished all the music at about midnight, when I went home. He showed up the next day with the finished product: lyrics, melody. He just walked in and said, "Hey, this is the title track to the next album.'"

For his first two albums, Prince had been promoted in both black and white markets at once, playing in new-wave rock clubs and opening for funk acts like Cameo. 'His first two albums were eccentric, he was trying out ideas,' says Dave Hill. 'Warner aimed him at the black pop market and he was written about in the black teen magazines. That's the only place he was taken seriously.' Prince, though, refused to take any of these early interviews that seriously. He asked one female journalist, who had been asking him all the regular questions, 'Does your pubic hair go all the way up to your belly-button?'

'The big change came with *Dirty Mind*: a bit punk, tinny organ, all that post-apocalyptic imagery, new-wave,' continues Hill. 'Suddenly he began to be written about by *Rolling Stone* in America, by *NME* and *Sounds* in Britain, initially in a laughing kind of way.'

The album, released in October 1980, had been a gamble. 'Sure it was a risky record,' recalled Bob Cavallo, a member of Prince's new management team Cavallo, Rufallo and Fargnoli, who had taken over from Owen Husney. 'Some thought we were losing our minds.' The gamble paid off, however, with *Rolling Stone* giving it four and a half stars out of five. Prince says he was depressed during the recording of *Dirty Mind*. 'A lot had to do with the band, the fact that I couldn't make people in the band understand how great we could be together if we all played our part,' he told *Rolling Stone*'s Neal Karlen. 'A lot also had to do with being in love with someone and not getting any love back.' The album was full of references to masturbation and incest. Compare the cover to that of James Brown's 1971 *Revolution of the Mind* – Brown is behind the steel wire of a jail. On *Dirty Mind*, Prince's backdrop consists of the upturned metal springs of a bed.

Lisa Coleman had replaced Gayle Chapman on keyboards in the summer of 1980. Chapman left because of her religious beliefs; she also couldn't take much more of the onstage making out. Lisa was the daughter of a Los Angeles studio percussionist, Gary Coleman, and was working as a clerk when a friend at Prince's new management firm told her that he needed a new band-member. 'I started composing when I was five,' says Lisa. 'I performed my first piece at a recital when I was seven. Prince didn't just want funk players. He had a gift for choosing slightly odd people.'

'Lisa was classically trained,' says Wendy Melvoin, Lisa's childhood friend, 'and when she was hired by Prince, right before *Dirty Mind*, the extent of Prince's exposure to classical music was Ravel's *Bolero*, the soundtrack to that film starring Dudley Moore. It was like, "Jesus Christ." Lisa was bringing Prince a lot of music back then.'

Prince had recorded *Dirty Mind* in his 16-track basement studio at home. Despite his band line-up (Matt Fink, Dez Dickerson, Bobby Z, Andre Cymone and Lisa Coleman), the album was again pretty much a one-man job. It didn't sell as well as *Prince*, but would go gold after the release of *Purple Rain*.

He had also decided to stop playing along with the media, a strategy of obfuscation he had planned from his very first interviews, when he had lied about his parentage. He says that it wasn't because he was ashamed of his background, but that he thought his personal life irrelevant to his music. Asked by Dick Clark, on the hugely popular *American Bandstand*, how many instruments he played, he replied, 'Thousands.' Asked how long he had been playing, he raised four fingers.

Black people, who were continuing to turn up at his concerts in large numbers, were more than a little surprised to be asked to sing along to 'Head'. The sight of Prince caressing the neck of his Telecaster guitar until it gave off a spurt of liquid owed more to punk than to Teddy Pendergrass.

Rhythm and blues was far more conservative when he went on the road with his album in 1980, now headlining and being mobbed by screaming girls for the first time. He wore high heels and black bikini underwear – even Sly never went that far. 'What was so different about Prince was he was so upfront about his sexual needs and desires,' says Kevin Powell, former *Vibe* columnist, now working on his first book, about growing up black and male in America.

'Prince did something really interesting,' says Vernon Reid, founder of black rock group Living Colour. 'He became the pimp and the whore in the same body. The long coat, the lingerie. The black bourgeoisie may be the last shockable people left on earth. Gender, aaargghh!'

Says bell hooks, 'He was the first African-American musician to deal with sado-masochism. He is still unprecedented in the kind of sexual issues he brought to the fore.'

'I think the biggest influence at that time was David Bowie,' says Greg Tate. 'I think the freedom, in terms of style and the way he looked, was down to Bowie, the great chameleon of pop.'

The *Dirty Mind* tour did get Prince to London, home of Bowie, punk and new wave, but his first performance, at the Lyceum in June 1981, wasn't to a full house – nobody in Britain knew who he was. 'It was a hip crowd, the Paula Yateses of this world,' says the journalist Tony Mitchell. 'Prince wasn't happy with the performance. I went backstage with a few mates thinking I could swan in and we could all have a nice chat, but it was all long faces and no one was speaking. He wasn't accessible or chatting to anyone. When I had interviewed him in Amsterdam the month before, it was all one-word answers and embarrassing gaps. Paula Yates got a trench coat, one with studs on, a real collector's item. I thought, bloody typical, I've given the guy a good review and a feature and she got the raincoat.'

Dirty Mind was doing the trick. A memo from Prince's publicist, Howard Bloom, to his manager, Steve Fargnoli, stated: 'Prince is a rock 'n' roll artist! . . . He is the first black artist with the potential to become a major white audience superstar since Jimi Hendrix.'

Dirty Mind was a definite move away from black audiences, but by the end of 1980, Prince had just had another bright idea. One track on the album, 'Uptown', described a thriving black musical community, with Prince as the high priest. He was about to make that fiction fact – and he was about to get seriously funky.

'How could a guy come out of Minneapolis and not only start a new trend in music but have the foresight to invent his own competition?' asks Susan Rogers. 'He realised that if he rose up on his own, it wouldn't have as much impact as it would if there was a black scene around him.'

The group Flyte Tyme had been around since the early 1970s, and were known around town as The Time. The core members were Terry Lewis, Monte Moir, Jimmy Jam Harris and Jellybean Johnson, all of whom had known Prince since high school. Alexander O'Neal, who had also been in Flyte Tyme, was Prince's first choice for lead singer of his new group. 'He said to Prince, "Hey, Prince, you know about this money thing, I need some paper, you know, I need a new car, I need some clothes,"' says Jimmy Jam. 'We knew we weren't going to make any money. Prince was very upfront: "There's not going to be a lot of money in this." For me and Terry Lewis, we didn't stick around for the third album. We were kinda booted out by then.' O'Neal went on to sing with local gospel group Sounds of Blackness, and to develop a successful solo career, despite his fondness for stone-washed denim. The job of lead singer went to Morris Day, who had played with Prince in Grand Central. Day had been born in the projects of Illinois, and moved to Minneapolis with his family when he was five. His mother brought him and his brother and sister up single-handed; he grew up on food stamps, the Beatles and James Brown. Day drafted into the band guitarist Jesse Johnson (no relation of Jellybean). Their first album, called simply *The Time*, has Prince as composer of all but one of the tracks.

Prince was already struggling with two different personalities. The shy recluse was also an exhibitionist, and the man who never gave interviews pored over every word written about him in the press. The funky descendant of James Brown, Sly and all the rest wanted everyone else to love him too.

Prince was warming up his new band. Andre Cymone had left in the summer of 1981, feeling he wasn't getting the credit he deserved, printer's error or no printer's error. He was replaced with another local musician, Mark Brown, soon to be known as Brown Mark, on bass. They were preparing to support the Rolling Stones for two shows in Los Angeles, the perfect opportunity for Prince to try out his rock credentials prior to the release of his fourth album, *Controversy*. Mick Jagger, of course, had been wearing eyeliner and frocks since the late 1960s. To the 100,000-strong audience at the Memorial Coliseum, though, the sight of a dimunitive black man in tights and leather underwear was too much. They showered the stage with objects and abuse. The show lasted twenty minutes before Prince strode off stage and on to a plane bound for Minneapolis. Only the long-distance pleading of Dez Dickerson persuaded him to return. The second night was even worse. He was pelted with pieces of chicken, and lasted for only three songs. 'There was this one dude right in front, and you could see the hatred all over his face,' Prince told Robert Hilburn of the *Los Angeles Times*. 'The reason I left was because I didn't want to play any more. I just wanted to fight. I was really angry.' But Prince was already planning his revenge, though he still had a little way to go before he could beat the Rolling Stones at their own game.

Controversy, released in October 1981, had mostly been recorded in Prince's home studio. *NME* called it 'Prince's first truly barmy record'. It was also the first for which he refused to give any inter-views – he was tired of the endless questions and answers. (Sales doubled that of *Dirty Mind*. He must have thought he was on to some-thing.) He had toyed with political statements on *Dirty Mind*, but here he really went to town: 'Ronnie, Talk To Russia' was at best naïve, at worst, as described by *Spin* magazine, 'wack'. Better was 'Annie Christian', in which he accused the Antichrist of the murders of black children in Atlanta and of John Lennon. The other tracks, though, covered familiar territory: 'Jack U Off'; 'Do Me, Baby'. The title track posed the questions 'Am I black or white? Am I straight or gay?' More apt might have been 'Am I always having sex or do I occasionally watch CNN in bed?'

'The big problem Prince faces as an artist is how to square the punky-funky cheesecake with serious statements on the state of the world and American culture,' said the Minneapolis publication *Sweet Potato*. 'It is precisely this schizophrenia that threatens to pull *Controversy* apart at the seams . . . There almost should have been a serious side and a sex side. Which would have made everything nice and cosy if the penis weren't a political tool in Prince's world-view.'

He had yet to cross over to white radio. That might not have been too irksome had he not lived in Minneapolis, a city with only a few hours of black music a day. Most local people hadn't heard of him by the time the *Controversy* show came to town in 1982. His local Met Center was less than a third full. But Prince was about to get busy with a global takeover, and he was about to release *1999*.

He put together a female trio by the name of the Hookers, which he soon renamed when he met Denise Matthews, whom he rechristened Vanity. Susan Moonsie and Brenda Bennett, who did most of the singing, made up Vanity 6 – the figure refers to the number of nipples. He wrote all but one track on their debut album, released in August 1982; Vanity says she co-wrote 'Nasty Girl' while sleeping behind a friend's couch in New York. Prince was taking no chances on potential audiences for their talents: the girls were Hispanic, black and white. He also worked on The Time's second album, *What Time Is It?*, again writing all but one of the songs. He christened his own band The Revolution.

That summer, he recorded *1999*, again in the basement studio of his purple house out in the suburbs. The studio was now called Uptown and equipped with 24 tracks. He threw away his live drums and bought a drum machine. 'I felt like an auto assembly-worker looking at a robot for the first time,' says Bobby Z, 'wondering if I still had a job. It was so early for drum machines, I didn't know what to make of it. It certainly kept good time. Prince said, "Here it is, figure out what you're going to do with it." The machine was on the record and I had to augment that and get it to work live. By the time we got to *Purple Rain* it was a big part of the show and disguised incredibly well. On the *Parade* tour, which was my last, we didn't use a drum machine – I really enjoyed that tour.' Peep inside the pale blue piano Prince would use on tour many years later, there were no strings and hammers, only a small computer chip. (All his pianos, incidentally, have reinforced lids, to withstand his leaps and lethal steel heels.)

The *1999* album was Prince's first real collaborative effort: he shared vocals with Lisa Coleman, and Dez Dickerson contributed the solos on 'Little Red Corvette'. 'On the title track, Prince, Lisa and Dez actually sang the entire song together,' said Alan Leeds, who had joined as tour manager during the *1999* tour. 'By the time he mixed it, Prince had changed his mind and decided to split up the lines, passing the baton among the singers like a relay race. The unusual approach accounts for how the melody keeps changing – as some of what are now lead vocals had been performed as harmonies.'

Prince played most of the instruments himself, but Vanity and his new protégée Jill Jones, who had been a backing singer with Teena Marie, Prince's support act on the *Dirty Mind* tour, helped out on vocals. Prince was in love with Jones's voice. She hailed from Ohio and grew up in a musical family – her mother was Teena Marie's manager – and listened to Janis Joplin and Sly Stone. 'When I met Prince I didn't like him. We didn't get along,' says Jones, who would play bit-parts in *Purple Rain* (she is the waitress who snarls in the club) and *Graffiti Bridge*, and would finally release her Prince-penned album in 1986 (she co-wrote 'G-spot' with Prince, a song originally intended for Vanity). 'He was a little arrogant 'cause he was shy. It's scary when you meet someone who's a lot like you, who's very naïve and a bit of a spoilt brat, to be perfectly honest. I think the reason we stayed such close friends for such a long time is because our relationship isn't physical. Everyone wanted to know if I was getting into his trousers but it's not like that at all. I've tried on his pants – they just about come up to my knees.'

Warner had to be persuaded to release *1999* as a double album; its European arm, WEA, thought better, releasing it as a single album in October 1982 and only relenting a year later. The title track was already being called a disco record by the British press, but it was in fact an eerie social commentary on the hedonism of the black community, who had nothing to do but party: no jobs, but plenty of a new drug – crack – on the streets. The album gave Prince room to address his favourite topics: rock critics, in 'All The Critics Love U In New York' (which also has him as a police car radio muttering, 'He's definitely masturbating'), and 'Lady Cab Driver', in which every sexual thrust is a chance to work out his aggression: 'This is for why I wasn't born like my brother handsome and tall.' Although the album reaped three hit singles and got him on to MTV with 'Little Red Corvette', it was also his most experimental, with three songs of over eight minutes' duration. Jon Bream called the album 'pornographic pandering. This intractable little guy needs a collaborator, a trusting friend, or just a little whisper from his Friend above to control his genius.'

'He was trying to become as mainstream as possible, without compromising,' says Matt Fink.

'*1999* amounts to me being in the third grade musically,' Prince told Steve Ivory, editor of *Black Beat*, years later. 'That's where I was then, and I had to grow musically from where I was before it to make it. I had to push aside *1999* to get where I am now. It's called growth. You wanna hear stuff like *1999* again, then listen to *1999*. I'm someplace else now.'

NME writer Barney Hoskyns tagged along with the 'Triple Threat' tour, headlined by Prince and The Revolution, supported by Vanity 6 and The Time. Jill Jones sang backing vocals for Vanity 6 from behind a curtain. Prince wore purple on stage for the first time, and had almost mutated into his look for *Purple Rain* (he had a shirt and a pair of trousers on). He has never explained his predilection for that colour, which he still wears today, on and off duty. All the videos for the singles were tapes of live performances shot during rehearsals. He wasn't being cheap; he was saving any form of narrative story for something much, much bigger.

When the entourage retired to a restaurant one evening, Hoskyns expected a big, happy, multiracial party. 'Rash assumption,' he recalled in *Mojo* magazine. 'Only when everybody is settled and ready to order does Prince, engulfed in the shadow of his giant bearded bodyguard, Chick Huntsberry, enter the restaurant, gliding silently past the row of booths and making his way over to the other side of the room – about as far away from his band members, protégés, crew and manager as is physically possible.'

Not only was it not exactly a party, there was dissension in the ranks. Jam and Lewis had begun collaborating on material they felt wouldn't be used in The Time, and had started flying to LA on weekends. They were caught in a freak snowstorm in Atlanta, where they had been working with the SOS Band, and failed to make a concert in Texas. Jill Jones stood in for Jam, while Jerome Benton, who acted as a valet in The Time's act, mimed to the guitar played offstage by Prince. Jam and Lewis fulfilled their tour commitments, but when the song they produced for Klymaxx, 'Just Be Good To Me', was a hit, they were out. 'We were fired,' says Lewis, 'because we were doing things outside the group. It wasn't something Morris or anybody in the group wanted. It was done without people's knowledge.' Prince says he didn't fire them; he merely told Morris Day what he would do if it was his band.

Local boy Paul Peterson, who resembled a young David Cassidy, was a new recruit, replacing Monte Moir on keyboards. Peterson comes from a very musical family: his late father was an organist, his mother is a jazz singer and pianist. His brother, Ricky, is a pianist; they now have their own producing/songwriting studio in Minneapolis. 'How I got to be in The Time is a mystery to me. I was still in high school when I got the call to audition,' says Peterson, now raising a family in his home town. 'Bobby Z's cousin is my sister's husband – it's a very incestuous musical community here – so everyone knew I was up and coming. I went in and did the audition. Jesse Johnson was running the show, he gave his approval and then Prince came in and said, "Yeah." Jesse Johnson is known as the Howard Hughes of funk now, you know. We don't see much of him around town any more. I see Jerome and Morris on and off. I play with Jellybean every Thursday night.'

Jellybean Johnson left, but returned to work on the *Purple Rain* film, and the next Time album. Even the ousted Jimmy Jam and Terry Lewis – now two of the most successful producers in the business with their Flyte Tyme label, which has reinvented not only Janet Jackson but gospel, with Sounds of Blackness – still live in Minneapolis and hang out with the old crew. 'We all got together in June 1996 for a benefit concert,' says Jimmy Jam, 'and just the other week, on Terry's birthday, we had a party over at his house and just jammed like the old days. Prince didn't show, [although] he was invited.'

In 1983 Prince cancelled his concerts at the Hammersmith Odeon and the Dominion in London without giving a reason, but he probably wanted to cash in on his continued success in America. *Newsweek* said that the tour made brilliant theatrical sense. 'A razzle-dazzle riot of erotic funk, featuring a band that includes black punks, a white boy in a green surgical gown and Lisa Coleman, a woman who writhes around her keyboard in slinky underwear and raincoat. He pantomimes making love, he hands out money to the crowd, which is 80 per cent black. He leaps before a lighted cross and raises his arms – a silly poseur, a pious martyr.'

He made the cover of *Rolling Stone* that year for the first time: he was photographed with Vanity, who has her hand down his pants, by Richard Avedon. The cover line was 'Prince's Hot Rock'. The magazine, who named him rock artist of 1982, had paid $10,000 to hire Avedon for the picture, on the condition that Prince be interviewed. Prince did the picture, but refused to talk.

But perhaps the most important new recruit to the posse was Wendy Melvoin, replacing Dez Dickerson, who had left to form his own band, Modernaires. (He would later turn to Christianity, sell his guitar through Prince's fanzine and go to live in Nashville.) Wendy, the daughter of jazz keyboardist Michael Melvoin, had grown up with Lisa Coleman in Los Angeles. She was just out of high school and an accomplished jazz guitarist, but had never played professionally before.

'Lisa and my father played together, we went to the same schools, we even had the same dentist,' says Wendy. 'Our families intertwined – there were three kids to each side, all similar in age. Lisa brought me in to the band totally.'

'Wendy had been around, coming to see me, so she already knew Prince,' says Lisa.

Wendy's live debut was at a benefit concert at First Avenue, a converted greyhound stadium in downtown Minneapolis. Prince premiered six brand-new songs. He hired a rock video director, Chuck Statler, to film him in concert and fooling around in his bedroom, because he wanted to try something. They used so much electricity they repeatedly plunged Chanhassen into darkness. Prince and the film crew were warned they would be disconnected if they blew the fuses again. That 16mm movie was never released. But the world was about to go crazy.

4

When U get it baby
nothing comes 2 hard

'I've never released an official live album. The bootlegs – some of these guys are making more off my music than I am,' Prince says today. 'I understand a fan's need: I wanted every note James Brown ever sung. But a live album is such a definitive statement. I will play my old stuff again, maybe "When Doves Cry" will sound right for once. Sometimes I get a better idea for a song, but it's already recorded.'

When Prince first finished recording 'When Doves Cry', it was much more conventional. He wasn't happy. He completely remixed it, stripping out all the bass. 'Prince took Bobby Z and me for a ride to hear this song. We thought the album was finished,' says Matt Fink. 'I didn't like it one bit.'

'A black song without a bass? You gotta be crazy,' the people at Warner told him. It gave him his biggest hit so far. 'He came in, cut it and mixed it in a day,' says Peggy McCreary, one of the two engineers who worked on *Purple Rain*. 'He was listening to it playing back, and just popped the bass out.'

'When I first joined Prince back in the days of *Dirty Mind*, he was already talking about his ideas for what would be *Purple Rain*,' says Lisa

Coleman. 'The album came together during rehearsals. Wendy and I both influenced "When Doves Cry".'

The music for *Purple Rain* was written in the last six months of 1983, and was the closest Prince would ever get to a live album. In August he gave the crowd at First Avenue a preview of the songs at a benefit for the Minnesota Dance Theater. He hadn't intended to use the live performances on the record, but decided to after listening to the playback. The last three songs on the album, 'I Would Die 4 U', 'Baby I'm A Star' and 'Purple Rain', came from that concert, captured on a mobile recording unit. 'It was very hot and humid,' recalls Alan Leeds. 'Prince took to the stage like a boxer to the ring. "Purple Rain" brought the house down. That's the version on the album. Thank God we got it on tape.'

The album was much more than a soundtrack for his new movie, and was the first to be a truly collaborative effort. 'The band really came together when Wendy Melvoin joined,' says drummer Bobby Z. 'Computer Blue' was written with Wendy, Lisa and Matt Fink. Lisa's brother, David, played strings on three songs, and Prince's father also received a composing credit. In the movie, during the scene where the fictional father tells his son that he, a truly great musician, never had to write his music down, the actor is actually playing one of John Nelson's own compositions.

The technicians working on the album also played a large part in its conception. Gone were the days when Prince could produce at home in Uptown. The complexity of the music he was making gave him the idea of building his own state-of-the-art studio complex. First, though, he had to make some serious money. (He was already a generous employer; those on his payroll that year got a bonus three times their annual salary. But all employees had to sign a document saying they wouldn't talk about their boss, unless with special permission.)

'I was a maintenance technician,' says Susan Rogers, 'and in 1983 I heard that Prince was looking for a technician, so I thought, I'm getting that job. I was a huge Prince fan. They interviewed me, said you'll be fine, and the first thing they had me do was to get Prince's home studio up and running. I let Prince know I was done, that the studio was ready, and he said, "Well, set up the mike, I'm going to record a vocal." I was expecting an engineer to come along, so I asked him, "Who's going to record it?" And he looked at me and said, "You, naturally." So I said, "Oh yeah, right, absolutely." So I started at the top. He had just finished "Darling Nikki" the night before, his equipment was breaking down, the person who used to work for him left, so I filled the shoes.'

'Let's Go Crazy' and 'Computer Blue' were recorded at The Warehouse in Eden Prairie, a Minneapolis suburb. It had been bought by Prince for $450,000, cash. Susan Rogers transformed the cavernous space into a working studio and rehearsal space. She manned the board in Minneapolis; Peggy McCreary did the job at Sunset Sound in California.

'He put the board in the middle of this huge, echoey place,' says Bobby Z. 'That gave all the tracks a live feel.'

'Jazz artists record very clean and tight-sounding,' says longtime collaborator Sheila E. 'Prince doesn't care what it sounds like. It's what you play from here [points to her heart].'

'There was a basic sound during the years I worked for him,' says Rogers. 'He liked the drums, the bass, the vocals a certain way – there were only two microphones he would use for his vocals. The production was his alone, but on the engineering side he was open to new ideas. He would work with other people occasionally, but always in tandem with me. We had a good rapport. There weren't many women engineers, and I think that's why he enjoyed working with Peggy McCreary and me. We broke the mould a little.'

Prince had been jotting down notes for his ideas for a movie during the *1999* tour. 'He had a vision in his mind of the film a year before we started shooting,' says Alan Leeds. 'When the tour finished, Prince called me and offered me a full-time position in Minneapolis. He was rehearsing not only his band but The Time and Vanity 6, writing upcoming albums. They were all taking acting and dancing lessons in preparation for the movie. He desperately needed someone to co-ordinate these movements. It was a bit of a handful.' Leeds had quit school to go on the road with James Brown, that other hard taskmaster. 'I went on to work with Bootsy's Rubber Band, George Clinton, Kool and the Gang, Teddy Pendergrass, Cameo. There were similarities between Prince and James Brown: they were both extremely talented, unique performers at the forefront of their genres in their generation. They had little else in common: they came from different parts of the country, different branches of culture. They were both perfectionists to work for, extremely focused. They both knew how to get the most out of the people around them – a good analogy would be a basketball coach, whose job it is to motivate each player.'

Prince expects miracles from everyone who works with him, and there were never enough hours in the day to meet his numerous deadlines. 'If I didn't get something done quickly enough, Prince would yell, "I'm losing my groove, Peggy!"' recalls Peggy McCreary.

'Prince doesn't make records like other people,' says her husband, David McCreary, also an engineer at Sunset Sound. 'Most people will get a band, cut all their tracks in one week, do overdubs and vocals over the next few months. Then they mix it. Prince will go in, record it, overdub it, sing it and mix it all in one shot. The song never gets off the board. He doesn't leave until it's done. Once, we'd gotten out of the studio at five or six in the morning and he wanted to be back at ten. Sleep is unimportant. He likes coffee. If you ask him to eat, he'll say, "No, it'll make me sleepy."'

'He would do Taja Sevelle's album for eight hours, then his band for eight hours, then go into the studio for six hours,' recalls Craig Rice, who worked with Prince as an agent/manager. 'He'd do this day after day after day.'

'When Prince was recording his vocals, he wanted complete privacy,' says Rogers. He also liked a little atmosphere in the studio. Even back in 1981, recording 'Do Me, Baby', he lit candles and draped soft fabric around the studio. Then he shut everybody out. 'There was a dichotomy between his shy natural persona and his outrageous public persona,' says Rogers. 'So I'd set up a vocal mike right in the control room, set up the tape machine so he had tracks to record on, he'd be all ready to go, and then everyone would leave the room and he would do the vocals by himself. He would come out and get us when he was done.'

It's comforting that Prince might blush while singing some of his more graphic love songs. He says he always prefers to sing in his falsetto because it hurts him to sing with any power in his lower voice. His high-pitched gospel shriek is as far from Michael Jackson's '*Oeeoww*' as Aretha Franklin is from Whitney Houston. There's something about Prince's voice that you feel in the pit of your stomach; he just sounds dirty.

He was also writing songs for the next Vanity 6 album, but there was a little bit of a hiccup when Vanity decided to walk out, not only on the album but with only six weeks to go before shooting started on the film. The official reason was that she wanted a solo career, and she knew that *Purple Rain* would have branded her for ever as just a Prince sidekick. Money was also cited as a reason, but she says now it was because she had been replaced in Prince's affections by his obsession with Susannah. And her personal life was spiralling out of control.

Vanity was replaced, after seven hundred women were auditioned, by Patricia Kotero, who would become Apollonia and take the film role that was a very fictional depiction of Susannah. Now that Prince had the money and the clout, he believed he could make anyone a star – his Midas touch would be enough. But even he couldn't bestow talent where there was none, and the more indulgent signings to his own label – the Carmen Electras of this world – meant that other, serious and very good albums – by Eric Leeds, say – were condemned by association.

'Yeah, the Vanitys and the Apollonias bothered me,' says Matt Fink. 'I thought, Prince, you could be surrounding yourself with and producing extremely talented people, not people who were there for their looks rather than their singing capabilities. The whole band found it annoying, but you had to bite your tongue and let it go. If you voiced your opinion, it usually didn't matter to Prince, and, believe me, I voiced my opinion more than once. He would just say, "Well, somebody's got to be the boss, and I'm him, that's it."'

'He was good at taking people and getting the right look, the right photos,' says Bobby Z. 'All those acts were just another outlet for him to get more music out, he had so many great songs.'

'There is no question that was very frustrating,' says Wendy. 'Prince would take these women who didn't have much of anything apart from the ability to emote a great amount of sexuality. I used to scoff at that – like, what are you wasting your time with this woman for? But then I realised he is not in the business just strictly for the music, no matter what he tells you. He's also in it to entertain. To me that is a mistake – leave entertaining to people like Michael Jackson. Okay, wear your weird clothes and all that kind of jazz, fine. You can be eccentric, but don't make that as important as how fabulous a musician you are.'

'He couldn't squeeze it all into just Prince, even extending it into Prince and The Revolution,' says Lisa. 'He needed other outlets. If he could have been Vanity 6 he would have done it; if he could have been The Time he would have done that. These were ways he could live different lives. His mind is out there, not just on another planet, it's in another galaxy.'

'Prince would put down guidelines for vocals,' says Wendy. 'He did that every time. You had to copy every lick, every breath, every sigh, no question, especially with his ghost bands. They had to follow everything he did, precisely.'

'Apollonia couldn't sing,' says Susan Rogers. 'The day we had to record "Take Me With U", Prince brought her to his house to rehearse. When recording vocals with other singers, there would be just him, as producer and engineer, and the singer, usually sitting in the booth in the dark. I remember thinking, this is gonna be a long night. He coaxed her into being more assertive. He has an incredible talent for recognising strengths and weaknesses. He has marvellous natural leadership, is very good at knowing just how to push you to get the best out of you, and he knew when to stop, in most cases. Singers, musicians, technicians, office people would rise to levels they hadn't thought possible. "Take Me With U" was perfect.'

After *Purple Rain*, Apollonia embarked on a solo career – 'He's married to his music, and no woman can compete with that' – releasing a self-titled album with Warner, which depicted her with ripped jeans on the cover and enlisted the help of eight producers. The album was never released in Britain. She is still acting, mainly bit-parts on TV.

Even though he was shooting his very first movie, Prince also found time to record an album, *The Glamorous Life*, with Sheila E, whom he had met while making his first album. The title track, about an ambitious girl who forsakes love for money, was Prince's little joke about Apollonia, originally intended for the album by Apollonia 6 – the new Vanity 6. She was less than pleased when he gave it to Sheila. (He also withheld 'Manic Monday' from poor old Pat, and gave it to the Bangles.)

Sheila Escovedo grew up in a poor part of Oakland, California. She started playing percussion at the age of five, with her father, Pete Escovedo, who played in a band called the Escovedo Brothers. She took violin lessons, but became more interested in running track and playing football. 'I changed my mind about going to the Olympics and decided to become a musician,' she told journalist Tony Barrell in 1984. 'I quit school and went on the road with my father with Azteca. He would tell me, "You have to play for money, you have to eat and help support the family."

'I came up against a lot of negative things from male drummers – they used to put me down a lot. I went on the road with Marvin Gaye on his last tour, George Duke, Lionel Richie – he wanted me to sing the Diana Ross part in "Endless Love", but I didn't want to. I met Prince because he was a George Duke fan, and he would come see me play. Then I heard from Tom Coster, who used to play keyboards with Santana, about this guy who was really young, who could play all the instruments and write and produce. I didn't know it was Prince until I went to see him play. We've been good friends ever since. When I got off that tour, Prince asked me to come into the studio and do "Erotic City". He thought I should have a solo career.'

The Glamorous Life, her debut album, took five days to record at Sunset Sound. 'It's not true Prince co-produced that album. He was too busy working on *Purple Rain* in Minneapolis while I was in LA recording. He'd call on the phone to see how I was doing, and on the last day he came to listen to it, but there was no time for him to put any parts on it. I have total control over everything I'm doing. Not a lot of artists have that. Prince is one of the few.' (Nonetheless, Prince does give the game away by giving a shout at the beginning of the title track; Sheila's father, Pete, admitted to *Rolling Stone* that everyone knew Prince was on the album, but she didn't want everyone to think she wasn't making it on her own merits.)

'I had heard all kinds of things throughout the years about what working with him was like, but all the negative things are lies,' she says now. 'He's the sweetest, nicest guy you'd ever want to meet. I never wanted to go solo. He makes you feel you can do anything. There are no rules, no limits. He sets you on a pedestal and says, "You can do it." We kept in touch and have been close ever since.' On their duet, 'Erotic City', he sings, 'I just want your creamy thighs.'

The Time made their third album, *Ice Cream Castles*, and this time the group actually managed to play on it ('Prince laid down guide vocals for Morris to follow,' says Susan Rogers). It would be their last album for six years. They were all tired of taking a back seat, and Morris Day had already decamped to California to pursue a solo career – which he achieved with some success, with TV sitcom work and a respectable album, *Daydreaming*, in 1987. By 1997, Day was living in Georgia, still on the road, touring with a new line-up of The Time.

*

Mookie to the Italian-American pizza-lover, Pino: 'Who's your favourite basketball player?'
'Magic Johnson.'
'Who's your favourite movie star?'
'Eddie Murphy.'
'Who's your favourite rock star?'
'Bruce.'

'Prince. You're a Prince fan. All you ever talk is nigger this, nigger that. All your favourite people are so-called niggers.'

'That's different. Magic, Eddie, Prince, they're not niggers. They're not black. I mean they're not really black in that they're more than that. They're different.'

'You know, deep down inside you wish you were black.'

From Spike Lee's *Do the Right Thing*

Just two years after Prince made his first film, *Purple Rain*, Spike Lee made his debut with another ground-breaking, small-budget film that recouped its money many times over: *She's Gotta Have It*. Lee credits Prince's film for paving the way for other black film-makers: that a film centred around a black character could be successful and knock mainstream films such as *Ghostbusters* off the top slot (in 1984, Prince was a bigger star commercially than both Richard Pryor and Eddie Murphy) made the financing not only of Lee's but of other black films much easier.

Prince's management team of Cavallo, Ruffalo and Fargnoli raised a budget of $7 million for the film; Warner Brothers were only brought on board as distributors when the film had finished shooting. Prince would later be one of the many black stars who offered money when Warner threatened to pull the plug on Lee's epic *Malcolm X*.

Prince would jot down ideas for the film in his little purple notebook. A scruffy little pad is never far from his side, whether he is on a stage, on a plane, in bed. Ideas come into his head with such frequency that unless he writes them down he would forget them. Prince also knew that Cavallo, Ruffalo and Fargnoli would bend over backwards to make the movie happen. Their contract with him was about to expire. 'It's simple,' Fargnoli reportedly told Cavallo. 'He wants a movie. If we don't get him a deal with a major studio, he won't stay with us.' They set about hawking their star around the majors. It wasn't easy persuading Hollywood players who had probably never even heard *1999* to part with their greenbacks. Richard Pryor was interested in putting up some cash. The film arm of

Warner were interested, but wanted to see more. Mo Ostin, head of music, who would go on to champion Prince throughout his career, agreed to stump up the cash out of his own pocket so that the production could start. Prince and his management spent $4 million of Ostin's money while they waited for Warner to come on board. The deal, that Warner would come up with the money upon receipt of the negative, wasn't sealed until cast and crew were celebrating at the wrap party.

Back in Minneapolis after the *1999* tour, Prince set about preparing himself and his musicians for their parts in the movie. Actor and director Don Amendolia gave The Revolution, The Time and Vanity 6 acting classes three times a week. William Blinn, then forty-six, who had won an Emmy for his screenplay for *Roots*, one of Prince's all-time favourite TV series, was brought in to write the script, based on conversations with Prince, and on Prince's copious handwritten notes. The only thing Blinn had in common with him apart from *Roots* was an admiration for Debbie Allen, one of the stars of the *Fame* TV series, of which Blinn was executive producer. The script, delivered to Prince in May 1983, was at that stage called *Dreams* (Prince would later tell Blinn he wanted the word 'purple' in the title). It was very dark, with quite a few explicit sex scenes (Wendy and Lisa were portrayed as lovers) and baffling flashbacks. Prince wasn't happy with the story and commissioned a second draft, which was written by Blinn before he returned to LA to continue work on *Fame*.

Rehearsals took three months. Amendolia told the *Minneapolis Star Tribune*, 'Jerome Benton was a hard worker. Morris Day wasn't as interested as some others, but he had natural abilities that the others didn't have. Vanity was lazy. She's so beautiful and she's good – but she didn't like to work hard. Prince was very, very good. He'd flip right out of his persona and be whatever character he had to be. He's very shy, as most actors are to a degree. He took direction well, probably the best. He asked a lot of questions.'

Choreographer John Command was enlisted. 'I was told by Prince to give the cast six years of dance training condensed into six months.'

He found Prince agile, limber, and good in the air. 'He would be able to suspend himself in the air like a ballet dancer.'

Prince's management, meanwhile, were on the lookout for a director. They travelled to LA to see a rough cut of *Reckless*, by a first-time director called James Foley. They offered him the job, but he said he was too busy. He recommended his editor, Albert Magnoli, whom he had known since they'd been at the University of Southern California's film school. Magnoli's only experience as a director was his thesis project, *Jazz*, an affectionate portrayal of jazz musicians in Los Angeles, with an entirely black cast. That short film had won the thirty-year-old Magnoli a student academy award. 'They called me up and told me they had enjoyed my film,' says Magnoli. 'I told them I had just made a deal at Paramount and wasn't available. Bob Cavallo was especially surprised. He said, "Listen, I'm offering you the possibility of getting behind this, and you're telling me you're too busy!"'

Magnoli was persuaded to meet Cavallo at a restaurant on Ventura Boulevard in the valley on a Thursday morning in September at 9 A.M. Magnoli wasn't impressed by the prospect of working with Prince. He had grown up in Connecticut in a very white, middle-class environment. He had gone to a Catholic school. His favourite directors in film school were Bergman, Fellini and Kurosawa. He was interested in music, though, and played the drums in a variety of high-school and college bands. But before that breakfast meeting, the only Prince songs he had ever heard were '1999' and 'Little Red Corvette'. He didn't own a TV, and had never seen MTV. 'I always had an affinity towards trying to understand other cultures. My interest in black culture came out of my appreciation for music, particularly jazz. So the prospect of working with Prince was a natural progression.'

He had read the Blinn script, but had no intention of either rewriting the story or directing the film. 'Cavallo asked me what kind of story it would be if I was to make a film with Prince. I just started telling him a story off the top of my head, and in that ten minutes I had outlined the concept of *Purple Rain*. The alcoholic father who hid the music, and the idea of the dysfunctional family, the psychology of observing your father hit your mother, and when you are with your back against the wall you lash out and hit the woman you are with, that all emerged from that cafeteria. I don't know where it came from.'

Cavallo put him on a plane on Friday, and he met Prince around midnight. 'We sat down, I pitched him the concept, and the first words out of his mouth were, "You've only known me for ten minutes, yet you tell me basically my story. How is that possible?" I said, "I'm not sure. But if you make a commitment to the emotional underpinnings of this story, you and I can make a movie." He said, "Let's do it."'

Within four weeks, Magnoli was installed in a Minneapolis hotel room, writing the script. He sat with Prince, Morris Day and Vanity, and talked about their backgrounds. Prince would play the Kid, a struggling local musician whose rival in love and on stage was Morris Day. Magnoli also immersed himself in the films of Bob Fosse, studying his editing techniques, his ability to bring dance to the screen. 'He made live performance emotional, erotic, sensual. I was able to realise how I could do the concert sequences for *Purple Rain*.'

The script took four weeks, and he finished it while flying back to LA to finish editing *Reckless*. On 11 September, he was back in Minneapolis. Pre-production started on 15 September. The script was still being revised: on 10 October, the Kid's parents were dead; by 14 October they had both survived the end of the movie. Vanity had by now left the cast and Prince wanted someone as physically similar to her as possible. Patricia Kotero says his first words to her were, 'Do you believe in God?' and 'Are you hungry?' She replied yes to both questions. She also fit the costumes and was a quick learner. Magnoli is unsure how much of Blinn's script survived, although both shared the writing credits; he thinks perhaps two or three of Blinn's scenes are in the final cut.

Shooting started on 1 November: not the best time of year to make a movie, with many scenes shot outside for the sake of economy. 'The day before we began shooting, there was eighteen feet of snow and the weather plunged thirty below zero,' Magnoli recalls.

'When Apollonia dived naked into the water, it was twenty degrees outside.'

The schedule was ten weeks, and some final scenes had to be shot in LA because the weather deteriorated even further. Prince couldn't resist popping into Sunset Sound to work on the Apollonia 6 album, and on three extra songs for the film: 'The Beautiful Ones', 'When Doves Cry' and 'Take Me With U'.

'"The Beautiful Ones" was his favourite song,' says Susan Rogers. It was the first song he ever wrote for Susannah Melvoin, Wendy's twin sister and his new girlfriend.

Although the script was fiction, all the inexperienced actors were playing roles not too far from their own characters – largely a result of Magnoli hanging out in the local clubs, eating dinner with them and watching them rehearse on stage at First Avenue, the club where a lot of the movie is set. Hollywood was invading their small town, and Magnoli's main objective was to ensure that the mechanics of filming were as unobtrusive as possible, so that everyone felt comfortable. All the cast and crew were warned: talk to the press and you're fired (Prince's stand-in did just that). Extras were paid $35 for twelve hours mostly spent standing around in the freezing cold.

'There really wasn't any kind of professional atmosphere about the acting,' recalls Wendy Melvoin. 'It wasn't a large stretch. We're not talking about a brilliant thespian film here, it's just a rock 'n' roll movie, no one had to go too far from themselves. The hours were a bit funny for musicians – getting up at 4 A.M. and being on the set at 5 A.M. at minus thirty. That was the tough part.'

'Our hope was that the film would become successful,' says Matt Fink. 'I had questions about it. I just didn't think it was there production-wise, but it made it anyway because of the music. They brought in a director fresh out of film school, who had no experience directing a motion picture, and the first-time thing meant I felt it could go either way. It was the attraction of Prince more than the content that made it a success. The plot was a little thin.'

'It's hard to believe it became the biggest rock 'n' roll movie since *A Hard Day's Night*,' says Bobby Z. 'You could sense it was the merging of MTV and a movie and a band. It was a real story, not just a band running around. Prince worked harder on the movie than I've ever seen him do anything. We rehearsed six to eight hours a day anyway, no matter what. It was really tough, but when you're twenty-something and you're making a movie, what else is there to do? We worked Thanksgiving, Christmas, New Year.'

How close to the truth was the depiction of Wendy and Lisa fighting Prince every step of the way to get their compositions heard? They both laugh loudly. 'That wasn't true at all,' says Lisa. 'It was the opposite. We always had ideas and he played them. That part was definitely fiction!'

Another piece of fiction was in the casting. The parents of the Kid were played by the only two professional actors in the cast, the black actor Clarence Williams III, and the Greek actress Olga Kartalos. Prince was portrayed as the offspring of a multiracial marriage partly to appeal to a wider audience, partly to remove the characters from his real mother and father. At the time he was worried that, because the film was so close to his life story – where he hung out, his friends – that his parents would be offended by their portrayal as heavy drinkers, always fighting and damn near killing each other. Making his screen mother white immediately distanced her from his real mother. Prince was on good terms with his father then, and didn't want him to believe his son thought of him as the drunken bully on screen. The casting, though, was perceived as Prince simply trying to cross over, as usual. 'Prince's father didn't have a gun. He didn't swear and beat up his mother, but Prince told me the basic elements of *Purple Rain* came from his life,' says Neal Karlen, who had interviewed him for *Rolling Stone*.

'It was clearly a story about one kind of de-Oedipalisation, the struggle over the social reproduction of patriarchy,' wrote Robert Walser in *Popular Music and Society*. 'His relationships with his father and with several women – his mother, Apollonia, Wendy and Lisa – propel the narrative.' The film contains one of the sexiest scenes in cinema, in which Prince caresses Apollonia before making love to her. (At the premiere, that scene was accompanied by hysterical screaming from the women in the audience.) It is also poignant: when Prince gets undressed, the ample Apollonia mocks his tiny body. The film's most dramatic moments are the scenes of domestic abuse: the Kid soon manifests his father's violent behaviour; his fear is that he will become just like him. He resolves that struggle by collaborating with Wendy and Lisa.

'Never has any black star been so adored and worshipped in a film,' wrote Donald Bogle of Prince's performance in *Toms, Coons, Mulattoes, Mammies & Bucks: An Interpretive History of Blacks in American Films*. 'The only rivals are Otto Preminger's fascination with Dorothy Dandridge in *Carmen Jones* or Berry Gordy's infatuation with Diana Ross in *Mahogany*.'

The premiere was held at Graumann's Chinese Theater in Hollywood. A number of fans won tickets and sat alongside the likes of Eddie Murphy, Steven Spielberg, and Prince's mother. Prince wore a purple trenchcoat and carried a purple flower. A thirty-foot canvas of him outside the cinema was immediately stolen. The party was held at the Palace Theater, with purple balloons, purple streamers, purple napkins. Sheila E played on stage, joined by Prince and The Revolution at 12:20 A.M.

Prince's role, in Bogle's words, was that of the 'tragic mulatto. Not even Lonette McKee's Lila in *The Cotton Club* seemed as tormented and troubled . . . as this poor racially mixed creature . . . He pouts, broods, flirts and struts like a 1950s screen siren: he's a coquette turned daredevil.'

The film took an incredible $7.8 million in three days, eventually grossing over $70 million, ten times what it had cost to make. Newspapers reported that they hadn't witnessed such scenes in a movie theatre since the Beatles' *A Hard Day's Night* twenty years before. 'In the Kid's world, women are there to be worshipped, beaten or humiliated, not necessarily in that order,' wrote Ed Naha in the *New York Post*. (After the scene where Prince tricks Apollonia into jumping into the lake and then speeds off on his motorcycle, instead of belting him one she smiles indulgently.) Prince was compared to both Orson Welles and Marlon Brando by the LA *Herald Examiner*.

'Filmed in the jazzily manic, staccato style favoured by every rock documentary since *Woodstock*. At the centre is the small, slight, nervous figure of Prince himself,' said the *New York Times*. 'With his mass of carefully tended, black curly locks and his large, dark doe eyes he looks, in repose, like a poster of Liza Minnelli on which someone has lightly smudged a mustache. Astride his motorcycle, the image suggests one of Jim Henson's Muppets. In the depths of depression, pacing back and forth in his dressing-room, he expresses all the pent-up rage of a caged mouse. The only cliché of the rock concert film it doesn't use is the split screen.'

Stills magazine put the film's success down to its astute marketing, but it succeeded despite Prince's insistence it open in the summer, going against advice from Warner that he hold off until the autumn to avoid competing with *Gremlins* and *Ghostbusters*.

The thriving, racially mixed scene portrayed in the film was also something Prince made up – it had little to do with growing up in his home town. In the late 1970s, when he and his friends started going out to clubs in their strange clothes, local thugs would chase them down the street, shouting, 'Faggots!' After the release of the movie, the atmosphere at the local clubs changed overnight.

'When the film came out,' Prince told *Rolling Stone*, 'a lot of tourists started coming to First Avenue. That was kind of weird, to be in the club and get a lot of "Oh! There he is!" I'd be in there thinking, "Wow, this sure is different than it used to be."'

'He knew the *Purple Rain* album was going to be big,' says Susan Rogers. 'He was ecstatic when we finished it.' It *was* big. It was released in June 1984 and spent twenty-four weeks on the top of the *Billboard* album chart, easily outselling Bruce Springsteen's *Born in the USA*. 'Purple Rain' the single was a number one in America, if not in Britain; on the B-side was 'God', a track he recorded in one take. It's pure gospel. You can imagine all those rock fans who had never bought a Prince track before flipping the record on the turntable and going, 'Oh no, not that church music . . .'

'Back in the 1980s, right after *Purple Rain*, Minneapolis was a

Mecca for black music,' says Jimmy Jam. 'That diluted the talent: people would move here from other places and say they were from here just to get a record deal. They didn't last long. So it was good for the area, but bad as well.' Jam and Lewis have launched a new label, having severed their links with A&M, and are now with Universal Records. 'We're gonna recruit local talent, put the town back on the map.' Indeed, local band Mint Condition are enjoying great success, and Prince himself was given a lifetime achievement award in June 1997 at the Minnesota Black Music Awards ceremony.

In the September after the album's release, Prince made the cover of *The Face* in Britain. The cover line was, 'Can Prince Take Michael Jackson's Crown?'. 'The difference of course is that Michael's sexuality is all-American freeze-dried, while Prince is a very dirty boy indeed,' wrote Dave Hill. Oh, how that perception has changed.

Although *Purple Rain* contained only one rather rude line, the one about Nikki in the hotel lobby masturbating with a magazine, such was the music's cross-over success it even reached the ear of Al Gore's wife Tipper, and prompted the introduction of parental guidance stickers.

The propensity of the media to mention Michael Jackson and Prince in the same sentence never failed to irritate Prince, who never felt Jackson to be a threat. Indeed, when Jackson named his son Prince in 1997, he was only deemed crazier than ever. 'I've never heard Prince mention Michael Jackson once,' says close friend Robin Power, sometime backing singer, who would get a bit-part in *Graffiti Bridge*. 'When Jackson signed with Pepsi, Prince was offered Coke but turned it down, even though it was a huge amount of money. He didn't want to be compared with Jackson in any way; he felt he should be compared with Miles [Davis] or [John] Coltrane.'

Jackson's *Victory* album had been eclipsed by *Purple Rain*'s sales. He was 'incredibly jealous' (the words of a friend) of Prince, especially of the Oscar Prince won for the movie, something Jackson longed to win. On a break from the *Victory* tour, he sat in on a Warner screening. How did someone who wore more make-up than he did have such a reputation for being a hot-blooded male? On 4 September 1984, in response to rumours, Jackson gave a press conference denying he took hormones or had had plastic surgery, and insisted that he planned to get married and have a family. Not long after, he invited Prince to his home at Hayvenhurst for dinner with his sisters LaToya and Janet. They exchanged few words, although Prince made several less than subtle passes at LaToya.

What about the rumoured duet between Prince and Michael Jackson on the 'Bad' single? 'The first line of that song is, "Your butt is mine",' says Prince. 'I said, who's singing that to whom? 'Cause you sure ain't singing that to me. Right there we got a problem.'

Prince was getting ready to take *Purple Rain* on the road. Karen Krattinger, a blonde Southern belle from Atlanta, who had been tour manager for the SOS Band and Cameo, was hired as production co-ordinator. She would be the most important woman in Prince's life for the next five years. 'I flew out to LA, working on stage designs, hiring vendors, then went to Minneapolis for rehearsals and building of props, several months before the tour actually started,' she says. 'I was working out of Prince's office at The Warehouse, and I remember someone telling me, don't look at him, don't talk to him. I thought, that's ridiculous. He would walk by me every day three or four times. I started saying, hello, how are you? And he'd say, fine. It was no big deal. Eventually we got out on the road, and I was working in the production office from eight in the morning until 1 A.M. after the shows, and at that time for some reason, our contract rider didn't call for a private phone in Prince's dressing-room, so when Prince wanted to use the phone, Chick [Huntsberry] would come in the office and say, "Everybody leave. Prince wants to use the phone." Then he'd look at me and say, "You can stay." So Prince got comfortable with me, I think because I didn't treat him like he was an oddity.'

When the tour was over, Krattinger was asked by Steve Fargnoli whether she would like to run Prince's company. 'Prince had asked me to sit in on meetings on the road, and I was very conscientious, so I'd take notes. He'd ask about something later and nobody would remember, and I'd say, well we said blah blah blah. I think he liked that.' She flew home to Atlanta, had a week to wrap up her personal

life, and moved to Minneapolis. 'It was really interesting that someone who had the type of success that he had, had no structure to his
company, he didn't have people taking care of the day-to-day stuff
who knew what they were doing. Prince was happy I was there. He
had so many people around him that, if he said he wanted something, they would just jump to it. Then it wouldn't be what he
wanted, and it would get trashed. Every time he'd tell me he wanted
to buy something or try something, I'd say, let me check it out. And
every time I gave him options, he would always choose the most economical, the most reasonable scenario. He was very hard on me and
very demanding, but he always said thank you. Always.'

'Prince ran the *Purple Rain* tour like it was the Marines,' says Eric
Leeds, who joined him on stage for the first time. Prince was by now
resembling a deranged hippie, looking as if he was dressed in his
granny's curtains, with a tasselled lampshade on his head. He had
been guesting at Sheila E's shows, and she would return the favour by
joining him for encores, dragging on Miko Weaver, a musician in her
band.

Although he had changed out of his tights, Prince really couldn't do
anything right in some people's eyes. Robert Hilburn, who in 1996
would say that he couldn't be bothered to get out of bed for him,
wrote in the *Los Angeles Times*: 'The conservative approach sacrificed
much of the challenge and provocation of his earlier performances.'
But Prince could never be that tame. He exposed his pubic hair on
stage in Detroit. And he stripped off on stage to get in that tub from
the video to 'When Doves Cry' That Christmas, 1984, he did what
he set out to do: he sold out five concerts in his home town.

'We could have kept touring with *Purple Rain* for another six
months in America, really milked it,' says Matt Fink. 'We just did a
six-month US tour. We didn't do Europe or Japan or Australia,
because Prince didn't want to go. He said, "I'm tired of the road –
that's it, guys, we're taking two years off." He said we'd be on the payroll, don't worry, you can all do whatever you want. Within three
months we were recording the next album.'

'Prince just couldn't wait to get *Around the World in a Day* out,' says Bobby Z. 'He was fed up with *Purple Rain*. You make the album, you record it, you mix it, you promote it and tour with it – you're sick of the music. It's a tedious process.'

But two bad moves on Prince's part started the roller-coaster of the mainstream press's campaign to have him perceived only as a preening madman rather than an innovative, if rather eccentric, artist. After collecting three American Music Awards in January 1985, he failed to turn up at the recording of the 'We Are The World' charity song in the studio round the corner. He was expected – his name was written on a piece of paper taped to the floor next to Michael Jackson's. The fact that he donated a song and a video to the *USA for Africa* album, '4 The Tears In Your Eyes' (they turned down 'Raspberry Beret'), a beautiful track recorded with just Wendy and Lisa on a tour day-off at the New Orleans Superdome, wasn't enough for the journalists keen to knock him off his frilly pedestal. 'We had talked to people doing *USA for Africa*, and they said it was cool I gave up a song for the album,' he said later. 'It was the best thing for both of us. I'm strongest when I'm surrounded by people I know. I probably would have clammed up with so many great people there. I don't want there to be any hard feelings.' And at the Brit Awards in London, where he picked up Best International Artist and Best Soundtrack, he was ushered to the stage wearing a multicoloured sparkly suit, accessorised with a pink feather boa, by his bodyguard, Chick Huntsberry, who was wearing a white beard and a snarl. The only words Prince uttered during the visit were 'Love God' at the microphone, and 'Show me some respect' as he flounced his way out at the airport. Big Chick might have looked like a monster, but even though he had a $1,000-a-week drug habit and left Prince's employ to kiss and tell the *National Enquirer*, Prince forgave him, kept him on the payroll, and even put a roof over his head (Prince's name remains on the deeds). When Huntsberry died, in 1990, Prince performed a $100-a-head benefit concert for his widow and family.

This was Prince's year for awards: he picked up three Grammys in February and an Oscar, for Best Original Song, in March. This time he was in purple sequins from head to toe and dragged Wendy and Lisa up to the podium. 'God, that's a weird memory,' says Wendy. 'Boy, that is just too weird. We were like these odd gargoyles following him up on stage, it was hysterical. We were like the grim reapers with the outfits we were wearing.'

'I remember feeling like I was on stilts,' says Lisa.

At the podium, taking the statue from Michael Douglas and Kathleen Turner, Prince turned to Wendy and asked innocently, 'Would you hold this?' 'I'd love to,' she replied. She got to take it home.

The whole world now knew about Prince. But, as he told *Rolling Stone* in 1985, 'I wish people would understand that I *always* thought I was bad . . .'

5

I can do whatever I want

So what did the biggest pop star on the planet decide to do next? *Around the World in a Day*. According to Eric Leeds, this was part of Prince's five-year plan. Show the Rolling Stones. Show the Beatles.

First, though, with The Time going their separate ways and with the talents of Susannah Melvoin waiting in the wings, Prince was about to start a Family. 'He wanted to put another group together,' says Paul Peterson. 'I was co-opted from The Time to be the lead singer, but I wasn't leader of the group. With Prince you never really have creative control, and I certainly wasn't making any money.'

Susannah Melvoin was also on vocals, Eric Leeds was on sax, Jerome Benton was a comic foil and Jellybean Johnson was on drums, while Miko Weaver played a funky guitar. The Family's eponymous album was largely ignored by audiences and critics – but then Prince kept his name off the credits; he is only mentioned in Susannah's thank-yous, after God and before Wendy, Lisa and her big brother, Jonathan. It did sound just like a Prince album: he composed every song, told Paul Peterson exactly how to sing the vocals – every lick, every breath, every sigh; no wonder Prince's version of the album's 'Nothing Compares 2 U' (recorded live in 1992 at a Paisley Park party, with Rosie Gaines) was so familiar, and no thanks to Sinéad O'Connor. The Family album also marked the first time Prince collaborated with Clare Fischer, who would subsequently work with him on almost every album. He would send tapes to Fischer and he (it is a he) would add his orchestral arrangements. The strings, and Eric Leeds's jazzy saxophone, were premonitions of Prince's later work. The album is a very obvious Valentine to Susannah – Prince hired Horst, more used to photographing Hollywood legends, to take the cover shot. Prince was starting to be fascinated by movies of the 1920s and 1930s, an interest that would soon be realised in his black and white homage, *Under the Cherry Moon*. The pictures inside the sleeve of *The Family* are mostly taken by Prince himself – Susannah by the lake, Susannah on a swing, Susannah in bed.

'By this time I'd moved to Minneapolis because of my involvement with Prince,' says Eric Leeds. 'I'd met him through my brother on the *1999* tour. I had really been into jazz since I was nine or ten, and what made me want to work with Prince was that he was a fabulously talented performer and player. When I was with him, playing and performing was his priority. It was a good time. The Family was the first big project I was involved with, and after that fell apart I was asked to join his band.'

Peterson's decision to leave The Family spelt the end of the band. 'He would tell me to talk to his managers, his managers would tell me to go blow,' he says. 'It was very difficult in the communications department because at the time he was so huge, and somebody dangled a carrot in front of my nose, and hey, every man has their price. I knew I had a talent and to this day I think I made the right decision. After I left, the others all joined Prince's band.' Prince's attorneys threatened to sue Peterson for $10 million for 'denial of contract', but he says he and Prince are now back on good terms. 'We had a meeting at the beginning of 1996 when he was putting a new band together, and he knows how I play, and we straightened out our differences and decided it would be best if I wasn't in his band. I have a lot of respect for the cat. I call him on the phone. We don't go to the movies, though.'

Peterson played on the 1994 *1-800-NEW-FUNK* album, a compilation of tracks from Paisley Park signings; his brother, Ricky, with whom he produces and records at their mini-studio in Minneapolis, later played on *Emancipation*.

Wendy and Lisa more or less ghost-wrote large portions of *Around the World in a Day* and the next album, *Parade* – they even posed on the cover of *Rolling Stone* with Prince, alongside the cover line 'Prince's women'. 'Wendy keeps a smile on her face. When I sneer, she smiles,' said Prince in 1985. 'It's not premeditated, she just does it. It's a good contrast. Lisa is like my sister. She'll play what the average person won't. She'll press two notes with one finger so the chord is a lot larger. She's into Joni Mitchell, too.'

'*Around the World* was the album we were most involved in,' says Lisa. 'We worked on the string arrangements, different sounds and instruments. My brother, David, and Wendy's brother, Jonathan, were also heavily involved. We called our brothers the original Wendy and Lisa – they were always writing songs together when we were kids – they had all these different bands.' David Coleman had already added strings to 'Take Me With U', 'Baby I'm A Star' and 'Purple Rain'.

'We knew Prince would adore our brothers,' adds Wendy (they often finish each other's sentences).

'We got a demo tape from them one day,' continues Lisa, 'and there was one song on it called "Around The World In A Day". Wendy and I flipped, and played it to Prince. There were a lot of different types of instrument on it, interesting sounds – Arabic music, the oud, cello, finger-cymbals, darbuka.'

The album was quietly political. Take 'Raspberry Beret', the first single to be released on the Paisley Park label (strings courtesy of Lisa), where he talks about his boss not liking his kind, ''cause I'm a bit too leisurely'. The track is also funny in that understated Prince way: 'Built like she was, she had the nerve to ask me if I planned to do her any harm.' The video, in which even his powder-blue shoes are covered in clouds, began with him clearing his throat rather loudly. 'I just did it to be sick, to do something no one else would do,' he told

Rolling Stone. The title track gave a little hint of the music that was to come on the next album.

'The influence wasn't the Beatles,' Prince said of *Around the World in a Day*. 'The psychedelic cover art came about because I thought people were tired of looking at me. I would only want so many pictures of my woman, then I would want the real thing.' His father gets a co-writing credit on the title track and 'The Ladder'. (Gil Scott-Heron's 'The Prisoner' failed to get its props for inspiring the introductory passage of 'Condition Of The Heart'.)

Prince released the album in April 1985, also on the Paisley Park label. It got lacklustre reviews but, on the strength of his *Purple Rain* success, sold nearly four million copies, staying at number one in the American album chart for three weeks. 'The sort of darbuka-and-finger-cymbals nonsense that Hendrix and Brian Jones might have put together stoned out of their minds in the Rif Mountains in 1968,' Richard Williams wrote in *The Face* (well, they'd called Prince the new Michael Jackson only nine months before). '"Raspberry Beret"'s sawing cellos and plodding beat suggest an attempt to remake "Strawberry Fields Forever".' The man said the influence wasn't the Beatles! 'It's subversive,' said *NME*. 'White pop can handle blackness as long as it's stereotypical. "Git down, party, do the funky chicken." On this album, Prince encroaches into the forbidden.'

Prince broke his silence to speak to *Rolling Stone*'s Neal Karlen that September. The cover photograph was a still from the 'Raspberry Beret' video, and very poor quality. Prince was happy with it, though; the cover still hangs, framed, on a wall at Paisley Park. According to Wendy and Lisa, the album achieved exactly the kind of success he wanted. 'We were really young. I'm thirty-two now; I was twenty or twenty-one then and we were like, is this selling millions or not?' says Wendy. 'We didn't really care. We just thought it was selling to the right people.'

'Coming after such a huge success, it was an incredible album to make,' says Lisa. 'We were all really cocky, but to come out with *Around*, which was experimental if self-indulgent, meant we still had enough sensibility, despite all the egos that had been stroked the year before, to try to grow musically, to make a statement.'

'Prince was by now hungry for influences to take him further,' says Wendy. 'So he relied heavily on Lisa and me to guide him in directions he couldn't think of himself. He knew he needed to go somewhere else – he just didn't know where he was going to go. Lisa and I had the audacity, or sheer stupidity, to try certain things, and he loved it.'

Prince wasn't happy with *Parade*. He felt it was rushed and that he could have done better. The music for the album and for his next film project, *Under the Cherry Moon*, was, once again, on a tight schedule, recorded in June and July 1985. He and the cast were needed in France in August to start shooting, and he was still finishing off the score in his hotel room in Paris, where he was ensconced with Jill Jones, Sheila E and Susannah Melvoin for some sightseeing. (The rest of The Revolution line-up – now expanded to include Brown Mark, Miko Weaver, Eric Leeds, as well as Jerome Benton, Wally Safford and Greg Brooks as dancers and backing singers – were later flown to Nice to make the video for 'Girls And Boys'. Atlanta Bliss, a trumpet player, was introduced to the band by Eric Leeds in November.)

'Recording *Parade* was the best period for me,' says Wendy. '*Around the World in a Day* was a very private experience – it was a lot more isolated. Everything about *Parade* worked out so well – it was a great blend of funky, songy, without being psychedelic; it didn't fit into a genre. To me that album spoke individually to Prince's musical abilities. It just didn't sound like anybody else – it was just Prince doing something different. Musically, it reflected him the best.'

'I remember being in LA a lot during that album, at Sunset Sound,' says Lisa. 'Prince would send us masters and we would work on them and send them back. They were skeletons. The melody and the lyrics, maybe a piano part, like "Little Wendy's Parade", which became "Christopher Tracy's Parade". He would send them to us and say, go for it.'

Clare Fischer was again indispensable, the string arrangements this time involving a 67-piece orchestra. Prince's father co-wrote

'Christopher Tracy's Parade' and 'Under The Cherry Moon'. Wendy and Lisa wrote much of the music for 'Mountains' and 'Sometimes It Snows In April'. Jonathan Melvoin also played on the album. Prince's French clothes designer, Marie France, rapped all the foreign bits.

'Prince was incredibly prudish,' remembers Kristin Scott Thomas, who was twenty-six when she landed the part of the female lead in Prince's next cinematic venture, *Under the Cherry Moon*. 'For the nude scene I was going to wear flesh-coloured tights, but they couldn't find any. The producers put me in a ridiculous bodystocking. I asked Prince if I could take my top off and do the scene in just my panties. He was incredibly embarrassed, and said there was no need for me to be naked in front of the crew.'

The film, shot on location in the south of France and at the Victorine Studios in Nice, was a love story, with Prince as Christopher Tracy, a piano-playing gigolo who falls in love with an heiress, played by Scott Thomas. She disobeys her father by falling in love with our hero. Jerome Benton played his sidekick, Tricky. And Prince would even get to direct his own death scene, one of the most self-indulgent and protracted since Brando popped his clogs in *Mutiny on the Bounty*.

Prince had had the idea for the movie while he was on tour with *Purple Rain*. This time, he wanted to play a dramatic role and shoot it in black and white on location in France. Steve Fargnoli insists the location was in the original script, but it was largely chosen because Prince had developed a taste for travel. Before he went to Europe in 1981, and briefly to London in 1984, he had never ventured outside the US. Fargnoli had taken him to Rio to sample the nightlife, and Prince couldn't wait to fly to Paris. He also wanted to be somewhere warm for a change – he certainly didn't want a repeat of the physical rigours of shooting *Purple Rain*. Although filming was scheduled to start in September, he flew over in June.

Becky Johnston, a New Yorker, wrote the script, although she had little screenwriting experience. She sent the first draft to Fargnoli, and was summoned to meet Prince and do a rewrite. The script was approved by Warner, who coughed up $10 million. After the returns on *Purple Rain*, they weren't going to question his judgment too closely. French photographer Jean Baptiste Mondino was first choice as director (he would later shoot Prince naked for the cover of *Lovesexy* and direct the video for 'I Wish U Heaven'), but he was too busy. Instead, Mary Lambert was brought in. She had directed some memorable pop videos, including Madonna's 'Material Girl', a homage to 1950s musicals, but this was to be her first movie. 'I was sitting round the house one day reading scripts I didn't like,' she says, 'when Prince called and asked me to meet him at Pacific Video. I prefer to work with someone who knows what he wants.'

That was certainly the case on this movie. Lambert was soon demoted to an advisory role. Prince was now in charge of an all-European crew, including Michael Barnhaus, who had worked with Rainer Werner Fassbinder, as cinematographer. Prince had originally wanted to cast Susannah Melvoin as the lead, but when it was discovered she couldn't act, she was replaced with Scott Thomas, a British actress living in Paris who had originally auditioned for only a small role. Terence Stamp was slated to play the father, but he was replaced by Steven Berkoff.

Francesca Annis played the older woman who employed Christopher's services. The former Royal Shakespeare Company actress says that Prince would often ask for her advice. 'Sometimes he took it, sometimes he didn't.' She found him quiet, shy, 'a little sweetie'. Scott Thomas says that she never once saw Prince fly off the handle, despite the difficult task he had on his hands: directing a movie with a crew many of whom didn't speak English.

When the film wrapped, Prince filmed the video for 'Girls And Boys', one of the first singles from the new album. Susannah and The Revolution were drafted in – they had all been enjoying a bit of a break watching from the sidelines, sunbathing, sleeping; a real change from the relentless schedule back in the Twin Cities. The album and the score for the film were finished in Minneapolis in December. The film was edited in March, but it was soon apparent that some new scenes had to be shot to make it work. So in April

1986, key cast members returned to France for more filming, and to make a video for 'Mountains' while they were at it.

Under the Cherry Moon won eight Raspberry awards, the alternative Oscars. It only lost one, to Madonna, as Worst Actress for her work in *Shanghai Surprise*. Scott Thomas actually came out of the film rather well – the way she delivers some of the lines, such as 'Don't you have any normal clothes?' and 'My God, he's gone mad' suggests they weren't in the script at all. She went on to enjoy a brilliant career of her own, being nominated for a (real) Oscar in 1997 for *The English Patient*. 'Scott Thomas was completely miscast [in *Cherry Moon*], but then you can't really blame Prince for not being Alfred Hitchcock, the only man who would have been able to understand and exploit her brand of sexiness,' observes Tom Shone, film critic of the *Sunday Times*. The two apparently fell out after the film wrapped – Prince tore up the invitation to her wedding. But they recently made it up over tea in London. He didn't seem to be aware that she was still in the acting business.

'Working on the film was fun – party all the time,' she recalled in *Harper's Bazaar*. 'There were all these limousines and handlers and managers, all kinds of glitzy stuff, but it wasn't my thing, and I was terribly disappointed in myself for not being able to get into it. What was I supposed to do? Sit there like a potted plant?'

The movie opened quietly, and to mostly derisive reviews, in Britain in August. In America, a twenty-year-old hotel worker by the name of Lisa Barber entered an MTV competition to have the premiere held in her home town of Sheridan, Wyoming. She also won the film's star as her date for the evening. She was very quiet and shy, and Prince was the perfect gentleman, driving her to the cinema in his car, putting his arm around her shoulders to guide her to her seat. At the party afterwards, attended by cast members including Scott Thomas, and Prince's long-time idol Joni Mitchell, he refused to let Lisa out of his sight, chatting in her ear, asking her to dance. All the winner could utter were the words, 'It was better-er than I thought it would be.' 'I gotta hot date,' he said as they left the party.

Part of the prize for Lisa Barber's home town was a Prince concert.

Trouble was, there wasn't anywhere to stage it. They ended up taking over the ballroom of the Holiday Inn. Prince refused to go ahead – the sound was going to be terrible. But when he saw the look on Lisa's face, he relented.

'Don't even turn up on the same continent where this is playing,' said *USA Today* of the film. 'However much you love Prince, you'll never love him as much as he loves himself,' said the *New York Daily News*.

'For all those who can't get enough of Prince, *Under the Cherry Moon* may be just the antidote,' wrote Walter Goodman in the *New York Times*. The review also stated that it wasn't so much a homage to B-films as to B-minus ones. 'The script is an adolescent's notion of sophisticated badinage,' it said, and went on to call Prince's character 'a self-caressing twerp'.

The film wasn't quite that bad. A great deal is actually very funny, even if the humour is unintentional. You even get to see Prince's bare feet as he leaps out of his bath to answer the phone. And when he kisses Scott Thomas (to the song 'Kiss') he puts Ralph Fiennes's love scenes with the actress in *The English Patient* in a league with Trevor Howard and Celia Johnson in *Brief Encounter*.

The movie would take only a third of its budget. Prince, though, says he learned from his mistakes. 'I learned that I can't direct what I didn't write.'

Two more tracks for the new album were written after the film wrapped. Released in March 1986, *Parade* went to number three in America, number four in Britain. 'Stunning in its scope, from the stripped-down rhythm and blues of "Kiss" to the trancelike psychedelia of "I Wonder U" and the orchestrated romanticism of "Venus De Milo",' wrote David Toop in the *Sunday Times*. But Jam and Lewis's work on that year's *Control* by Janet Jackson kept Prince off the top of the charts.

The biggest hit from the album – his third American number one – was 'Kiss', recorded in June 1985 and originally intended for local funk group Mazarati, a band David Z and Brown Mark were producing for Paisley Park Records. It was a song so ahead of its time that

Prince had sat on it for ages. It was only added to the album as an afterthought, and to this day he isn't completely happy with it, one reason why it sounds different every time he performs it live. 'I had that song for a long time,' he says. 'Changed it around a lot. Happens all the time.'

Not only was Prince kneeling at the altar of Curtis Mayfield's voice, the drum machine was the offspring of the one used on Sly's 'There's A Riot Going On'. David Toop, this time writing in *The Face*, couldn't believe his ears. '"Kiss" is the best thing anybody could release right now. Bass drum like someone rushing furniture around; Prince singing in a new Curtis Mayfield voice; chicken scratch guitars; wah-wah guitars; snare drum that sounds like it's sitting next to you in the living room. Brilliant.'

The video wasn't bad either. Prince's apology for the male strutting in *Purple Rain* was to cast himself as the half-naked sex object, Wendy Melvoin as the woman who looks like she might tell him to go jump in the lake. The song is grounded on a 12-bar blues progression, yet he slows it down, producing an erotic trance. The video uses mirrored doubling and vaginal imagery, both from women's art of the time. He and the dancer are in high heels. He wears a black, midriff-revealing outfit inspired by flamenco (he also had one run up in pink). His voice trembles with desire. The only deep, male sound, a 'Yeah', comes out of the mouth of the female dancer. He looks askance at this, as surprised as we are. Brilliant.

'That was an interesting time for Prince and me personally,' says Wendy. 'The video was an opportunity for the two of us to experience each other away from everybody else. The two of us would walk into a room together and it seemed very powerful. Making that video, and I'm not trying to toot my own horn at all, I could give two craps about that, but it seemed a powerful combination.'

The video, which won an American Music Award, also marked the start of Prince's collaboration with Rebecca Blake: 'Kiss' was the first video she had ever directed. 'I first met Prince when I was on a shoot photographing Sheila E,' she says. 'He didn't say a lot, but I knew he was watching me. A month later I got a phone call. They gave me the music and I envisioned what the film would be – I made drawings, wrote a treatment and gave it to him. We had a conversation on the phone about it – it was mysterious and humorous at the same time. On the shoot, his performance was so extraordinary, his ability to take direction on a moment's notice. Prince didn't want a choreographer, but eventually he came around. I had a rapport, because I was a woman. It was magical, metaphysical, he knew me.'

Blake would go on to direct videos for the *Diamonds and Pearls* album, and says they plan to make a movie together one day. She had been Prince's first choice to shoot the video for 'The Most Beautiful Girl In The World' in 1994. 'I had already staged and made plans for it to be an enormous production,' she says, 'but we were caught in the middle of the Los Angeles earthquake and the whole project, on which we had worked so hard, was literally blown to pieces. The one he ended up making, where different women are watching themselves achieving their dreams, was pretty hurried and off the cuff.'

'The time leading up to the release of *Parade* was a time when Prince was interested in seeing where he could go artistically,' recalls Eric Leeds. 'After *Purple Rain*, he decided, okay, I've done that. We spent a lot of time out in LA, where we were doing the bulk of our recording. He was growing as a composer, getting involved with Miles Davis. We were doing a lot of spontaneous stuff, particularly with Sheila E. It was the closest we ever got to a jazz concept. Most of that music was never released, was never meant to be released, but it laid the groundwork for *Parade*, *Sign o' the Times*, *Lovesexy*.'

As part of that movement towards jazz, Prince attended sessions for Davis's *Tutu* album, and recorded a track for it. He had written to Davis, saying, 'You gotta hang out with me and Sheila E, 'cause a lot of people have to find out who you are.' He signed it 'God'. That cracked Miles up. 'When we sent him the tape and he heard what was on there, he didn't think his tune fit,' wrote Davis in his autobiography. 'Prince has high musical standards, like me. So, he just pulled his song meant for the album until we can do something else at a later date. Prince also records for Warner, and it was through people over there that I first found out that he loved my music and considered me one of his musical heroes. I was happy and honoured that he looked at me in that way.'

'The *Parade* tour was the high point. Lots of other musicians who were with him over the years say the same thing,' says Eric Leeds. 'It was the most performance-oriented tour we ever did – we just came out and played music.'

The tour began in March 1986, the same month the album was released, and Prince looked his happiest, throwing grins bigger than he was in the direction of Susannah, who was sharing the microphone with her sister. The event was less a rock extravaganza, more a stripped-down soul revue, with Prince the leader of an eleven-piece band decked out in a succession of primary-coloured zoot suits.

'By the time the music was played live it was bigger than life and everybody was involved musically – the train just fit perfectly together,' says Wendy.

'We really all looked forward to the club gigs after the shows,' says Eric Leeds. 'That was when we could be spontaneous: it was the antithesis of what we were doing on the concert tour. I was in the band as Prince's instrumental foil; Cat, in the next tour, would be his dance foil – he always likes someone to bounce off. Prince was interested in taking advantage of my jazz background, the improvisation. While he has never claimed to be a jazz musician, he listens to a lot of jazz. That was the feeling he wanted to put across on that tour.'

Prince finally came to Europe, reaching London in August, beginning a long and affectionate relationship with British audiences. Celebrities fought to get into the after-show party at the Kensington Roof Gardens, where Prince took the opportunity to get down on the drums.

At the end of the tour, he decided to disband The Revolution. Said Brown Mark, ousted as bass player: 'He wanted to go back to funky things, back to where he started. I didn't need to go back – I wanted to go forward. If he was going to do something new, I'd be there.'

Prince had become so reliant on Wendy and Lisa that he fired them halfway through recording his next album, *Dream Factory*, which was never finished. One much-bootlegged track from those sessions, 'Power Fantastic', would eventually surface on his greatest-hits compilation in 1993: 'At one of the first sessions in his sprawling new house, separation gained a whole new meaning when Lisa Coleman found herself playing the grand piano in the upstairs living room while the rest of the band huddled into the crowded basement studio,' wrote Alan Leeds on the compilation's liner notes. 'Connected only by mikes and earphones, The Revolution still managed to pull off the exquisite song in a single take – even the jazzy intro that Prince suggested just as tape was ready to roll.' Without any credits on the bootleg version, the incredible horns were initially attributed to Miles Davis. They were in fact by the hugely talented Atlanta Bliss, who, along with his Pittsburgh music school collaborator Eric Leeds, comprised the Paisley Horns. When Bliss was plain old Matt Blistan, he and Leeds played in various jazz-rock bands in the early 1980s. They both moved to Atlanta in 1983 (hence the name) and when Prince needed a trumpet player, Leeds suggested his old friend. Bliss joined the band during the last days of the recording of *Parade*.

The *Dream Factory* sessions did provide a handful of tracks that made it on to his next album, *Sign o' the Times*: 'Starfish And Coffee' (co-written by Susannah) and 'Play In The Sunshine'. 'Strange Relationship', a track Wendy and Lisa say they had a major part in composing, also made it.

'The last show we did with him was at Yokohama Stadium,' says Wendy. 'We did "Sometimes It Snows In April" as an encore. It was heartbreaking. We had been having problems during the tour leading up to his disbanding The Revolution. Lisa and I knew psychically there was something wrong. He was treating us differently, he was doing a lot of avoiding. So it wasn't a real big surprise when he invited us over to dinner and gave each one of us pink slips. You're never really prepared for something like that, but if it hadn't happened, I couldn't imagine where Lisa and I would be right now. When you're working with Prince you have to go to the limits of your abilities twenty-four hours a day, and it's exhausting – the only people who can survive that kind of schedule aren't terribly stable. It's easy for someone to dictate rules and regulations when you're not a very stable person. If you have a certain amount of stability, that schedule is impossible, it will break you. We're better off not being part of that.'

'He told us he wanted to go back to recording the way he used to,' says Lisa. 'It was painful to listen to *Sign o' the Times* and hear something we'd worked so hard on and not feel a part of it.'

'Not only not feel a part of it, he didn't put our name on the record!' adds Wendy.

Prince's music was never quite the same after they left, after just four years. 'I felt we all needed to grow, we all needed to play a wide range of music with different types of people . . . No band can do everything,' he told *Rolling Stone* in 1990. 'For instance, this band [the New Power Generation], this band I'm with now is funky. I just keep switching gears on them, and something else funky will happen. I couldn't do that with The Revolution. They were a different kind of funky, more electronic and cold.'

'Wendy and Lisa were close to Prince, but they had a major fight with him in the fall of 1986, and he said goodbye,' says Matt Fink. 'He let Bobby [Z] go because he wanted to bring Sheila E into the group. Prince gave me the option to leave or stay, and when I stayed, Bobby wasn't upset with me, because he would have done the same thing. Lisa and Wendy were a little bit resentful of me. I tried to stay in touch with them. They worked with Bobby on their first solo record, then during the *Lovesexy* tour they came to the party at Paisley Park, but I haven't seen them since. I tried very hard to get hold of Wendy last summer [1996] when she lost her brother, because I knew him very well, but Bobby said they're not ready to talk to anybody. I called them in January, but they won't return my calls. I'm a little disappointed.' Jonathan Melvoin, as well as contributing to Prince's music, had played briefly with The Time before joining the Smashing Pumpkins on keyboards. He died aged thirty-four of a heroin overdose.

'I'd been with Prince eleven years,' says Bobby Z, whom Prince had long described as his best friend. 'I knew Sheila wanted to take the job, and what a great replacement! It wasn't like I was replaced by somebody who did what I did. I was replaced by somebody who was one of a kind, one of the five best drummers in the world. It was like splitting up after a marriage; some days Prince and I were close, other days it was Wendy and Prince. There are many great memories – Prince was as much a part of the fun as anyone. I met Ringo Starr many years ago; I met a Beatle, so I guess I'm okay.'

Bobby Z went on to produce an album for Boy George, as well as working with Wendy and Lisa, whom he still sees when he is in LA. His Minneapolis-based company has most recently produced the debut album by Anna Voog. Neither Matt Fink nor Bobby Z kept in contact with Andre Cymone – after a seven-year relationship, he married Jody Watley, formerly of Shalamar, in 1991; they divorced in 1995. He is now based in Los Angeles, but frequently pops back home to Minneapolis to visit his mother, Bernadette. In 1996 he got together with Paul Peterson with the idea of forming a band, but that didn't materialise.

Levi Seacer had been in Sheila E's band before she joined Prince, along with the musicians who would eventually become Tony Toni Toné. He played on her second album, *Romance 1600*. He came from the Bay Area of San Francisco, like Sheila, and started out playing in his grandmother's band in church – both his grandparents were preachers. When Sheila joined up with Prince, she took Boni Boyer, a singer and keyboard-player, with her. 'Prince said to me, "What are you going to do now, Levi?" I was feeling a bit left out. But when Brown Mark left, he invited me to join the band. I became his band leader, and I was with him for years. He became more and more involved in the business side: he'd go off to LA for two weeks, and I would carry on and rehearse the band. *Lovesexy*, particularly the tour, is the best memory for me of my time with Prince. I learned so much. He's the most incredible musician I've ever worked with.'

After Wendy and Lisa left, relations between them and Prince deteriorated. 'I still hear a lot of hurt from them, and that bothers me,' Prince said. 'I don't know what they are so hurt about. I wish I did, but I don't.'

'Prince was very close to both of us, like a brother–sister thing,' says Wendy. 'It was difficult when he fired us because we'd seen him let go of a lot of people, and he was very good at, once you're out, not maintaining the friendship. You don't maintain anything. Prince thinks memories aren't healthy, so when we were let go we knew we were *really* out. It was like, "Don't mention their names around here, I'm trying to forget them." Over the years it has been difficult to try to reconcile that kind of childish attitude. We would work with him again, but the circumstances would have to be completely different.'

Wendy and Lisa went on to record three albums, two with Susan Rogers, before they were dropped first by Columbia and then by Virgin. They were with the independent label ZTT for a while – an album recorded during that time is still sitting idle in the vaults. They have since contributed their not inconsiderable talents to albums by Joni Mitchell, Me'shell Ndegéocello, Nona Gaye and Seal, and have composed two film scores, for *Dangerous Minds* and *Soul Food*, a film financed by the most successful R&B composer of all time, Kenneth 'Babyface' Edmonds. 'Lisa and I have been masterminding putting a band together of very powerful women, and we searched Me'shell out for that. It will happen; none of us has had the time to do it yet. We don't want huge success, we don't want someone to say, "Oh, that was the year they competed with Alanis Morissette."'

'We want to make another album together, just us. We're always writing, but we're looking for a record deal,' says Lisa. 'We come up with ideas, titles, everything but a deal.' Prince dedicated *Emancipation*'s 'In This Bed I Scream' to them, perhaps feeling a little guilty: 'How do we ever lose each other's sound? . . . A thousand times I feel whatever I put U through.'

'He asked us to work on that track, you know,' says Wendy. 'Then he never called back. To be with Prince during that time was incredible. It was too bad, there was no controlling the relationship – like Lisa says, it was his card. If he wanted it he could have it; if he didn't it was gone. Lisa and I aren't two-year-olds, we're adults. The ball's in his court.'

ó

All sisters like it when
U lick 'em on the knees

I ask Prince if he always wears make-up. 'On a normal day, I'm clean,'
he says, meaning when he isn't doing interviews, making a video,
rehearsing, or in the studio – meaning no, never, he always gets out of
bed and draws the liner across his eyelid, the mascara wand across those
limousine lashes. His taste in clothes, such as the canary-yellow
crocheted jumpsuit he wore to the MTV Awards one year, which
incorporated a cut-out for his buttocks to peep through, has tempted
many to label him as some kind of freaky cross-dresser. 'Hey, whatever floats the boat,' he says when challenged about his sexual
orientation. Self-parody is perhaps the most important ingredient of
his success: every time he comes out with a dirty lyric or an outrageous outfit, he is, in a way, poking fun at his own creation. 'One
minute he's the drooling, hip-pumping, sex-crazed deviant, the next
he's ethereal in white diaphanous lace,' observed Andrew Graham-
Dixon in *Vogue*. 'His genius is inseparable from his schizophrenia.
His gender-bending has never called into question his heterosexual
orientation, perhaps because it is so obviously narcissistic – acting
female is merely a way of playing out his own fantasies, becoming the
object of his own sexual desire. Visually, he's a contradiction: the

dandy whose bare, hirsute chest suggests an animal lurking under the surface of all this refinement.'

'Prince is a ladies' man in the classic tradition, he likes women, likes to shop with women,' says Vernon Reid. Prince insists he wears high heels because women like them, but they immediately make him more feminine – less of a threat, more of a confidant.

'I really did think Prince was gay when I first met him,' says Denise Smith, née Matthews, who very nearly went by the name of Vagina until Prince changed his mind and opted for Vanity. 'I didn't know who Prince was. I'd been in Japan working and didn't know he was famous and a brilliant musician, so I wasn't attracted to any of that. Then we went out and I realised he was definitely *not* gay.'

She first met Prince in 1982 at a party after the American Music Awards in Los Angeles. She was a year younger than Prince, was of Scottish and Eurasian descent, and had grown up in Niagara. She had already enjoyed a certain notoriety of her own – after working as a model in Toronto, she made a film in Montreal, a soft-porn effort called *Tanya's Island* in which she wrestled with a gorilla – before moving to look for work in New York.

'At the party, Prince sent someone over to talk to me. He took my number and gave it to Prince, who called me the next day. He came to pick me up that night in a white limo and we went out to dinner. He was with Morris Day – I had insisted on a double date because I didn't know if I could trust Prince. Then we began to see one another. He asked me to come out and see him on the road. We began our little affair. And I became Vanity.'

As a child, she says she was 'very abused back then'. Her family were Hispanic and very poor, and after her father died when she was fifteen she decided she was going to be rich and famous. 'The only thing I wouldn't do was sleep with someone to get what I wanted. I fell in love with Prince because of who he was. He told me he was going to make me a star, so I moved to Minneapolis to live with him. I remember looking the word "vanity" up in the dictionary. It said, worthless, lack of real value, trivial, pointless. Oh yes, I was learning to love myself! I was told, it's wonderful, just get out there, take off all your clothes and run around naked and people will love you and give you money. Prince was really young then too, but he still thinks the same way today. He's still the rude boy but he's trying to turn it into a spiritual thing. When I look back at Vanity, I just think, oh, you poor thing.'

She is talking at her home outside San Francisco. She is out of breath, sweating, having just completed several miles on her treadmill. You recognise the beautiful face that stared out from behind Prince on the cover of *Rolling Stone* in 1983, her hand reaching inside his trousers. Yet only two and a half years ago, she had been told she would be dead in weeks. 'I'm three years sober on 26 March 1997,' she says. 'I had been smoking cocaine for twelve years, on and off, and I ended up in hospital with kidney failure. I had already lost one kidney because of my drug abuse, and I had been on dialysis for the remaining kidney for two and a half years. I went blind and lost my hearing – I didn't know if I was going to see again. When it's dark for six months you don't think it's going to come back. I had a stroke. I was bleeding internally. My blood pressure was 250 over 190. I prayed to God, don't let me die. When I was Vanity, I pictured that I would die somewhere strung out on drugs without anybody knowing.'

She says that she took drugs the entire time she was with Prince. 'I did it on the sly, but nobody tried to stop me. There were a few of us in the band who were doing that. Prince couldn't help me. How could he say anything to me? "Well, I don't think you should be Vanity any more." I mean, come on!'

Her ability to function normally deteriorated during the *1999* tour, when Vanity 6 and The Time supported Prince. 'Nobody seems to remark on how peculiar it is,' wrote Barney Hoskyns, recalling the tour in *Mojo,* 'that Vanity, supposedly enjoying pride of place between the little chap's sheets, actually has her own bed in a separate bus and scarcely exchanges a word with him through the three days I'm on the tour.'

She says she was jealous of Prince being with other women, and was unable to control her drug-taking. She was tired of the constant rehearsing and travelling from venue to venue. Her exit three weeks before filming started on *Purple Rain* was explained at the time by her ambition to pursue an acting career on her own merit, and also a dispute over money. The truth, though, was that she wasn't physically able to make it through the punishing shooting schedule. Cast members had to be on set at 5 A.M. (Vanity struggled to get out of bed at 5 P.M.). They also had to look good on camera.

'I left for me – it wasn't about Prince,' she says now. 'He was upset. Yes, I really do believe he loved me. We were very alike – we even looked alike. But I wasn't making any money. I wrote the lyrics for "Nasty Girl" – I never got paid for any of that. Who cares! I'm glad for the road that I took. I might never have known God.' Her performance on that track is on the 1996 compilation Prince put together for Spike Lee's film *Girl 6*. The credit reads, 'Written by Vanity.' She says she never got a cent.

After leaving Prince, she got a few acting parts – *Action Jackson*, *Miami Vice* – and a short-lived deal with Geffen Records. She married LA Raiders football star Anthony Smith, from whom she is now separated. She is now a preacher, and travels all over America spreading the word of God and warning about the dangers of drugs. She spoke in Washington on Martin Luther King Day, and attended President Clinton's inauguration in 1997.

'The hospital said, pray God gives you a kidney that matches you so well, we're not allowed to give it to anybody else. I said, "How often does that happen?" They said it would be like winning the lottery. I was about to die, and they said I could be on the waiting list for four years. I was six weeks on the transplant list when they told me, "You've won the lottery!"'

She says she once wanted fame and fortune and love at any cost. When she left Prince, she felt she had lost all of those things. Did he try to contact her, help her out? 'It got to the stage where I wouldn't answer my mail, I certainly wouldn't answer the phone, I stopped paying bills. The only reason I needed electricity was to pop a rock in the microwave and zap it. All my life I wanted out of pain. An album couldn't fix it, a film couldn't fix it, sex couldn't fix it.'

*

'I fell in love with Prince when I was thirteen years old. He was just this attractive guy with a light complexion,' says Robin Power. 'I never slept with him, but with Prince there's always the possibility it could go the other way. He has a temper. We disagreed over a song and he didn't talk to me for a month. I saw him every single day and he would look past me like I was never born. One day he called and said, "Do you want to come to the studio? We'll pretend we just met so I won't be mad at you any more." I have been defending Prince since I was thirteen. You see him with the most beautiful women in the world and you ask, is he gay? He adores women. When we go to a club a man would talk to him and he'd have nothing to say. With a woman, it's "How you doing?" His dad always has a beautiful woman on each arm as well.'

Prince will cite his father leaving his mother, and the fact that he didn't get on with his stepfather, as reasons why he loves to be around women. He says he had a girlfriend when he was eleven, and that his first love was a white girl but her parents didn't approve of him. He says that being small didn't call into question his ability to get dates in high school. 'It questioned my ability to shoot hoops, though.' He does admit that he found it hard to keep a relationship going for very long. 'I was insecure and I'd attack anybody. I couldn't keep a girl-friend for two weeks. We'd argue about anything.'

Oprah Winfrey asked him if his sexually provocative songs meant he was just really into sex. 'We have this image of you behind purple doors just kind of having sex,' she told him. 'Oh, my goodness,' was his only reply, and he actually blushed.

'Prince's whole issue with white women was about marking his transgression,' says bell hooks. 'Prince wasn't about staying within boundaries of male/female, black/white, but within the strange boundaries of freakishness. I identify him as a black artist who wants to be self-defining and decolonised.'

The politics of slavery denied black men the freedom to act as 'men'. Slave narratives describe men who longed to assume patriarchal responsibility. 'Given this aspiration and the ongoing brute physical labour of black men it is amazing that stereotypes of black men as lazy and shiftless became common,' wrote hooks in her book *Black Looks*. 'In the early nineteenth- and twentieth-century representations, black men were cartoon-like creatures only interested in a good time, an effective way for white racists to erase the significance of black male labour from public consciousness. These same stereotypes were evoked as reasons to deny black men jobs. They are still evoked today. Many black women who endured white supremacist patriarchal domination did not want to be dominated by black men.'

Black men have been constructed and mythologised, according to the author and cultural critic Michael Eric Dyson, as 'peripatetic phalluses with unrequited desire for their denied object – white women'. Writes bell hooks: 'As the story goes, this desire is not based on longing for sexual pleasure. It is a story of revenge, rape as the weapon by which black men, the dominated, reverse their circumstance, regain power over white men.' Who can forget the words of former Black Panther Eldridge Cleaver in his autobiography, *Soul on Ice*, on the need to 'redeem my conquered manhood' by raping black women as practice for the eventual rape of white women?

Prince has refused to fit the mould of the black man as ultra-macho loverman – perhaps one reason he has been so loved by black women, even if he didn't seem to love them back. 'I saw him on the *Dirty Mind* tour, and as a black woman he was the kind of guy you're not supposed to touch,' says Robin Power.

'In songs like "Strange Relationship", Prince reflects on the contradictions built into dominant narratives about gender,' wrote Robert Walser in an essay for *Popular Music and Society*. 'In other songs, "U Got The Look", "Darling Nikki", he sometimes succumbed to patriarchal structures of pleasure. Deconstructing gender boundaries and liberating desire do not automatically lead to better lives for real men and women. Michael Jackson is the perfect example: though he has seemingly slipped the moorings of sexual and racial identity, his songs are filled with misogyny and gynophobia.'

Prince is threatening, mostly to men, not because he is explicit but because his work is so outside the norm. He invites men to imagine a different way of relating to women, and invites women to imagine men who could imagine such things.

After Vanity, his next serious relationship was with the Californian, all-American valley girl Susannah Melvoin. She was barely twenty when they met. The love affair would inspire him to compose some of the most moving songs ever written – their entire relationship is mapped out in his music, from infatuation, desire, pursuit, conquest, to heartbreak and loss. But band members and studio technicians who had to watch the affair played out before them each day say that Prince was compelled to create torment and drama. How else would he know they loved each other? Those close to him say he never quite got her out of his hair.

'I'm a twin, so it's very difficult for me to be any distance from Susannah for any length of time,' says her sister, Wendy. 'So when I joined Prince's band, Susannah would visit me in Minneapolis, and that's when Prince met her. As a matter of fact, he met her at a party at Dez Dickerson's house – the guy I replaced in the band. Remember that, Lisa? We were like, oh my God, Prince is outside with Susannah!'

Susannah was almost identical to Wendy, with curly light blonde hair. She was curvy, statuesque, but a departure from Prince's usual type of Latin American Barbie doll. She came from a stable middle-class home. She was educated and articulate. She argued back and he wasn't used to that. He wasn't able to manipulate or dominate her in the way he could Vanity or Apollonia. He told everyone she was the love of his life, and everyone thought they would get married. He even bought her an engagement ring.

'Prince had a very tumultuous relationship with my sister, and he would take that to work with him. It was the beginning of the end,' says Wendy.

'It was hard. We couldn't take sides,' says Lisa. 'Prince was trying to draw the lines all the time. He's still like that: this is my friend, this is my employee, this is my family. He'll have his brother working for him, then he's not working for him and they're not speaking. The lines were always shifting.'

'They were very blurry, depending on the day,' says Wendy.

'One day he'd want you to be his confidante, he'd say, "Oh, I'm in so much pain, she's doing me wrong," and the next day it's none of your business, you're not involved in my private life, stand over there and play your instrument,' says Lisa. 'It was always coming from him – he'd feel we were failing him and we thought, it's your design, buddy, where do you want me to stand?'

'Lisa would be bold enough to say, that sounds like shit,' says Wendy. 'She'd do that more than anyone – she would just go right up to him, absolutely fearless.'

Did the enormous fame of *Purple Rain* change him, make him always want his own way, harder to live with?

'Prince had changed before *Purple Rain*: there was something inside him, a horribleness,' says Lisa.

'The devil inside,' adds Wendy. 'All Lisa had to do was give him a hairy eyeball and he'd respond to her. She was much better at that than I was.'

'Prince used to say I laughed in the face of danger,' says Lisa, 'because I would laugh at him and he'd be evil. I'm like, you're kidding me, that's not going to work.'

But Prince respected Wendy and Lisa as musicians, as friends. He likes to work with women – not only as band members but as engineers, video directors, musical arrangers, photographers, personal assistants. And he seemed to respect the women he wasn't sleeping with more than the ones who found him irresistible.

'I didn't want to have a sexually intimate relationship with the guy, so it was very different for me,' says Wendy. 'I don't know whether or not he respects people because they don't screw him.'

'Prince is the most gorgeous man I've ever seen,' says Karen Krattinger. 'Everyone would ask me, is he a fag? I'm like, "No! He's all man."' Even though Krattinger was never involved with Prince, he liked the fact that she was at his beck and call, and became jealous and demanding if she was ever unavailable. 'There were occasions, maybe because there wasn't anyone else he felt he could call, when he would phone me at three or four in the morning and say, Karen, you gotta come hear this song I just wrote. And I'd run over to his house – it was really special. This may sound arrogant, but in those days I felt like he was the prince and I was the queen. He did tell me one time that he loved me – he knew I was particularly angry at him that day. I was completely immersed in every aspect of his life – it was like I was one of his women. I did things above and beyond the call of duty, because I cared about him. He was very dominant and possessive of me. I met a man in Switzerland, we got engaged, and I started taking a little more time off. I told Prince I was going to Switzerland for a week and he would just have a fit.'

He once again used the 'I can make you a star' pickup line on Susannah, and created The Family so that he could keep her close, write her songs. He wrote all but one of the tracks on their one and only album, including the instrumental 'Susannah's Pajamas', and his unabashed declaration of love, 'Nothing Compares 2 U'. He directed the video for their single, 'Screams Of Passion'. When that group dis-integrated, he incorporated her in his band as a backing singer. Her photograph adorns the sleeve of the 'Kiss' single; most people thought it was Wendy. She watched him shoot *Under the Cherry Moon* – and endured seeing him grope co-star Kristin Scott Thomas. But Scott Thomas wasn't really his type – far too brittle and bony.

The atmosphere on stage during the *Parade* tour made the audi-ence feel like several thousand mothers-in-law at a honeymoon. Their affair undoubtedly inspired 'Strange Relationship' and 'If I Was Your Girlfriend' on *Sign o' the Times*. (Susannah also sings back-ing vocals on that album, on 'Play In The Sunshine' and 'Starfish And Coffee', for example; her credit went on the liner notes, even if Wendy and Lisa were pointedly left off.) 'If I Was Your Girlfriend' was his desperate plea to Susannah that he would be different, he'd stop seeing other women, he'd be like a sister to her, if only she would have him back. 'Being a twin, she's very close to Wendy,' says Susan Rogers, who engineered that track. 'It was a way of asking, "Why can't I have the closeness you have with your sister? Why can't we be friends too?"'

'Looking back on it, it was an impossible situation,' recalls Wendy.

'It was impossible for her as well. Their pain and love produced some amazing songs, no question about it, but he was nasty. Horrible.'

'Prince bought some land, a little over 200 acres, in Chanhassen, and I helped him renovate the house,' recalls Karen Krattinger. 'He put me in charge of decorating Paisley Park, which was just being built. At that time, Prince was engaged to Susannah, and she and I were very close friends, still are. I was real surprised when Prince got married – I didn't see him as the marrying kind. I just thought Susannah was so wonderful. When we first heard "Forever In My Life", which turned up on *Sign o' the Times*, with the line about a man getting tired of fooling around and wanting to settle down, I said, "Susannah, that's got to be about you." That's my favourite song. There was no engagement party – it was never official – but he gave her a beautiful ring. We all thought they'd get married. Susannah and I were doing up his house together, and we stayed there while Prince was away – he had rented a house in LA and flown to Paris. He phoned and told her he had changed his mind. It was devastating for her – he just told her it was over. I knew I had to be careful because I loved her so much, but I worked for him.'

'I still keep in touch with Susannah,' says Paul Peterson. 'We were great buddies. The last time I saw her was in September 1996, when I flew to New York for the memorial service for her and Wendy's brother.'

Although Susannah would never work with Prince again, she is still singing, and was on tour at the end of 1996 as a backing singer with Seal.

'I'm sick of being asked whether I had a relationship with Prince,' said Sheena Easton, talking to Lucy O'Brien in her history of women in music, *She Bop*. 'I think it's a sexist attitude, assuming that if a man and a woman work together they can't have a friendship and mutual respect.'

Prince did work with a lot of women, but if he wrote you a song, he wasn't necessarily telling you he wanted to get busy. If he had slept with every woman he has been linked with by the press, he would never have got any work done, let alone produced two or three albums a year. When Rosie Gaines joined his band, despite the fact she was a happily married woman, she was immediately called 'his new girlfriend'. The same happened when he worked with nineteen-year-old Nona Gaye, daughter of Marvin. The same thing happened when Cathy Glover, alias Cat, joined the band prior to the *Sign o' the Times* tour in 1987.

'Cat was about twenty when I first met her in Chicago,' says the journalist Tony Mitchell. 'We discovered we were both big Prince fans. She was dancing in black clubs – a street dancer, tall and willowy. I introduced her to another dancer, Toni Basil, and they worked together on a video album. Cat went to LA, was seen by Prince and flown to Minneapolis. She was "his new girlfriend", although she never was. She was very close to him, and he was very fond of her. Still is.'

The first Prince single Cat bought was 'Soft And Wet'. She was fifteen and she was hooked. She saw *Purple Rain* over and over again. She wanted to be just like Jennifer Beals in *Flashdance*. She moved to LA and won *Star Search*, a TV talent show, seven out of eight times, with her partner, Pat – they were Pat 'n' Cat. 'I used to try to look like Prince. I wanted to be like him. He's different, he's funny. He's *so* beautiful,' she gushed when I interviewed her in 1989. She had just come off the *Lovesexy* tour and was about to embark on her solo career. 'Prince only goes out with people he wants to know for life, meaning his bodyguard or me or his dad.'

Cat first met Prince in a club called Dingbats in LA. He asked her to dance. His manager, Steve Fargnoli, who had known Cat in Chicago, introduced her to Vanity 6. Her first job was to choreograph their stage act – no easy task, as Vanity immediately saw Cat as a rival. Cat told Fargnoli she wanted to dance with Prince. She was told to be patient. A few years later she was still dancing in the front row at his shows, and when the tour came to LA she made a beeline for Tramps. She knew he'd turn up. They danced to 'Addicted To Love', and she was glad she wore her flat pumps – she's 5ft 7in. Prince asked her to audition, and she flew to Minneapolis on New Year's Eve. For the first rehearsal she wore a tu-tu dress. He was in polka dots. 'That's a whole lotta dress,' he told her. 'That's a whole lotta polka dots,' she replied. She made her debut on the cover of the 7- and 12-inch singles of 'Sign O' The Times' and on the inner sleeve of the album. Her name wasn't listed on the credits. But her first real job was to choreograph the *Sign o' the Times* shows and videos – Prince must have thought she was good.

Prince was shy with Cat for about five months. And then she wouldn't go over to his house – 'I was afraid of doing something stupid' – but eventually relented and went round to play pool. He'd tell her not to eat so much. She told him off when he was grumpy. The customised denim jacket worn during his live performance of 'The Cross' was her handiwork – she got bored while nursing a torn ligament in Stockholm (the tour was tough on everyone – Sheila E fractured her elbow but still carried on playing). He put a TV and a video in Cat's hospital room. 'Prince brought all my shy parts into the open,' she said. 'I was like a child on stage – I was one of the fans, so I knew what they wanted. I *was* that person.' Cat, and her bone-shuddering body shake, were indeed very popular with the fans – she would sign autographs tirelessly, reply to their letters and even phone them up. They wouldn't believe it was her on the end of the line.

'When Prince split with Fargnoli after *Lovesexy*, Cat had to take sides,' says Tony Mitchell. 'She had seen what happened when you stay a Prince girl. Do I stay with Prince and be in his shadow? Her solo album was distributed through Warner, but Fargnoli as her manager signed her to his own label. She was very fond of Steve.'

Cat turned to British producer Tim Simenon, of Bomb the Bass fame, and all quirky tracks with a Princely feel were ironed out to produce a bland, housey sound. The first and only single, 'Catwoman', bombed; the album, *I Am Energy*, was never released, despite huge publicity on account of her Prince connection – she was even photographed by Snowdon for the *Sunday Times Magazine*. Prior to the shoot in a West London studio, the titled photographer ('Is he really related to the royal family?' Cat asked) professed not to have heard of either Cat or Prince. Cat locked herself in the dressing room with her make-up artist for hours, only peeking out to yell over the tape of her music (Snowdon was by now looking for earplugs), 'Do you like my music?' She eventually emerged in a short skirt, stilettos ('I can wear heels all the time now') and those stay-up white leggings from *Lovesexy*. 'They're the type worn by basketball players. They're Prince's favourite thing. You can't buy them this long – he had them specially made.'

She was clearly missing her mentor. 'We keep in touch. I send him tapes and he offers advice. He offered to produce the album but it wouldn't have worked out. He keeps telling everyone, "She's gonna have a *lotta* hits, a lotta hits."'

'Cat spent a lot of her own money on that album,' says Tony Mitchell. 'Thousands of pounds. I remember meeting up with her and she was looking for a place in London. I said, "How much are you willing to pay?" She said, about £300 a week. I thought, she's not got any income to speak of – she's living off what she earned on her Prince tour. How long is her money going to last?'

When she parted company first with Warner and then with Fargnoli, Cat went back to dancing in clubs – at Prince's Glam Slam nightclub in LA, until it closed down. She then moved back home to Chicago. She would choreograph the odd performance for Prince, such as 'The Beautiful Experience', a TV special for the album *The Gold Experience*. As she talked to me in 1989 she twisted a *Batman* ring around her finger. It had been given to her by the film's star, Jack Nicholson, whom she had met when visiting the set with Prince. She was already well aware what Prince was giving one of the other cast members.

'Last time I spoke to Cat,' says Prince, 'she walked up to Mayte and me and said to us, "I like you two dancing together, but she'll never be what I was with you." The *very* last time we spoke,' he laughs.

Prince flew to London to visit the set of *Batman* at Pinewood Studios. He couldn't decide whether or not to record the soundtrack, despite the fact that the director, Tim Burton, and Nicholson were begging him to do it, and the 1960s TV show had been his favourite programme as a kid. What changed his mind? The part of Vicki Vale was being played by Kim Basinger, the star of *9½ Weeks* – one of Prince's all-time favourite movies, along with *Barbarella*. Basinger was older than him by five years, blonde, already a star in her own right. Back in America, they were soon having a romantic dinner together at the Chaya Brasserie in Hollywood, and both covered their faces when they were spotted by a photographer.

Basinger wasn't a singer, but Prince still enlisted her talents (several moans and squeals) on 'The Scandalous Sex Suite', a 12-inch single, and promised to make an album with her. Cleaners who went into the studio at Paisley Park the morning after the 'Scandalous' session were confronted with the task of cleaning honey off the console.

Basinger was already married, to make-up artist Ron Britton. She paid him £5 million for a quick divorce so that she could marry Prince. She moved to Minneapolis to be with him, and the couple were seen around the city, now very open about their relationship – causing the residents of the town she planned to buy, Baselton in Georgia, to lodge a complaint, saying that she was an unsuitable owner because of her involvement with somebody they likened to the Antichrist. She even changed her management company, hiring instead Albert Magnoli, who was by then handling Prince's affairs.

But Prince and Basinger's relationship was tempestuous and only lasted six months. She reportedly discovered him with another woman. Her older brother, Mick, even told a tabloid that he had to fly to Minneapolis to almost kidnap her to get her away from Prince, who, he said, had begun driving her around Minneapolis at great speed and through red traffic lights, with some strange kind of death wish.

Basinger and Prince hadn't only been experimenting with Gales honey and getting traffic violations. They had written a script that would eventually (after a heavy rewrite) become his sequel to *Purple Rain – Graffiti Bridge*. Basinger pulled out at the last minute when she realised he wasn't about to stay faithful, let alone marry her. When they split up, he banned all members of his staff from mentioning her name. 'She's a sore subject round here,' said Craig Rice, co-producer of *Graffiti Bridge* and facility director at Paisley Park.

On stage soon after the break-up, Prince joked into the microphone that he had given up dating blondes. 'I really don't know her that well,' he told *Rolling Stone* when asked about their relationship. 'I never publicise [who I'm dating]. My friends around town are surprised when I introduce them to someone I'm seeing.'

Still, he must have had some feelings for her. When she was sued for pulling out of the film *Boxing Helena*, he offered to help with the bill of nearly $10 million. There is no denying how deeply upset he was at being dumped. Basinger left Minneapolis in such a hurry, she left her car parked at Paisley Park. Prince called the police and had it towed.

Prince may not have had relationships with all the women he has worked with, been linked with or pursued. And the introverted, shy, workaholic musical genius, even if he says he never had any trouble getting dates, could never have dreamed that he would have a relationship with a real-life movie sex symbol whom he considered the very ideal of blonde, prom-queen beauty (four hundred years of conditioning is indeed a powerful thing). But in America, if fame gets you anything, it gets you women. And by 1992, he also found it hard to believe that any woman would turn him down.

The second convention of Prince fans held in Minneapolis attracted a lot of attention. Local TV stations and MTV covered the events – concerts at Glam Slam, trips to Paisley Park. Prince made sure he had an itinerary of the events and would put in an appearance at every one, giving fans ample opportunity to see him.

'He took a shine to one young fan on the trip. She was a very pretty young girl from England, a lovely person,' says Eileen Murton, president of the Controversy fan club and organiser of the convention. 'She said Prince had been phoning her at the hotel. He told her he wanted to photograph her.'

The girl, by now almost hysterical with excitement, told Murton that Prince wanted her to go over to Paisley Park to meet him. 'She'd already phoned her mother, who said it would be okay for her to meet him as long as I went along as chaperone,' says Murton. 'What a choice: make a fan's dream come true or possibly make a superstar tetchy. But I felt responsible for her. Everyone was travelling home that afternoon, so we were caught in a deadline, but we drove out to Paisley and waited in the reception area. As Prince approached, he phoned ahead and was told that someone was with the young girl and that she had a flight to catch. He instructed the receptionist to send the girl out to his car. Prince was driving his little yellow sports car and there was no way I was about to ask if I could hang on to the roof to chaperone anybody, so I just stayed in the reception area and prayed that all would work out well.'

Shortly after getting in his car, the girl told Prince, 'I came with Eileen.' Prince simply replied, 'Eileen Murton?' and she confirmed. He then took her on a short spin before delivering her back to reception and driving off, his wheels spinning on the gravel.

Another close encounter came in June 1997, when the *Minneapolis Star Tribune*'s Cheryl Johnson bumped into Prince as he was driving his sports car. He recognised her and pulled over on the road between his house and Paisley Park. Winding down his tinted windows, he leaned out and called her 'Billy' – a reference to the song he wrote about her, 'Billy Jack Bitch', on *The Gold Experience* album: 'What distortion could U let your pen forget 2day?' – and also said she was 'his worst enemy'. When asked why she didn't like him, Johnson said she didn't like the way he behaved, and wondered why he wasn't more 'normal', like Jimmy Jam or Terry Lewis. 'I thought you hated me because you were an old girlfriend,' he replied. Johnson took off her sunglasses and told him, look, I'm not exactly Apollonia or Mayte. 'It's what's inside,' Prince said, tapping his chest.

Mayte Garcia, of course, was the woman one of the most famous bachelors in the world eventually married. Like his other former lovers, she inspired his songwriting: in her case, 'If I Love U 2Nite' (in Spanish) and 'Latino Barbie Doll'. She also inspired a line on 'Peach' – 'She was dark, she was tan, she made me wanna be a man' – and almost all of the thirty-six songs on *Emancipation*.

'I was with Prince the day he met Mayte,' says Rosie Gaines. 'She was a child when she met him, and she took on a lot. Prince was never happy with just one woman. Mayte was very patient. She has calmed him down a lot. She's good for him.'

'I think it's wonderful Prince married – it's wonderful he's in love,' says Denise Matthews. 'I saw what happened to him as a child, and that's an ugly, depressing thing for someone to go through. I just hope she is not involved in his lifestyle.'

'I don't think it is just fame that has created what's going on with him,' says Wendy Melvoin. 'I don't think he feels very good, that's all I'm going to say – I think there's something going on. I think the older he gets with the less help, the worse he'll get – and that's very old, nothing to do with his fame. Except the more money he has or whatever, the fame only allows him more isolation. I truly believe he loves Mayte, I really do – he's not one to fake love. He's a very sensitive and feeling person, but I don't know if he realises it's not going to cure every ill he has. As a matter of fact, the longer you're married the more your ghosts come up, so I'll be interested to see what happens after ten years of marriage.'

Prince and Mayte are talking on the eve of their first wedding anniversary, having lost their first child. 'She was either my sister, or we were the same person or something in another life,' Prince says. 'There's a closeness that you know is right and you don't argue with.'

Do you run into your old girlfriends? 'Very seldom.' What's your relationship with them? 'None.'

Will it be for ever?

'Yes, it will be for ever,' says Mayte.

Come midnight in LA's Culver City, Prince and Mayte seemed closer than ever after all the months of grief, strain and media intrusion in their lives. They had just come from the Image Awards ceremony at the Pasadena Clinic, where Prince had been given a Key of Life award by Stevie Wonder, and were on their way to the Smashbox studios for a photo shoot with Patrick Demarchelier for the May 1997 issue of *Harper's Bazaar*. Prince had planned on bringing a lot of clothes and accessories with him, but his luggage had been lost between Minneapolis and LA – though as it was purple, it is hard to see how it went astray. He had let the stylist, Alison Edmond, know that he was interested in British avant-garde designers, so she had lined up lots of John Galliano.

'Prince and Mayte would choose an outfit, then both disappear to the loo to try them on,' she says. 'You could hear them giggling like a couple of kids. They were completely at ease with each other – Mayte was very calm, very beautiful with a great body, not too thin or over-worked-out. She had definitely got her figure back after the baby. Prince fitted the women's sample sizes perfectly; I put him in men's Gucci but had to gather it up at the back for the photo. He had a big necklace on that made an outfit look too messy. I thought, shall I dare to ask him to take it off? But he was cool; he said, "Of course." I finally managed to persuade him into a red and white leather Galliano jumpsuit, but Mayte laughed so much he took it off. They were really conservative, which surprised me. I put Mayte in a sheer dress, but Prince asked me to sew a body inside it. He didn't want her nipples to show.'

The shoot went on until four in the morning, but husband and wife were still giggling as they disappeared together into the cold LA night.

7

The dream we all dream of

'"If I Was Your Girlfriend" was an accident on my part,' says Susan Rogers. 'Prince wanted to do his vocals alone as usual, so I set him up with his mike and left the room, and I just inadvertently had something switched the wrong way that day and when I came back in and heard the finished vocal, I thought, oh no! It was so distorted. I thought, he's going to kill me. He never said a word. He had this attitude, well, maybe that was meant to be. He was good about those things.'

The song is so detailed and so observant, trying so hard to please ('Baby can I dress U, I mean help U pick out your clothes before we go out, I ain't saying you're helpless . . .') and so touching that it revealed a new and complex side to Prince, the lyricist. He sobs. He begs. Most women can't believe a man would be able to say those things. ('Listen, for U naked I would dance a ballet, would that get U off? Then tell me what will.')

'I encouraged him to release it as a single. I'd never heard a man say that before, [it was] wonderful, a good thing to say, a good thing to put out there,' says Rogers. 'There was a very different atmosphere when we started making *Sign o' the Times*,' she continues.

'Prince was going through the transition of the break-up of The Revolution, the incorporation of Sheila and some of her former band members, the break-up of his relationship with Susannah Melvoin, which was a pretty long relationship for him, and it was the beginning of a serious dispute with Warner Brothers. He wanted to release a triple album, *Crystal Ball*, and they flatly refused. He was someone who had sold millions of records and he wasn't prepared to have his label say, "You can't do this." So he was coming up against a lot of barriers. During that time he was particularly courteous of the people who were still with him. I was still there, Alan and Eric Leeds. He was appreciative.'

It would be almost ten years before Prince would realise his dream of releasing a triple album. *Crystal Ball* contained some tracks from an earlier project, under the name of Camille, which had got as far as a test pressing and a catalogue number and was planned to be released in January 1987. Camille tracks would surface over the years – one, 'Shockadelica', was the B-side to 'If I Was Your Girlfriend'. *Crystal Ball* was mastered, complete with a twelve-minute title track, before being shelved by Warner. At the company's behest, it was trimmed to a double album and a new title track added – a stunning song, even more amazing when you learn that it was written, recorded and mixed in a single day. The double album he would finally release, *Sign o' the Times*, contained tracks from both aborted projects. Other left-over songs would eventually surface – 'Joy In Repetition' on *Graffiti Bridge*, for example. (He not only produced his own material in the last few months of 1986 and the beginning of 1987, he wrote much of his new signing Madhouse's first album, Sheila E's third, and Jill Jones's debut.)

Eric Leeds, Susannah, Wendy and Lisa and Sheila all appear on *Sign o' the Times*, but Prince played or sang nearly everything. 'I co-wrote "It's Gonna Be A Beautiful Night",' says Matt Fink of the track that was recorded live in Paris, with Susannah and Jill Jones on backing vocals, 'and I played on a couple of other songs on the album, but when Prince is pretty much playing everything, when you're left out of the creative process, it's difficult to deal with.'

'There was a refreshing feeling about making his own music unen-cumbered again,' says Alan Leeds. 'I think it showed an artist who had really grown.' With Prince's own studio not quite ready, much of *Sign o' the Times* was recorded at his home and again at Sunset Sound. But he was impatient to christen his Paisley Park complex in Chanhassen (complete with custom-made studio floors – wooden for the piano, concrete for drums), and recorded 'The Ballad Of Dorothy Parker' before his brand-new high-tech console was up and running. 'Prince says he dreamt that song,' says Rogers. 'I noticed there was something wrong: there was no high end at all, half the new console wasn't working. It could have been remixed, but Prince loved it the way it was.'

A chance visit by Sheena Easton, who had popped by in the hope Prince could work on her next album, revived her career in another way. She was asked to do the vocals on 'U Got The Look'. 'Prince didn't feel like socialising,' says Rogers. '"U Got The Look" had gone through a million changes, and he was really struggling. It worked.' (He can't have been that unhappy to see her. He had penned 'Sugar Walls' for her, a thinly disguised homage to her vagina. Easton returned the favour by co-writing 'La La La, He He Hee' as a B-side, featuring the barking of a dog.) The aching 'Adore', sadly never released as a single, was inspired by all the Luther Vandross albums he was listening to at the time – he wanted one of his own tracks to get busy to. That meant Eric Leeds and Atlanta Bliss also had to get busy: they were summoned to the studio in LA to add horns to the song. It was Thanksgiving. 'Prince has seldom behaved as if recording was a job,' says Alan Leeds. 'It was simply what he did – day in, day out.'

The reviews for *Sign o' the Times* were ecstatic – the album wasn't the commercial success of its predecessors (its highest chart position was number six), but it established him as a true 'artist'. If David Bowie had produced an album like this, music critics the world over would have spontaneously combusted. It was likened to the Beatles' *White Album*, and one track was described as a 'Springsteenesque bar-room bop'. *Rolling Stone* called the album his *Exile on Main Street*. Is that an improvement on the Bee Gees?

Prince might have started to write songs about AIDS – one of the first – and gang warfare and how black teenagers smoking marijuana get far stiffer sentences than their white equivalents, but this was also the Daisy Age. *Spin* magazine noted: 'Isn't this man a musician? Five minutes and thirty-four seconds into "Adore": listen to the piano arpeggios, the harpsichord dipping and spinning under the multi-tracked voice of Prince. But who needs musicianship? We want beats.'

For the *Sign o' the Times* European tour, Prince retained some of the old Revolution line-up: Eric Leeds, Miko Weaver, Matt Fink, Atlanta Bliss, Greg Brooks and Wally Safford. Sheila E was now on drums; she had already brought on board her old band members Levi Seacer on bass and Boni Boyer on keyboards and vocals. Despite the fame Boni would enjoy as a full-time member of Prince's band, when she died suddenly of a brain haemorrhage at the end of 1996, her mother appealed to her original fans to send money to help pay for her funeral.

Last but not least came Cathy Glover. 'I can't believe people thought that was Prince,' says Cat of the headless picture on the sleeve of the 12-inch 'Sign O' The Times'. 'You know his legs ain't that big.'

As usual, the home crowd got a sneak preview in a performance at First Avenue in March 1987, on the eve of the album's release. That was about all America was going to get. His most accomplished and commercial show so far only toured Europe, even missing out Britain. He did rehearse here, though, at the Birmingham NEC, staying in nearby Clifford Manor in Warwickshire. He had flown into Gatwick Airport with his entourage, which included his new bodyguard, Gilbert Davison, who would be running Prince's affairs by the end of the decade. The *Sun* gleefully reported that 'Potty' Prince had even brought a woman 'just to do his ironing'. Very unusual for a show with a cast of up to twenty to have a wardrobe mistress. The fact that Prince disguised himself in a beard to go to a pub in Stratford didn't put anyone off the scent. The imposing, ponytailed figure of Davison at his side was a bit of a give-away.

'*Sign o' the Times* changed every night,' says Eric Leeds. 'Everything he does is a work in progress.' Prince used the sell-out 23-date European tour to film footage that would later be a substitute for the real thing in the US and in Britain, where he had been booked to play in the open air at Wembley Stadium and cancelled with a week to go because he feared bad weather. He took the opportunity of Sheena Easton guesting on stage at the Omnisport in Paris to shoot the video for 'U Got The Look'. 'The storyline for that video, the choreography, was all my idea,' says Cat. 'Sheena and I are rivals, and I win out by dragging Prince off by his hair. He got really bruised doing that.' Her work earned her a Grammy nomination.

'Just before he played his three dates at Ahoy stadium in Rotterdam, Prince decided he wanted to film the rest of the tour, including the final concert in Antwerp,' says his sound engineer on the tour, the long-suffering Susan Rogers, who was called in to make it happen. In the end, very little real live footage was used; the sound was good but the quality of the pictures wasn't – the crew had been given only five days' notice. He filmed the bulk of it back home on the newly completed Paisley Park sound stage, again enlisting Albert Magnoli as director. It was premiered in Detroit in October. For once, Prince managed to get the notoriously slow-moving movie industry to keep up with his pace: he persuaded distributors to place the film in thirty cinemas at six weeks' notice, though the process normally takes months.

Photographer Dave Hogan, invited to Minneapolis to shoot the star during the live performance of *Emancipation* in 1996, remembers a time when Prince wasn't quite so co-operative when it came to photo opportunities. 'I was at the *Sign o' the Times* show in Paris, and we'd been told not to take in any cameras. Well, I took my camera out, and immediately a huge hand was on my shoulder. My camera was taken away, but instead of being escorted outside I was taken backstage, out the front into the pit and placed with Duncan Raban, who had also been busted, right at the foot of the stage. Now, for a photographer, being placed within inches of the best pictures you could imagine, but without your camera, is the worst torture you can imagine. I guess that was Prince's idea of a joke.'

Prince did achieve one lifelong ambition that year. At a New Year's Eve benefit for local homeless people at Paisley, attended by John

Nelson and Mattie Baker, he made his jazz-loving parents very proud. He played drums on stage with Miles Davis.

'Prince was pretty overawed,' remembers Eric Leeds. 'Miles was the guy who not only changed my life, he changed Prince's life. There's no other musician you can say that about.' When Davis played at Prince's Glam Slam club in Minneapolis in 1991, not long before he died, he kept urging Prince to join him on stage. Prince, who was watching from the balcony, refused. Perhaps he just wanted Miles to have the spotlight all to himself.

'Prince was stunned by the criticism of *Sign o' the Times*,' says Susan Rogers, 'that he had lost his funkiness, that he was crossing way too far into pop. He wanted to say, wait a minute, check *this* out.'

She says that *The Black Album* was never meant to be a proper release. It was during the recording of *Sign o' the Times* that he decided he wanted to make some music for a birthday party he was throwing for Sheila E. The tracks would be the last Rogers worked on. She is now one of the most respected producers and engineers in the business. 'I gave up a lot to do what I did. It's a hard career for a woman – the hours are so long. I'm forty now, and haven't started a family because I chose to do this. With Prince, music was all there was. We would all hang out together, talking, but you always got the feeling Prince was thinking, I've got them all here anyway, we might as well be working.

'I engineered all of *The Black Album*, except "When 2 Are In Love". The tracks were odds and ends, things we would do on a day off. When he was making an album, sometimes he wanted to break away and do something just to get it out of his system, like "Le Grind" or "Cindy C". So there were tracks he'd record but never intended to release. He got an acetate pressed for the DJ to play for Sheila's party – that was it.'

'Prince showed up with this record one day at rehearsal and said, "Here's a tape, start learning." So I learned the whole thing and we never played it. Ever,' says Matt Fink.

The Black Album did get as far as being given a catalogue number,

WX147, and a release date of 7 December 1987 – Prince had mooted releasing it anonymously as a club record. Fat chance. The general consensus was that he was having second thoughts about the lyrical content of tracks such as 'Rock Hard In A Funky Place'. He stated in a 1991 interview for *USA Today* that he had had a vision of a field with the letters GOD hovering overhead, which prompted him to replace *The Black Album* with the far more spiritual *Lovesexy*. In his notes for the *Lovesexy* tour programme, he wrote: 'Camille set out 2 silence his critics. "No longer daring" – his enemies laughed. "No longer glam, his funk is half-assed . . ." So Camille found a new colour, the colour black . . .'

According to Rogers, though, it was the quality of the tracks that he was unhappy with. Bootleg copies were on the streets almost as soon as Sheila E had blown out her candles, which perhaps accounts for the poor sales of the official version when Warner released it in January 1995, reportedly against Prince's wishes. And the unreleased album still got official reviews. 'His most avant-garde and funky LP to date,' said *Melody Maker*. Prince would later sing the songs 'Superfunky-califragisexy' and 'Bob George' during his *Lovesexy* tour. 'Bob George' is hilarious, his voice slowed down to that of a foul-mouthed hoodlum who berates his girlfriend, played by Cat, for eating TV dinners and dating a creep who manages rock stars, notably Prince, 'that skinny motherfucker with the high voice'.

'Prince called me when *The Black Album* was on the docks waiting to be shipped,' says Karen Krattinger. 'He said, "Karen, we've got to stop this album. It's evil." So I got on the phone to Alan Leeds and Steve Fargnoli and told them, this is what Prince has just said. What are we gonna do?'

'We really were just kidding around,' says Cat. 'He didn't want everyone listening to it.' But the mystique about the record didn't do him any harm, and it seemed made for endless duplication on cassette: the bass just got funkier. The video for 'Alphabet St', the first single off *Lovesexy*, contains a not too subtle message up the side of the screen: 'Don't buy *The Black Album*, I'm sorry.'

*

We very nearly weren't able to buy *Lovesexy*, released in May 1988. The cover shot features Prince wearing only a cross, seated coyly next to the rather aroused stamen of a lily. Some record chains in America, including Wal-mart, refused either to stock it or to display it. Warner actually defended the cover. 'We don't see anything wrong with it,' said its VP of sales, Lou Dennis. 'Prince loves it,' said Karen Krattinger.

The album, which Prince says he made in seven weeks, most of the songs recorded in the order in which they appear, dealt with his loneliness and with his dismay at the black-on-black violence increasingly evident on America's streets. 'How many young brothers must die?' he asks on 'Dance On', his sequel to '1999'. 'His continuing fascination with the female psyche, which surfaces on the single "Alphabet St" and the haunting "Anna Stesia", is most plainly revealed by the cover photograph, where he poses nude with slender, girlie grace,' wrote David Sinclair in *The Times*, in one of the many positive reviews of the album. One of the exceptions was by David Toop, who wrote in the *Sunday Times* that it was 'a turgid collection of inconclusive riffs and weak melodies, decorated to distraction by harsh and flashy ornamentation. His lyrical preoccupations of the moment are fascinating. He shares the growing panic about drug abuse and violent crime in America and his answer, also shared by many Americans, seems to be religious.' Prince was disappointed that *Lovesexy* didn't sell better in the US, reaching only number eleven, which reinforced his decision to concentrate on Europe and the Far East for his live tours. It remains one of the albums he is proudest of. 'People still write to me telling me *Lovesexy* changed their lives,' he says.

A local Minneapolis performance poet, Ingrid Chavez, makes an appearance on the album as 'Spirit child'. Mostly, though, the band in the same one from the *Sign o' the Times* tour, with Cat the most prominent, contributing the rap to 'Alphabet St' ('Prince heard me rap one day and he just freaked out'). Eric Leeds says he contributed the jazz feel, suggesting snatches of Charlie Parker and Duke Ellington in the live show.

Prince was now spending more and more money on his videos, shot on the sound stage at Paisley Park. 'Alphabet St', made from start to finish in one evening on new, high-tech equipment, features his father's old T-bird and Prince batting his long lashes in slow motion. 'I was meant to be in that video,' says Cat, 'but I had the weekend off for a change and went away. When I got back there was a message on my answering machine saying, "Come to Paisley Park, I'm making a video." I was in "I Wish U Heaven", where me, Sheila and Boni had to look very pale and pure. All those parts of the body, the lips, the hand, are all mine. Prince always said that if he was a woman he'd want a body like mine.' (The B-side to that track was the rather less than pure 'Scarlet Pussy'. The lyrics didn't really bear translating, but so many fans were puzzled that he sent *Controversy* magazine a handwritten note headed 'From the desk of Prince', explaining the more baffling ones, and signed with a smiley face that was, in fact, a self-portrait.)

The *Lovesexy* tour was his most ambitious, costing $2 million and boasting an entourage of ninety people. Despite selling out in Europe, he barely broke even, still refusing to be sponsored. The tour kicked off in Paris at the Palais Omnisport, followed by a late-night jam at the Bains Douches, where Prince was joined on stage by Mavis Staples. He would later record tracks for her new Paisley Park album in London. 'We go back to the dressing room and I had no idea this man was shy and bashful,' Staples told Dave Hill. 'He blushed and smiled all the while. I couldn't get a word out of him. His little mind's a genius. You gotta think about the way this child's kickin'. Look at Picasso: one eye up here, one eye down there – don't ask why. See, he's different.'

At last, Prince came to London, and his seven-night run at Wembley Arena and two nights at the Birmingham NEC sold out almost immediately to fans who had only seen *Sign o' the Times* in the cinema and were desperate for the real thing. The show was per-formed in the round, giving those unable to get into his after-show jams some idea of what they were missing. 'Within five minutes we had had simulated sex, simulated oral sex and the star had dragged himself across the stage behind Cat, sniffing her in a manner that would have had the most inquisitive dog expressing reservations,' commented the DJ John Peel. It was named by *Q* magazine as one of the best live shows of all time: 'From the first moment, when a huge pink Cadillac delivered him to the middle of the arena, it was fantastic. He kept changing guitars and costumes and at the start of "Raspberry Beret" he played a complex arpeggio on piano, then paused and crowed, "Sometimes I just frighten myself." A quintessentially Prince moment.'

Polka dots, Prince's favourite fabric pattern at that time, weren't easy to come by, so he had the material specially printed. Months ahead of a tour, contracts are sent out to specialist dry-cleaners in every city on the itinerary, so that each costume can be cleaned overnight. A wardrobe assistant hand-washes the more delicate items every night.

During the tour, which was far more complex than any he had undertaken before, four wardrobe assistants would have special responsibilities for the costume changes of each artist – much in the way that models have dressers who are as quick as mechanics at a Grand Prix pit-stop. For this tour, he drew designs for every costume, as he had always liked to do. For the *1999* tour, he had drawn a design for what Brown Mark would wear (a trenchcoat) down to the precise shade of purple ('Same material as light purple, lavender, baggy suit for Prince,' he wrote), the position of the studs on the lapel and the number of hanging chains.

He is most obsessive, though, about his shoes, handmade since 1990 by Costas Kyriacou, a cobbler whose father owns the City Cobbler in Old Street, London. 'They were having trouble with their shoe-makers in California and brought in some pairs to repair while they were in London on tour,' says Kyriacou. 'I offered to make his shoes. I was sent his measurements, along with drawings of his feet, and we did a fitting in the back of a taxi. They send us the material from his outfits. Prince always has the same heels made. It all starts with the heel; he's very fussy about the heel.' The boots are reinforced with steel to survive high jumps and splits. Prince wasn't satisfied with one candy-striped pair: he sent a ten-page fax with detailed instructions and modifications. If he ever gets short of footwear, he could borrow some of Mayte's – they have the same shoe size.

'For *Lovesexy*, the length of the word that would appear along an arm or a thigh depended on the proportions of the wearer,' said Helen Hiatt, then head of wardrobe. 'He even decides on the size of the buttons on the clothes, and considers the wearer's face symmetry before deciding where the buttons should go.'

The *Lovesexy* tour repaired his relationship with his British fans. He even turned up in polka dots in London's Oxford Street to sign copies of his album. On 25 July, he performed an after-show gig until four in the morning at Camden Palace, duetting with Mica Paris and impersonating Mick Jagger while sharing a microphone with Ronnie Wood. Although Prince would write 'If I Love U 2Nite' for Paris, she wasn't as generous. 'No way am I going to make out with that little man in front of thousands of people' she said.

The real reason for the party was that it was Cat's birthday, and he serenaded her alone on stage before giving her a cake, complete with twenty-six candles and the message 'Happy Birthday Darling'. Then the rest of the band joined him, leaving Cat to watch the show. She spent the entire night leaning over the guard rail, transfixed. 'Did you have a nice birthday, darling?' he asked. 'Yup,' she said, blushing.

After dates in Milan, Oslo, Rotterdam, Copenhagen, Frankfurt, Hamburg and Dortmund, Prince went home. The Met Center, Minneapolis, was only half-full, even though it had been three years since his last major tour. Cat and Sheila tirelessly did TV interviews and press conferences to promote the show, but Prince lost a lot of money and vowed never to tour on a grand scale in America again.

'We'd learn the show and next day he'll change it as if we didn't learn anything and start again,' says Sheila E. 'I think it was one of the best bands he'd had in a while. It was unique, what we had with *Sign o' the Times* and *Lovesexy*.' Prince still found the energy to party at Paisley Park, with Miles Davis, Jam and Lewis, Brown Mark, Jill Jones, Wendy and Lisa and many others. Cat was already on a plane, on her way to London, and out of Prince's life.

*

Prince is seated at his purple piano at Paisley Park. 'I'm gonna do the first tune I ever taught myself to play,' he says. It is the theme to the 1960s TV series *Batman*.

You might think he would have jumped at the chance of writing the soundtrack for the movie, but it took Tim Burton and Jack Nicholson months to persuade him.

'I was called by Mark Canton, president of production at Warner,' says Albert Magnoli, then acting as Prince's manager. 'Bob Cavallo had already had some preliminary conversations about the idea of Prince doing the music, but when I heard about the movie I felt in my heart that Prince was perfect for it. When Mark called, I looked up on my bookshelf and I had all of the *Dark Knight Returns* comic books. That was the image I had in my mind when it came time to shoot the videos for "Batdance" and "Partyman".'

Burton used '1999' and 'Baby, I'm A Star' on set to get the actors in the mood while Prince started writing and recording at the end of 1988, sweetened by a fee of $1 million, plus royalties. Jon Peters, the producer, had had an idea to use both Prince and Michael Jackson on the soundrack – Prince for the dark side, Jackson for the light. Jackson didn't get a visit. In January, Prince and Magnoli flew on Concorde to London at Canton's behest. They watched six scenes being made at Pinewood Studies – 'We just walked around the set,' recalls Magnoli, 'and Prince talked to Tim and Mark, and met Kim. Seeing the sort of movie they were making really decided him.' Said Canton, who had worked on both *Purple Rain* and *Under the Cherry Moon*, 'Prince went berserk.'

Prince had planned to spend the next year at Paisley Park after the long, hard *Lovesexy* tour. He had already recorded tracks for his next planned album, *Graffiti Bridge* – the title track and 'Elephants And Flowers'. But it would have to wait. Warner didn't want a 'Prince' record until Christmas 1989, another reason why he agreed to make the *Batman* soundtrack – it would sell on the back of the movie, and would give him something to do until Warner let him put out *Graffiti Bridge*.

'I think he's confused and a little frustrated over what's been going

1. *Overleaf* A promotional shot for the release of his second album, *Prince*, in 1979.

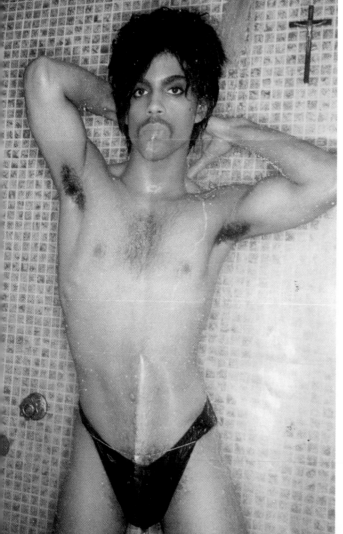

2. *Above* The Nelson family. Prince and Sharon flank their father, John. 'We could be bigger than the Wayans or the Jacksons.'

3. *Left* The infamous shower photo, prior to the release of *Controversy*. He may be crucified by the critics for his dirty mind, but at least he has a clean body.

4. *Above* Andre Cymone, Prince and Dez Dickerson in 1980 during the very first tour. Prince had managed to overcome his initial on-stage shyness.

5. *Right* Vanity on stage during the *1999* tour. 'Prince told me what to wear, how to sing, how to move on stage.'

6. *Opposite* Prince in his own creation: a purple trenchcoat, designed for the release of *1999*.

7. *Above* On the road with *Purple Rain*.

8. *Right* As The Kid, with Apollonia, formerly known as Patricia Kotero, in his 1984 film, *Purple Rain*.

9. Jerome Benton and Morris Day taking time out during the filming of *Purple Rain*.

10. The *Parade* tour: more an old-fashioned soul review than a rock show, with Prince at his best.

11. Prince in *Under the Cherry Moon,* as Christopher Tracy – a character one critic described as a 'self-caressing twerp'.

12. Lisa Coleman (left) and Wendy Melvoin. 'We were young when we were with Prince,' says Lisa. 'And fearless,' adds Wendy.

13. *Opposite* Prince and
Cathy Glover making the
1987 concert film, *Sign o'
the Times*. Audiences at the
live shows in Europe were
instructed to wear only
peach or black.

14. *Above* With drummer
Sheila E, arriving in
London for the *Lovesexy*
tour, 1988. 'She plays
pretty good, for a girl.'

15. *Right* Cathy Glover and
the late Boni Boyer on stage
during the *Lovesexy* tour.

16. *Above* Prince and his manager, Steve Fargnoli, on board the *Lovesexy* tour bus.

17. *Left* Susannah Melvoin on stage. 'Sometimes I trip on how happy we could be.'

18. *Opposite* Carmen Electra, Prince's 'rapping' protégée, who went on to have a career as a centrefold and calendar girl.

19. *Above* Rosie Gaines and the NPG during the recording of *Diamonds and Pearls*. Left to right: Tommy Barbarella, RG, Michael Bland, Kirk Johnson (front), Sonny T, Tony M, Levi Seacer and Damon Dickson.

20. *Right* During the ♀ tour of 1993: 'What's my name?' he asked the baffled audience. 'Mr Nelson!' someone shouted. 'Yes, I suppose it is.'

21. *Opposite* 'If I was a woman, I'd want a body like yours.' These days Prince ensures that Mayte, now his wife, keeps covered up.

22. *Above* Prince and Mayte open the ill-fated NPG shop in Camden in 1994. It closed within two years.

23. *Left* When it all started to go wrong. Prince adopts a red scarf during a visit to London in 1995.

24. *Opposite* Prince pencilled the word 'slave' on his cheek with eyeliner. The public merely thought him barmy.

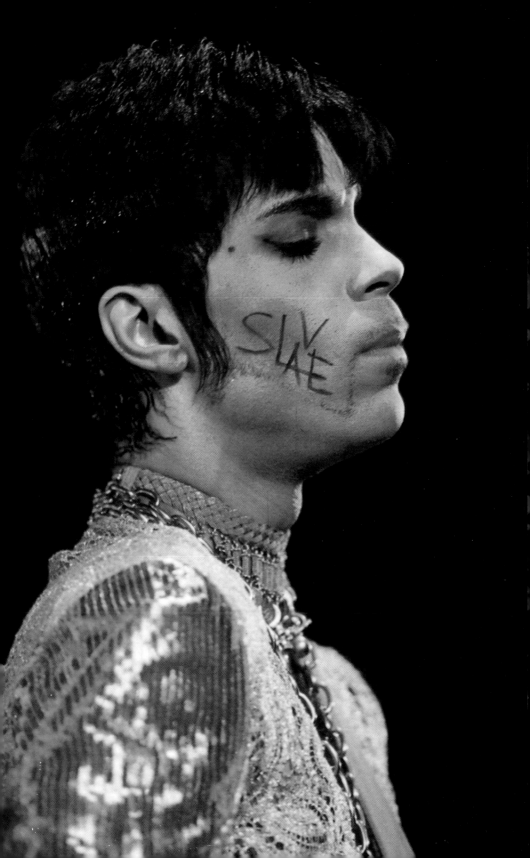

25. *Above* At the Brit Awards in 1997 with his new band. Left to right: Mike Scott, Rhonda Smith, Mr Hayes, Kathleen Dyson and Kirk Johnson.

26. *Left* Prince and Mayte at the NAACP awards. 'It will be for ever,' says Mayte.

on in his career since *Purple Rain*,' Michael Ostin, then an executive at
Warner, told *Rolling Stone*. 'As brilliant as he is, the audience has a
hard time keeping up with him.' Prince is quick, but Tim Burton
didn't realise quite how quick. One month after visiting Pinewood
(during which he played eight nights in Japan), he played the director
eight songs, including an instrumental, 'The Batman Theme', that
was later discarded. 'Rave To The Joy Fantastic' and '200 Balloons',
which was released as the B-side to 'Batdance' and was actually about
condoms, were also rejected, so he went away and came up with
'Trust' and 'Partyman'. Only three songs on the album – 'The Arms
Of Orion', 'Lemon Crush' and 'Batdance' – aren't heard in the film.
He shared publishing rights – the first time he had done so – for the
six songs that appear in the film with Warner Brothers Music Corp.
The songs were unusual in that they were inspired by the characters
rather than by specific scenes in the movie. An instrumental score, by
Danny Elfman, was released as a separate album. 'There was so much
pressure on Tim that for the whole picture I just said, "Yes, Mr
Burton, what would you like?"' said Prince. He shot the first of the
lavish videos to accompany the singles: 'Batdance' was directed by
Magnoli, with choreography by Barry Lather, and features fifteen
dancers and a chorus line of Basinger lookalikes. He crawls between
their legs, like the cat who got the cream. 'Batdance' would be his
fourth American number one. It battled with a release from the
second *Ghostbusters* film, 'On Our Own' by Bobby Brown; it had
been another *Ghostbusters* track, by Ray Parker Jr, that had knocked
'When Doves Cry' off the number-one spot.

Prince was again busy on myriad projects: he took George Clinton
on to his label and worked with him on *The Cinderella Theory*. He
hired Michael Bland, a giant of a man who still lived with his parents
in Minneapolis, to replace Sheila E as drummer; Candy Dulfer, the
Dutch saxophonist, was also drafted in, and made her first appearance
in the video for 'Partyman'. She decided not to go on his next tour,
the 'Nude' tour, and returned home to work with her band, Funky
Stuff, as well as other jazz musicians, including Maceo Parker. 'The
only contact I have had with Prince since,' she says, 'was when he sent

me a demo tape with different songs on – they're my style but don't have the funky Prince sound. When I received the tape my album was almost finished, so I chose one song for it. Prince wanted to produce my whole album but I don't want to get the name of another artist who became popular by Prince. I found it great he sent me a tape, unexpectedly, after all that time – a good sign that he still follows me, even though I decided not to tour with him a few years ago. I hope he liked our version of "Sunday Afternoon", because we changed it a little bit.'

Prince recorded a third Madhouse album at the end of 1988, mostly with Eric Leeds. Mavis Staples, whose voice was legendary in the late 1970s when she sang with The Staples Singers, released an album with six songs by Prince and others by her former Stax colleagues Homer Banks and Lester Snell. *Time Waits for No One* was a critical but not a commercial success.

Partly because it was riding on the coat-tails of a much-hyped film, *Batman* was a huge hit, selling over six million copies. It was pretty much Prince as a one-man band again, but included nice touches, like the Sounds of Blackness gospel choir, brought in by Jam and Lewis and engineered by Sheila E, and the song 'The Arms Of Orion', with Sheena Easton. 'Scandalous', largely an ode to Kim Basinger, was co-written by the ever-broadminded John Nelson, the video featuring Prince in red getting intimate with his microphone. (Two B-sides to *Batman* singles were the tracks 'Feel U Up', on the flip of 'Partyman', and 'I Love U In Me', the B-side to 'The Arms Of Orion'. Now you can't tell me Prince wrote *that* one.)

'After *Purple Rain* and *Under the Cherry Moon*, after "Thriller" and Eddie Murphy's "Delirious" tour, after MTV, house and new jack swing, after *Raising Hell* and *It Takes a Nation of Millions* and *Straight Outta Compton*, after *She's Gotta Have It* and Tracy Chapman and Living Colour and CDs and Janet Jackson's *Control*, it's amusing to listen to Prince singing and Morris Day playing drums on a song called "New Power Generation". New? These brothers are both over thirty. Day is married and on the wack ABC sitcom *New Attitude*. And baby-faced

Nelson recently gave up shaving, surely a sign of encroaching old age.' So wrote Nelson George in New York's *Village Voice* in 1990. He was referring to a track on the new Prince album, *Graffiti Bridge*, the soundtrack to his fourth movie.

The new Time album, with the original line-up, was called *Pandemonium*. Released in 1990, it was again essentially a Prince album but this time with far more input from The Time themselves. Prince had saved all the best tracks from the *Pandemonium* sessions for himself, and *Graffiti Bridge* owes much to Levi Seacer, who co-wrote, co-arranged and co-produced it. Guests include Mavis Staples, George Clinton, yet another Prince protégée, Elisa Fiorillo, and his old friend Robin Power, and the album also features Clare Fischer's orchestral arrangements, vocal icing by soon-to-be band member Rosie Gaines (a diva from Oakland who had been summoned by her former band colleague Seacer), and the thirteen-year-old Tevin Campbell, hailed as the new Michael Jackson but who on maturity has turned out to be more like the old Michael Jackson.

The real gem of the album is 'Joy In Repetition'; not surprising, as the *Sign o' the Times* leftover was recorded and mixed by Susan Rogers. It remains one of Prince's favourites – he chose to perform it at the launch of *Emancipation*.

The *Graffiti Bridge* album, released in August, was moderately well received, which was more than could be said for the movie, co-starring the insipid Ingrid Chavez (thankfully not on the record). The film took six weeks to make and thirty-six weeks to edit by FedEx and a hotel-room VCR (Prince was by now on his European tour: 'One of these days I'm going to work on just one project, and take my time') and was universally described as a turkey. Even today, though, he doesn't accept it was a failure. 'It was non-violent, positive and had no blatant sex scenes,' he says of the movie that was released in American theatres in November 1990 but only made it to video in Britain. 'Maybe it will take people thirty years to get it. They trashed *The Wizard of Oz* at first too.'

Chavez, whose solo album co-written by Prince and entitled *May 19, 1992* was released the next year, wasn't on the *Graffiti Bridge* album because she wasn't supposed to be in the movie. Chavez had only got the part at the last minute when Basinger and Prince went their separate ways.

Chavez had met Prince in a Minneapolis club. She was Hispanic but had been brought up by a white family. She was twenty-eight, writing poetry, and had a young son. 'I passed him a note. It said, "Hi, remember me? Probably not but that's okay because we've never met." Prince liked my poetry,' she says. 'He said, "You're one of the only girls I know who is smaller than me." He went on tour with *Lovesexy*, came back and did *Batman*. Then he pulled out tracks from a couple of years before and said, "Do you want to work on it again?" I said, "Cool." Just because you create something with someone, people assume you're sleeping with them. Prince is a pretty normal friend. Not everything we do is good, but everything unfortunately Prince does is put out in such a big way it gets criticised. *Graffiti Bridge* wasn't *Purple Rain*.' Chavez was supposedly the inspiration for the *Lovesexy* album. Her main claim to fame since has been her assertion that she co-wrote Madonna's 'Justify My Love' with Lenny Kravitz, her ex-boyfriend. She sued Kravitz for 25 per cent of the publishing rights and won. She says that Kravitz had her sign away the rights to stop his then wife, Lisa Bonet, finding out about their affair. 'I had to fight Prince to do my own thing. I hired my own manager, which the others didn't do.' She insists that it was her idea to pose naked for *Interview* magazine.

Chavez did manage to get the film's only commendation, as 'Prince's first female movie lead who doesn't look like she was ordered out of a catalogue'.

'I had just finished shooting *Tango and Cash*, with Sylvester Stallone and Kurt Russell, and I was going to start writing the screenplay for *Graffiti Bridge*,' says Albert Magnoli of the movie that was conceived as a sequel to his record-breaking debut, *Purple Rain*. 'But my idea for the new film was for a higher-budget, more elaborate concept. But Prince really wanted a lower-budget approach and to get the film out within a year. So I said, why don't you do that, 'cause I'm shooting for the moon here. I hadn't done any work on the script at all.' He adds to to set the record straight, 'I also wasn't involved in *Under the Cherry Moon*.'

Magnoli might have been able to rescue *Graffiti Bridge*, but the film was doomed from the start. Prince did indeed want to shoot a kind of sequel to *Purple Rain*, but this time featuring The Time as the main characters.

He had already started work on a new Time album, initially without Jesse Johnson, Jimmy Jam and Terry Lewis, but the project was put on hold by Warner. They were adamant that the album and movie (the title came from a real bridge in Eden Prairie, a suburb of Minneapolis, that was used by local graffiti artists) feature the original Time line-up if they were going to put up the money – just under $10 million. 'Prince called us up,' says Jimmy Jam. '[In a little voice] Can you come to Paisley Park for a meeting? We said, yeah. The meeting was about a script based around The Time. The pitch for the new movie was that it would tell The Time story, whereas *Purple Rain* had told Prince's story. We said, "That sounds kinda good, P. Cool. You going to write it up?" It turned into a Prince movie with a cameo by The Time.' (Prince says that he pitched the Time movie to Warner, with himself as director and not appearing in it, and they didn't buy it.)

The version of the script shown to Warner had largely been written by Prince (the earlier draft co-written by Basinger was deemed unusable). Basinger had agreed to take a cut from her usual fee, but Warner still weren't happy. The departure of the leading lady when she dumped Prince only delayed filming by a week: he merely merged her role and that played by Jill Jones, who was relegated to a smaller part as his girlfriend, and gave the new part to Ingrid Chavez.

Filming started in February 1990 at Paisley Park on a set specially constructed to re-create the jazz Mecca that was the Seven Corners area of Minneapolis in the 1950s. The set resembled that of an old MGM musical. 'Yeah, cheap!' Prince laughed to *Rolling Stone* while on the 'Nude' tour in Europe. 'That's okay. That's how we did *Dirty Mind*. But, man, what I could do with a $25 million budget.' He said he wasn't trying to be Francis Ford Coppola. He succeeded.

Once again, it was a closed set. None of the 500 extras or 40-strong crew were allowed to talk to the press. As well as Prince and The Time, the cast included Mavis Staples and George Clinton. One person who was allowed to drop by was Spike Lee, who wandered around the set with Prince one afternoon, their arms around each other's shoulders, one in high tops and the other in high heels. They agreed that Lee would direct him in a video one day. Jimmy Jam also chatted to Lee, and tried to persuade him to direct the next Time video. That job went to Julien Temple, the British director whose movie *Absolute Beginners*, another surreal musical fantasy, was panned almost as much as *Graffiti Bridge*.

Just as Warner had brought in Tommy Vicari to oversee their rookie signing in the recording studio, they now brought in Peter McDonald, a fifty-year-old director who had had experience of handling singing stars who directed – such as Barbra Streisand in *Yentl*. The dramatic scenes often took a dozen takes; the musical numbers took just one or two.

Prince again worked harder than anyone, spending fourteen hours on set before going to watch the day's rushes, and working on the musical numbers in his studio until the early hours. His co-star was a little more outspoken than the rest of the cast. Chavez told British journalist Chris Heath that she would try to make Prince take time out to do normal things, like take a walk in the woods. He would make excuses, or simply ask, 'What for?' When Prince read what she had told Heath, he phoned her up, hurt and angry.

Eventually Prince had to cancel a show in Rotterdam to fly home and rescue his movie. Test audiences had given it a thumbs-down. They found it incomprehensible – especially the scene where he lifts up his rather chunky love interest in an alley for a passionate kiss. Warner brought in their own experienced film editor, Steve Rivkin, to oversee the production. Steve was the brother of Prince's drummer, Bobby Z, and engineer/producer David Z, and had been a friend of Prince's for many years. Prince was still reshooting come September. After many delays, the film was premiered nearly three months after the release of the album at the Ziegfeld Theater in New

York on 1 November 1990. Prince wore a white scoop-neck top with matching, and very revealing, white leggings. Even that sight wasn't enough to distract attention away from what was on the screen.

'I saw a trailer for *Graffiti Bridge* this summer before *Another 48 HRS.*,' wrote Nelson George in the *Village Voice*, 'and enjoyed it more than the feature, though the word out of Cali is that it's a dog.'

The 'Nude' tour, which began in June 1990 and took in Europe and Japan, was a resounding success, a greatest-hits package that forsook the more complex and esoteric staging of *Lovesexy* (a large portion of the *Lovesexy* audience, who hadn't managed to buy *The Black Album*, had been perplexed by his rendition of 'Bob George'). The band now consisted of Levi Seacer, Miko Weaver, Michael Bland, Rosie Gaines and rappers and dancers Damon Dickson, Kirk Johnson and Tony Moseley. The only chance America got to see it was at the Chick Huntsberry benefit concert at Rupert's nightclub in Minneapolis, followed by a final dress rehearsal at the Civic Center, for which tickets were $10 as long as you brought along food for the local homeless.

Only 'The Question of U' and 'Thieves In The Temple' were aired from the new album – 'Thieves' appearing only as a pre-concert video. This was a real departure for Prince, who loved to try out his new tracks. 'Kids save a lot of money for a long time to buy tickets, and I like to give them what they want,' he says. 'When I was a kid, I didn't want to go hear James Brown play something I never heard before.' One song he hadn't performed before but which was familiar to his audience was 'Nothing Compares 2 U', written for Susannah Melvoin back in 1985 (he would later release it with his greatest-hits collection). The song had already been a huge hit for Sinéad O'Connor that year. O'Connor accused Prince of threatening her when she visited him at his Los Angeles home. She told the Irish music paper *Hot Press*, 'He continually said that he was going to beat the shit out of me.' She said he had found her language, when she refused to sing the American national anthem, offensive. She said he sent her limo driver away, leaving her with no way to get home at 5:30 in the morning. 'He started laughing at the fact that I was crying, saying that my big mouth had got me into trouble again. I don't see why he had to threaten me with physical violence and use the fact that he is a man to intimidate me and be quite amused at the fact that I was frightened. His problem was that I did a song of his without him being involved in it. He's jealous. And he did say to me that he wished I'd never done his song . . . I think, frankly, that that song saved his fucking ass. He was in serious financial trouble until that song happened.' Prince denied her accusations. It is true, though, that her manager then was Steve Fargnoli, still not on the best of terms with Prince after being replaced by Magnoli, and it had been Fargnoli's idea to cover the song. He doubtless made a huge sum from the release, though Prince's royalties, too, would not have been small. But physical violence? Built like she was?

Prince couldn't win. He had been criticised for the overblown and often incomprehensible *Lovesexy* tour, but on the 'Nude' tour one critic remarked that 'a trio of male dancers trundle on to the stage, causing no sensation whatsoever. There's no Cat. There's no Sheila.' But Prince broke all the records with a remarkable eighteen nights at Wembley Arena at the end of June. Robert Sandall singled out Rosie Gaines in his review in the *Sunday Times*: 'In the past the role of singing duets on stage with Prince was an unenviable and frequently undignified task, involving a lot of extra-vocal services – getting pawed a bit, bumping and grinding on revolving beds, and so on. By replacing his usual squeaky sex kitten with a lioness like Gaines, Prince has added maturity to his sound.'

The show, and the itinerary, were physically exhausting. One journalist who joined the band for part of the tour was *Rolling Stone*'s Neal Karlen. 'At four in the morning, flying into their third country in the past twenty-four hours, the band and the entourage of about thirty are sacked out in what looks like the sleep of the dead. But while his band mates and support staff snooze around him, Prince keeps air-jamming beneath the glare of his seat's tiny spotlight. Listening to a tape of his own performance that day, Prince stays up all night, all the way to London.'

One member of the audience in Barcelona who would later admit to being 'dragged' to the concert was one Mayte Garcia. No Cat. No Sheila. Now wait a minute . . .

8

Maybe U think I'm being a little self-centred

By the time *Diamonds and Pearls* was released, in October 1991, Prince was chasing trends rather than creating them. The 1980s' most innovative musician was looking over his shoulder at the commercial viability of hip-hop: he wanted this record to sell, and made an effort to promote it, performing at record industry showcases, the tenth birthday party of MTV, and on Arsenio Hall's television show. He also employed a clever marketing trick that had certainly got the world intrigued back in 1987, with *The Black Album*. He released an unnamed record into clubs on the morning of his birthday, 7 June 1991. He quoted lyrics from James Brown's 'Mother Popcorn', and the only clue to its identity was the purple scribble on the white jacket. That particular record, of which only 1,500 were pressed, is now one of the most sought-after pieces of vinyl among record-collectors. The track? 'Gett Off', from his new album.

He was already working hard that summer with his new rapping discovery, Carmen Electra, who hailed from Cincinnatti, Ohio. He lavished millions of dollars on promoting and making videos for her (she was the support act on the *Diamonds and Pearls* tour; Prince would sometimes travel in her tour bus, with Mayte following in the one behind) but her album never sold and pushed the Paisley Park label further into the red. He was furious, blaming everyone – pluggers, marketing men – except Carmen and himself. She later moved into acting, appearing in *Baywatch Nights*, posing naked in *Playboy* (May 1996) and getting the job as the hyperactive host of MTV's dating show, *Singled Out*, in February 1997. She is short with enormous breasts. She had auditioned for Prince when he was toying with the idea of putting together another band, her audition piece consisting mostly of a demonstration of her ability to 'booty shake'. 'He was putting together an all-girl band and was looking for females. He asked if I could sing or dance. I didn't hear from him for two months, but then he called and said, "You should go solo, move to Minneapolis and I'll write an album for you."' She has even brought out her own near-naked calendar for 1997 – MC Lyte she most definitely is not.

After the 'Nude' tour, Miko Weaver and Matt Fink decided to go solo. On tour, band members were on about $850 a week; Weaver felt it wasn't enough, although, unlike other musicians hired for a tour, Prince's band were always kept on the payroll. Matt Fink still lives in Minneapolis; he built his own house with a studio downstairs, where he produces numerous albums for the Minneapolis-based K-Tel label, among others. The line-up that would become the New Power Generation – Tommy Barbarella (né Elm), Sonny Thompson (now Sonny T), Michael Bland, Rosie Gaines, Levi Seacer, rapper Tony Moseley (Tony M), and Damon Dickson and Kirk Johnson as dancers and percussionists – all worked on the new album. They soon discovered that their working week would only give them Sunday off. They had all been hired with a personal call from Prince along the lines of 'Would you like to think about it?', and when they said yes, they were put on to his assistant, who booked them on the next flight to Minneapolis. Michael Bland was playing drums down at the local Bunkers Music Bar and Grill. 'Prince had just come off his *Lovesexy* tour and he sat in with the group. He never took his eyes off me,' says the man whose arms are thicker than the entire body of the drummer he replaced, Sheila E. 'Months later he called me at my house. His demands on me were exactly the same as his demands on himself. There's no separation. He only wants to work with people who have the same work ethic he does. On a daily basis he's switching things around and organising and writing new music. He's made me very unaccepting of slackers.'

The rapper who had the misfortune to be featured on the new double album was Tony M, who had long been on the sidelines waiting for his big chance – when he was plain Tony, he used to watch Prince in his band Grand Central at local school parties and fêtes. 'Prince was very quiet, and when he appeared with that contract from Warner, a lot of people would have loved to see him fall flat on his face,' he says. 'I first met him in 1983, when me and Damon were in a talent contest.' They were hired as extras in *Purple Rain*, but wouldn't get their starring roles for almost seven years. But Tony M was certainly no Snoop Doggy Dogg. One of his better ideas was that the band should all wear roller skates on stage. The trio of male dancers just looked leaden and out of date.

'For years, everyone was listening to Prince to see what he was doing, but there came a time when he began listening to rap and said, "I can do that, and I can do it better,"' says Eric Leeds.

Prince desperately wanted a hit single, and hired Rebecca Blake, who had made the video for 'Kiss', to shoot the promos for 'Diamonds And Pearls' and 'Cream'. Two dancers who auditioned looked so much like sisters that he decided they should become Diamond and Pearl. 'The other girl, Laurie Elle, and I look a lot alike so they paired us as twins,' says Robia La Morte, a.k.a. Pearl, who had trained in ballet, tap and jazz from the age of twelve. 'We were flown from LA, where we both lived, to Minneapolis a lot. We had no idea it was going to happen – first it was one video, then we wound up doing the shoot for the album cover, then Prince was talking about taking us on tour. We were used to long hours, being dancers, but he works crazy hours. We'd get a call saying, "Can you get on the red-eye?" So Laurie and I would run all over town, getting our stuff together, fly there, report to the set at, say, eight at night and shoot all the way through till morning. The choreographer was Sean Teasman, and Prince picked everything up straight away. He's never

had formal training, but for the type of dancing he did he was phenomenal.' La Morte enjoyed two seminal video moments: Prince
licks the cream off her finger at the beginning of the video of that
name, and rips her dress off in 'Gett Off'. 'You wouldn't think he was
sexy if you saw him walking down the street,' she says, 'but see him
sit at a piano, see him being really good at what he does – that blows
you away. We were on tour with Mayte, and it was her first professional job, so she kind of looked up to us. She was very young and
inexperienced, we were like her big sisters.' The shy sixteen-year-old
who had been introduced to Prince in Germany was now a fully
fledged member of the band.

The *Diamonds and Pearls* show began with a spaceship-style lighting
rig in the shape of the soon-to-be-familiar male/female symbol.
There were up to eighteen musicians and dancers on stage at once.
The only thing missing seemed to be George Clinton himself, so
closely did the show echo his P-funk-mothership extravaganzas. The
P-funk shows, though, were funky jams, happenings; this show was
tightly choreographed. Bob Fosse would have been proud.

Days off were few and far between. A normal day consisted of a
ninety-minute soundcheck, with more energy expended than in most
performers' real shows, then a two-hour performance, followed by
an after-show gig at a club. The next day, a flight to the next city. It
was more Broadway than James Brown, but it went down well.
Prince toured Australia for the first time, with fourteen sell-out dates
culminating in an outdoor show at the Sydney Cricket Ground in
front of 45,000. During his trip to Australia he was seen by 200,000
people and received the best live reviews of his career.

By the time the show got to Britain in 1992, with eight nights at
Earls Court in London, followed by Manchester's Maine Road and
Glasgow's Celtic Park, it was polished to perfection. The event,
though, wasn't the cool, in-thing to be at. No after-show gigs took
place, as a bomb had gone off near the planned venue, and at one of
the Earls Court concerts I stood in front of Lulu. She couldn't see a
thing. Notably absent at the London shows were black faces – at Earls
Court, it seemed they were all at the altar of evangelist Morris

Cerullo next door. The most exciting thing to happen was Prince's hair-dryer catching fire in the dressing-room. A fire engine pulled up outside, having driven at great speed through west London; someone had already pulled the plug out.

'I'd never been to a concert before I went on tour with Prince,' says La Morte, 'but after I got home I went to see some other concert and realised the show we had been doing was phenomenal. I had no idea all shows weren't like that. People just stood at the microphone singing, and I'm like, wait a minute!' She retired from dancing after the tour – 'after Prince, there was really nowhere to go but down' – and is now an actress, appearing in *Beverly Hills, 90210* and *Buffy the Vampire Slayer*. Laurie Elle joined Michael Jackson's troupe for his 1996–97 tour.

The 'Cream' single turned out to be Prince's most successful since 'Batdance' – indeed, the *Diamonds and Pearls* album produced four top-thirty hits in the US, his best performance since *Purple Rain*. Like that record, it was a group album with a live feel, with contributions from everyone, most notably Rosie Gaines.

'When Boni left the band to go solo,' says Levi Seacer, 'Prince was reluctant to take on anyone new; he didn't want someone who would up and leave. With his music, you need to feel like family, real close. But I knew Rosie Gaines from San Francisco. I had been in a band with her, and I persuaded Prince to listen to her sing Marvin Gaye's "What's Going On". He couldn't believe what he was hearing.'

Gaines co-wrote 'Money Don't Matter 2Night', the one track with a social conscience on the new album – it mentions the Gulf War and came with a video directed by Spike Lee (he left all footage of Prince off the video; a more MTV-friendly one, interspersed with shots of the star at the piano, was made later). 'Rosie is like a tornado,' Prince says. 'There's never enough hours in the day for her voice, never enough tape for her voice.'

Of 'Money', Gaines recalls: 'There's got to be more to R&B than partying! I sang this melody to Prince and he immediately wanted to put a demo down. So I was up all night, all the next day. Prince makes you want to work. I know how tough it can be to get people to work together. We didn't really socialise, though. I wanted to ask him over to my house to meet my husband, have a barbecue.' The only time he did make it to her house was to park outside and call her on the phone from his BMW. She came out to sit from his car while he played her some new tracks on the stereo. He wouldn't come inside.

'Prince made me feel good about myself – I didn't even want to be in the videos – and now I really would rather have this voice than be skinny,' says the woman with the Arethafied alto. 'People think Prince discovered me, but my band was well known in the Bay Area. I always made it clear to Prince I wanted to do something on my own.' She officially left the band in 1992, after the Sydney leg of the tour.

Rosie Gaines's solo album for Paisley Park was never released – a casualty of his escalating dispute with Warner. 'Prince taught me so much. He took a month or so to get to know me, but we became very close. We would go for drives and he would play me music. *Diamonds and Pearls* was the best time for me, because the whole band wrote that album with him.' Prince composed the title track for Gaines. The reason he has never performed it since is that he vowed never to sing it with anyone else.

Gaines's tours with the NPG, however, had not proved to be a happy experience. 'Prince would be with Mayte, Diamond and Pearl, and I would be the only woman with the band. And there were members of the band who were jealous of my friendship with Prince, who would call me names and disrespect me. Michael Bland was cool, and a couple of others, but the rest of the band were horrible. I told Prince that he had to get rid of these people, they were no good, he shouldn't have them around him, they were bad for his health. But he wouldn't address the problem, so I decided to leave. I had no money in my pocket; my husband and my daughter just got in our car with our U-Haul behind us and drove back to California. We didn't even know where we were going to live. But Prince didn't want to let go of me. He wouldn't let me out of a three-year contract, which meant I couldn't sign with Motown.'

After she was finally able to sign with that label, her one and only album with them, *Closer Than Close*, went almost unnoticed when Motown were taken over by Polydor, and staff were either shuffled or made redundant. Since then, tracks from the album have been bought by a Scottish record company, Big Bang, remixed and re-released – they were even on Radio 1's playlist in May 1997. Her new album on her own label, Arrival, is available only on the Internet (at *www.rosie-gaines.com*). Now where did she get that idea?

Gaines did, though, return to add her voice to *Chaos and Disorder* and *Emancipation* – a rare occurrence in the Prince world, where if you're out, you invariably stay out. 'We hadn't talked for a year, and then Prince phoned and said, "This is stupid. We love each other." Working on *Chaos* was different – he had fired all those people in the band, it was much calmer. He was so happy making *Emancipation*, he had Paisley redecorated, Mayte was pregnant. Everything suddenly seemed to be going right.'

Diamonds and Pearls was Prince's attempt to move towards more melodic soul. 'Everybody else went out and got drum machines and computers,' says the man who back in the late 1970s had used the very first Linn drum machine, 'so for this album I threw mine away.' Alan Leeds, VP at Paisley Park Records at the time, says: 'He was embracing the fact that young kids today would have musicians, as well as rappers and scratchers, to look up to.'

But the album was released in 1991, the year he cancelled an open-air concert at Blenheim Palace in Oxfordshire with only a week's notice, and he was keen to get back in people's good books. The album was critically well received, but it wasn't anything new, mixing pop and funk and rap and soul. 'You know when you buy someone's record and there's always an element missing,' he said at the time of the album's release. 'The voice is wrong or the drums are lame or something. On mine there's nothing missing.' Perhaps this was part of the problem. 'Producers like the Family Stand have out-funked Prince, and bands like Living Colour have taken his fusion of rock and funk and catapulted it into the next galaxy,' wrote David Browne in *Entertainment Weekly*.

The homeboy-in-heels stance wasn't really working. 'Nubian princes strutting their stuff, out of the ghetto and into many other neighbourhoods. This is the new black music power. No androgyny, all masculine brawn,' said *Spin* in 1991. 'Who stood up to say that Prince's sex and race and faith debates filtered down through the minds of those hip-hop nationals? All these black men, adopting new names, flaunting their difference, grabbing their thangs, and talking about it? They were the nephews of one Prince Roger Nelson.' Trouble was, they didn't know it – yet.

His next album, released in October 1992, was known only by the symbol that would soon become his name. It was released right after his renegotiated multimillion-dollar deal with Warner. *Rolling Stone* called the record a high-concept muddle, 'the last seven songs wrestling with stardom, sacrifice and salvation – the same hodge-podge that made *Sign o' the Times* so incomprehensible'.

Mayte was on backing vocals, and was dressed in the videos as an Egyptian princess. The video for '7' has her and Prince destroying all his former trappings, with the message that Prince is dead – a pre-cursor to the announcement that he would no longer be known by that name. 'Sexy MF' was his birthday present to us for 1992, a live recording he loved so much it prompted him to swear he would only ever record with live instruments. The song was a moderate success as a single, even if the version released for radio play made the whole concept a bit of a non-starter. 'The music I make is reflective of the life I'm leading,' says Prince, 'and "Sexy MF" came during the period I had the Glam Slam disco. There was a dance troupe there, and the sexier the dancers, the bigger the revenues and the noisier the crowd.'

His rapping on 'Love 2 The 9's' can't really be called that – rapping is too straightforwardly male for him; it's more slurred, seductive. He's not taking himself too seriously. '3 Chains O' Gold' starts beau-tifully – 'U say you'll call me and then U don't / I'll want to kiss U and then I won't / We both do nothing and call it love' – and then dis-appears under pomp. Missing, though, were the huge vocal cords of

Rosie Gaines; now that she had left the fold, her voice was re-recorded by Prince. Mostly, the songs are serenades to Mayte, sex, spirituality and sex – except 'The Sacrifice Of Victor', his condemnation of the abuse of children, a story continued in 'Papa' on his next album.

This was the last album that Levi Seacer played on. He is now the band leader with Sounds of Blackness, the choir formed twenty-five years ago on the campus of Macalester College in St Paul, and another institution in Minnesota, much like Prince. Seacer composes many of the tracks on the Sounds' 1997 album, *A Time for Healing*, their first without Jam and Lewis. He even hooked Prince up with the Sounds' guitarist. 'Prince loves Sounds of Blackness,' he says, 'but then he was raised on gospel. They're from his home town.' Seacer has now settled with his family in Minneapolis. 'We all just stick around,' he says. 'Tommy Barbarella, Tony Moseley, all the old NPG are still here. We've just formed a new band, called Mpls, and we're bringing out a new album. Not on Prince's label, though.'

Prince played a small-scale tour in America – the band was joined by Morris Hayes on keyboards – including three nights at the Radio City Music Hall, with Madonna in the audience, and a show at the famous Apollo in Harlem, where he jammed with Lenny Kravitz to an invited audience of disadvantaged children. After a performance of 'My Name Is Prince' he held up copies of the bad reviews for the ♀ album and set light to them. The tickets for Radio City sold out in nine minutes – they hadn't seen him for five years – so Prince paid for the shows to be broadcast simultaneously on the giant Sony video screen right outside in Times Square.

During that limited tour, he was spotted at the Sinatrabar in Florida going for a quiet drink. 'Prince was lifted by his bodyguards over the Miami Beach bar's back wall into the courtyard,' said the *Atlanta Constitution*. 'That way he avoided the mere mortals who were straining at the bellropes out front. The tiny pop star disguised himself in a gold jumpsuit with matching gold platform shoes and a rhinestone-studded cane. He wanted to avoid drawing attention to himself.'

The ♀ tour, basically another greatest-hits package, went to

Europe in the summer, and at last he appeared at Wembley Stadium – a venue not really suited to Prince, who is hard to see at the best of times – and Sheffield Arena. His little joke was to dress Mayte as himself – you know, the usual peaked cap with chains over the face – and have her strip off his clothes to reveal a woman's body. His manipulation of gender used to be so much more subtle. (And most people had already spotted that it wasn't really Prince: the slightly thicker waist and clumpy shoes gave her away.) When he came out at the Sheffield gig, he asked repeatedly, 'What's my name?' There was Prince – 'No.' Victor – 'No. Definitely not Victor.' Mr Squiggly, Symbol, etc. Then someone shouted, 'Mr Nelson!' Prince laughed and replied, 'Yes, I suppose it is.' And at Wembley Stadium, imagine 72,000 people singing 'sexy motherfucker'. Even the security men were laughing.

'The NPG have gotten noticeably tighter from all this old-fashioned stage sweat, funkier than any of his previous groups,' said Alan Light, editor-in-chief of *Vibe* magazine, of the San Francisco show. 'Watching him cue them, stop on a dime, introduce a new groove, veer off by triggering another sample, you can only think of James Brown burnishing his bands to razor-sharp precision, fining them for missing a single note.'

'I love this band,' said Prince. 'I just wish they were all girls.' When he is asked to loan out the NPG by other artists, he always says no. 'That would be like letting another man make love to my woman.'

That September, he performed live on Radio 1 at the BBC Radio Concert Hall in front of two hundred competition winners, the first time a pop star had played live there since Jimi Hendrix twenty-five years before. He wore a blue jumpsuit and was as thin as a rake. He had phoned Radio 1 only the day before. His only requirements: a hundred towels, a limo, six bottles of Evian, a bottle of freshly squeezed orange juice, twelve large oranges, a coffee-maker and an electric kettle, six Earl Grey tea bags, six herbal tea bags, two whole lemons, one sharp knife, a cutting board and some sugar.

Nineteen ninety-three was a turning point in Prince's career. Warner wanted to recoup some of that spectacular advance; in

September they put out *The Hits/The B-Sides*, with two new singles, 'Pink Cashmere' and 'Peach', the last new tracks he would ever release under the name of Prince. 'Cashmere' charted, but 'Peach', containing a sampled yelp courtesy of Kim Basinger, sank. For such a long-awaited greatest-hits release it didn't do well. Prince certainly wasn't behind it. Warner had by now closed his Paisley Park label, and he responded in 1994 by giving them *Come*, largely recordings from his vaults that had been given a once-over (the orgasm on 'Orgasm' is by 'She knows'), with a picture of his funeral on the album cover. It is in many ways superior to ♀ : there's his sweet rap on 'Space', the slowed-down version of 'Letitgo' (his apology for his old self: 'Lover here, lover there, who cried, who cared?'), and 'Come' itself, during which he discusses how he gives oral sex. It was his last album as Prince. That same year he released 'The Most Beautiful Girl In The World' (Warner said he could, but only if he picked up the tab), a brand-new song composed for the by now fully matured Mayte.

Alan Light interviewed him for *Vibe* in Monte Carlo in May 1994. Prince was on a high from his independently released hit single, keen to put his side of the story and to release what he believed to be his best album ever, *The Gold Experience*, but doubtful Warner would ever let it see the light of day. That's why he was appearing at the World Music Awards, a tacky ceremony with pseudo-celebrities the old Prince would have avoided like flat shoes. 'We have a new album finished,' he told Light. 'But Warner doesn't know it. From now on, Warner only get old songs out of the vault. New songs we'll play at shows. Music should be free, anyway . . . There's just a few people with all the power. Like, I didn't play the MTV Music Awards; suddenly, I can't get a video on MTV.'

The cover shot and the photographs to accompany Light's piece in *Vibe* were taken in Paris by Dana Lixenberg, and turned out to be among the best in his career – he's vulnerable, beautiful, far from the rather preening, petulant pictures of old. He looks like a fawn. Lixenberg was just beginning to make a name for herself; for one of her first projects she went to Los Angeles to photograph gang members, and she went on to specialise in portraying rappers and other musicians – Tupac Shakur, whom she photographed while he was in prison for assault, Gil Scott-Heron, Al Green. 'It was my first cover for *Vibe* and I was very nervous,' she says. 'Prince was only going to be in Paris for one day, after the Monte Carlo awards, and at the last minute I got a call from Karen Lee, his publicist, saying he wasn't gonna make it. Then she called to say he was on his way, and when he arrived I wasn't prepared for the fact he doesn't shake your hand or make eye contact, but I thought, fine. He cleared the studio, so there was just my assistant and me. He put on his own music, and asked if his make-up was okay, because it was already done when he arrived. He really paid attention while I explained what I was going to do – he's very focused. You don't really have to talk. I started by letting him do his poses, then slowly I toned it down. I asked him to put his arms down, his hands away from his face. The pictures took an hour and fifteen minutes, amazing for a cover and several spreads, but he's so quick to pick up what you are doing. I was a little worried, because he wanted to do some pictures with handcuffs, so we had to wait for those. We had to send the images for his approval, but, unlike most of the new stars, he approved everything. I saw him again in New York after a concert at the Palladium. The magazine had just come out, and he had a little gathering at the back. People were brought in one by one, and he shook my hand and said he liked it very much. It was nice he remembered me. Mostly, you shoot someone and they honestly don't remember you.'

He would not release *The Gold Experience* until September 1995. It was a commercial success (it finally went gold in the US in December 1996), in no small part because it contained the single that had gone to number one in Britain, and it had been heavily trailed in the *Gold* European tour in 1995. Most of the album was previewed at a party at Paisley Park in February 1994 to commemorate the release of the 'Beautiful' single. At that time, Prince and his band were virtually in residence at Erotic City, upstairs at Glam Slam, where they would start at 2 A.M. and jam for hours playing Stevie Wonder and Sly Stone covers.

'I had been going to those gigs before *Gold* came out,' says Jim

Walsh, who had followed Prince's career in the local *City Pages* and then at the *St Paul Pioneer Press*. 'No one was paying him attention, but I was going to these shows all the time. They were phenomenal: they'd start at 2 A.M. in a club, then carry on at Paisley and I'd get home at like five in the morning.' Walsh was invited to write the liner notes for the *Gold* album. 'People were surprised he ran the liner notes as is, because they are fairly critical.' In them he writes that, only a year before, 'The word on the street was that Prince was old news.'

When the album was finally released, the reviews were largely positive. 'The songs are stripped-down, taut, funky as hell, full of sex and bite. "319" is rocking, roaring and dirty,' wrote Alan Light. 'The most cohesive and most fun Prince album since *Sign o' the Times*,' wrote Jon Bream. Except this wasn't a Prince album. It was his first under his new, and as he readily admits, unpronounceable, name.

Word on the street in 1995 was that Prince had lost his mind.

9

What's this strange
relationship?

Prince came to the end of his performance of 'Dinner With Delores'. He flounced away from the piano, his long black frock-coat twirling in his wake. The only words he would speak that night in July 1996 on the David Letterman talk show were: 'Free TLC.'

His new band were seen for the first time – Kirk Johnson on drums, Mr Hayes on keyboards, Rhonda Smith and Kathleen Dyson on guitar, with a guest appearance by long-term collaborator Eric Leeds on sax – and the word 'slave' pencilled on the singer's right cheek was, thankfully, making a final appearance. For this was one of the last obligations to his record company of almost twenty years, a relationship that had generated $300 million in revenue: a petulant plugging of *Chaos and Disorder*, his last album for Warner. And he couldn't resist a final swipe at a recording industry he saw as strangling the creativity of its artists.

TLC, the three-woman group whose *Crazysexycool* album had sold five million copies, had filed for bankruptcy court protection at the end of 1995. That a lot of their troubles stemmed from the fact that they were merely singers, not writers or publishers of their own material, and from the decision by one of the group, Lisa Lopes or

'Left-Eye', to burn down an ex-boyfriend's house (which couldn't be put out by firefighters because of the toxic fumes from his burning athletic shoe collection), seemed to matter less to The Artist Formerly Known as Prince, than solidarity among musicians and a desire to see the entire recording industry overthrown.

As far as the general public were concerned, the superstar who had seemed the most likely, out of the 1980s triumvirate that also included Madonna and Michael Jackson, to see most of us into the next millennium, had seriously lost the plot. By the summer of 1996, his two releases so far that year – *Girl 6*, the soundtrack for the new Spike Lee movie, which was a greatest-hits package with only three new tracks, and *Chaos and Disorder* – had sold fewer than 100,000 copies each: his worst-ever figures. *Chaos* also received his worst reviews (Prince himself admitted the album had only taken ten days to record with some of the old New Power Generation line-up, including Rosie Gaines). It was short, only forty minutes, but perhaps that was a blessing. It was described by *Rolling Stone* as 'a half-hearted transaction from a self-pitying celebrity . . . The lyrics gracelessly confuse the personal with the political'. It reached number twenty-six on the US *Billboard* pop top 200 (significantly, it wasn't classified as R&B, the chart where his music has traditionally fared better). It dropped from sight after four weeks. The one and only single, 'Dinner With Delores', wasn't even released in the US; in Britain, the album reached number fourteen, dropping out after four weeks. The single reached number thirty-six, and disappeared after a fortnight. On the day the album hit the stores, an employee at the Virgin Megastore in London's Oxford Street recalled the days when a new Prince release automatically meant queues outside the door at opening time. On the first day of *Chaos* going on sale? 'We sold four copies.'

'It was a spiteful, contract-breaking album,' says Charles Aaron of *Spin* magazine. 'Prince can't punish Warner, but people who buy the record will think him even more irrelevant than they did before. In the history of rock 'n' roll, so many albums are bad because they were a way of getting out of a contract.'

'It's easy for the artist to go out and act like they're the wounded one,' says David Fricke, senior editor of *Rolling Stone*. 'You see Prince walking around with "slave" on his face. Can you imagine an executive at Warner walking into a shareholders' meeting with "We were fucked" on his face? They can't do that. He *can* do that. He can generate sympathy among fans. But he can also generate scorn from people who think he's just a whining rich guy who has mis-spent his talent and possibly his fortune. His situation is analagous to what Frank Zappa went through, and he was suing people up the butt for years because they didn't treat his music right. Prince is a quality control freak. I can understand why he is pissed at Warner, I can see why they can't deal with him. How willing is he to take advice, to bend a little?'

'There were lots of people in the early days who protected Prince,' says Owen Husney, his very first manager. 'There were times when Russ Thyret [Warner's CEO] put his job on the line for him. Prince has had to fight for everything he has, so I can see both sides. But I don't think writing "slave" on your face is the way to deal with people like Mo Ostin or Lenny Waronker or Russ Thyret. These people believed in him and would have given him anything, and did give him anything to get him off the ground. I would have dealt with Warner completely differently. I would have convinced them, as I did when Prince wanted to be his own producer, that they should let him put out as much as he wants. I would have said to Prince, you need to understand your audience is going to shrink, 'cause even too much lobster is going to get to you, but I know you can't stop yourself. I'd have said to Warner, look, the guy's Beethoven, in 200 years people will look back on his body of work and say, my God, he's a genius. A war played out in the press never does anyone any good. Prince has to understand that there is a little kid in a basement right now who will explode and Warner will sign him. Warner will find fifty more to replace Prince. As far as I'm concerned, Prince is in the top ten of all time, but he takes himself too seriously.'

'To be honest, we're glad of a break from him,' said Bob Merlis, the Warner vice-president who had handled Prince's media relations for many years, on the day Warner announced the divorce. And it looked as if the record-buying public had finally lost their patience as well.

Prince's personal crusade seemed to have backfired badly. He had overestimated his fans' loyalty – even those in Britain, who had supported him at times when he was misunderstood in his home country, had had a bellyful. His UK visit in 1995 had been the final straw, for Warner and for the general public.

In the first two months of 1995, you couldn't move in London without bumping into Prince, or rather The Artist Formerly Known as Prince. The *Sun* renamed him the Liz Hurley of pop. At the Brits on 21 February he took the opportunity to attack his label for not releasing his new album, *The Gold Experience* – he had wanted it out on his birthday, 7 June, the previous year. As he accepted the award for Best International Male Artist, he whispered, 'Prince – in concert, perfectly free. On record, slave.' But Warner did have a point. Only the previous month, it had officially released *The Black Album*, the work shelved by the star in 1987. He still didn't want it released, but Warner wanted a hit. *Come* hadn't sold well in 1994, and nor had the compilation album *1-800-NEW-FUNK*, his independent release of tracks by NPG artists including Nona Gaye, Madhouse and the Steeles. Yet here he was, telling British tabloids that 'a lot of the guys [at Warner] who caused me problems have gone now, but I'm still waiting to see if things change. I still believe that *The Gold Experience* will never be released. They wouldn't even let me release a ballet I had written.'

He told *Q* magazine: 'All they know is marketing. You know what one of them actually said to me? [In a stupid, goofy voice:] "So, uh, do you think this hip-hop thing is gonna last?"' He told the *Evening Standard*: 'They're only interested in money, not music. The old bosses like Mo Ostin may have been smiling when they took my records, but the result was the same . . . If my fans are worried or confused, should I really care? Surely they want me to be true to myself.'

He soon found out he should have cared. His seven nights at Wembley Arena in March failed to sell out, and at Sheffield, only 3,000 out of 10,000 tickets were sold – a first for him in Britain. Sections of the arena were even curtained off. This was a blow: as his UK publicist, Chris Poole, revealed at the time: 'This tour is crucial for him. He has a small cashflow problem. He's not broke, but he has always been known for spending his money on his music.'

The *Gold* tour was renamed the 'Gimme Your Money' tour by fans. Each night at the arena, fliers were passed along the aisles naming the venue for the after-show party. Those who had already shelled out for tickets for the official show felt short-changed: was he cutting the gig short in order to be fresh for later on? Those who did make it to the second show, at the Astoria or the Emporium, found they had to pay cash, at least £20, on the door.

He also found he had Warner checking up on him. After the Brits outburst and all the newspaper stories about how they were keeping the *Gold* album prisoner, they sent Karen Lee to London to keep him quiet. Lee had been co-opted from Warner to become Prince's in-house publicity person at Paisley Park; she had left him, and been persuaded to return, on more than one occasion. She was now back at Warner, as vice-president of media relations. Her arrival at Wembley wasn't welcomed by Prince: he sent her a ticket but no backstage pass of any description – the ultimate insult in record company land. 'I wish Prince well in everything he does,' she says now from her office in Century City, California. 'But what he does with his career is no longer my concern.'

Warner were by now threatening to sue him. They claimed he performed on a new single and album by his backing band, the New Power Generation, which included his girlfriend, Mayte. The album, *Exodus*, had been released on his new NPG label. The legal wrangle meant that when he turned up to play on Channel 4's *The White Room* in April, he was introduced as 'Tora Tora', and proceeded to sing the offending single, 'Get Wild', with a scarf concealing his features. (If Warner executives failed to notice it was Prince they were even more stupid than he thought.) Most viewers, however, were unaware of this particular battle and just thought he was bonkers.

That was surely the opinion of sometime supermodel Veronica Webb, who conducted what was touted as Prince's first TV interview for thirteen years, on BBC2's *The Sunday Show*. 'I always fantasised about Prince when I was at school,' she says. 'I had seen him at the Brits a couple of weeks before – I rushed over to introduce myself and felt like a Catholic meeting the Pope. I could have kissed his ring and been happy for the rest of my life, but he offered to be interviewed. There were just two conditions: he wouldn't have to speak and he wouldn't show his face.' Webb, increasingly annoyed, had to make do with him whispering in Mayte's ear, who would then relay the replies – he wasn't going to return to the US until 1999, when his contract expired; and being in the record industry was like working for The Firm. When he maintained that the reason for not speaking was that he had lost his voice, Webb said, 'Don't tell me you lost your voice – I heard you speak five minutes ago.' When she asked him about the mask, Mayte said it was because he was too ugly to look upon. Webb was at the end of her tether, completely unfazed by his celebrity: 'You got to do better than that. You get out there and shake your thang every night.' She asked him about his music and the 'reply' was 'Who does your hair?' When she called him Prince, he threatened to 'give her a kick'.

When Warner did release *The Gold Experience*, it was to mark the end of his creative tenure there. A relationship that had produced some of the most memorable music of the past two decades was about to shatter.

The success of the soundtrack to the movie *Saturday Night Fever* made 1977 a very good year for the record business. Black music, notably funk, had by default given the industry an enormous boost in the form of disco – a mutation that was embraced by white audiences. So, when Minneapolis studio owner Chris Moon turned up at the offices of Owen Husney with a three-track demo he had co-written with a youngster whom he described as a 'sixteen-year-old [*sic*] who will be the next Stevie Wonder, except he's not blind', Husney probably thought he would be getting a surprising new twist to disco, or at least a black artist who could perhaps tap into the lucrative market being milked by the likes of Michael Jackson. 'I put the demo in the tape machine and I said, God, that group is fantastic,' says Husney. 'But it was one person writing everything, singing everything, playing all the instruments.'

Warner weren't known for signing black acts – they were a 'vanilla' label, home to mostly country and rock – but signing Prince in June 1977 was their attempt to be up with the times, and that deal was the first of its kind for a black artist. He would deliver three albums for $1 million. And Warner agreed to the terms: he would produce his debut album, *For You*, released in April 1978, himself. 'We took him into the studio one day,' recalls Lenny Waronker, then an A&R man at Warner, now at Dreamworks SKG Music. 'We said, "Play the drums," and he played the drums and put down guitar and bass parts. And we just said, "Yeah, fine, that's good enough."'

Although Warner imposed the restraining influence of Tommy Vicari as 'executive producer' to oversee recording, the bill for the first album, about $170,000, used up the budget for the next two albums as well.

But Warner were understanding, indulgent even, of their new signing – they stumped up more cash to finance his first tour. 'Warner Brothers has defended artistic freedom since the beginning,' said the rapper Ice-T in his book *The Ice Opinion*. 'Warner is the number-one hated label by the Parents Music Resource Center. They've been fighting Tipper Gore for years. They put out every one of my records without censoring them. Dig this, they put out "Cop Killer".' Ice-T claimed it was the police who forced Time–Warner, the label's parent company, to recall the record, by withdrawing police pension-fund money from the company. The controversy cost Warner $150 million.

The climate in the industry today is very different from the 1970s. 'It's become corporate America up here in Rockefeller Plaza,' a Warner vice-president says, referring to the company's Manhattan headquarters. 'Nothing has been the same since Mo Ostin left. It's all about money. If they don't like what you're doing, you're out. These guys aren't star-struck. We used to be seen as the artists' label – look, we've held on to Joni Mitchell all these years. Not any more. And artists like Prince aren't going to be happy in that environment.'

Mo Ostin and Lenny Waronker, who became respectively CEO and president at Warner Music, had been regarded as two of the few executives to put the music first. Together they had built up an artist roster and back catalogue other labels only dreamed about. Then it all started to go wrong. Time–Warner lost its chairman, Steve Ross, who died in December 1992. After that, the power of the mighty corporation was wielded by Robert Morgado, Music Group chairman. At that time, only Warner/Reprise, headed by Ostin and Waronker, was doing well. Morgado put Doug Morris in charge of all the labels. Ostin left on 31 December 1994, after thirty-one years. Waronker left his job at the end of 1995. Michael Ostin, Mo's son, left his job as senior vice-president. Their new home? Dreamworks SKG Music. There are no job titles at the new label, part of the Steven Spielberg, David Geffen and Jeffrey Katzenburg empire, and they already seem to be taking recalcitrant artists under their wing – their first signing was George Michael, whose freedom from Sony they bought for $40 million.

From 1958 to 1962, the Warner record division lost money and the film company considered closing it down. Then albums from comedian Allen Sherman, folk group Peter, Paul and Mary, and actor/comedian Bill Cosby, turned it around. CBS and the foul-mouthed Walter Yetnikoff now had a rival: the short, bald and media-shy Mo Ostin, who had started out as Frank Sinatra's accountant. In 1963, Sinatra sold his label, Reprise, to Warner, and Ostin was chosen to run Warner/Reprise. With the signing of the Grateful Dead, Warner was on its way to becoming a rock label. Mo Ostin might have been faceless, but Warner had other, more high-profile star-makers: Jerry Wexler at Atlantic, David Geffen at Asylum. Warner's nurturing of acts including Prince, Madonna, Talking Heads, Tracy Chapman and Anita Baker means it has the best reputation for A&R in the business. Other labels tried to lure artists away with bigger and bigger advances. The bidding war started by Warner and CBS upped the ante and set in motion the crazy numbers game that still operates today.

In the late 1970s, about the time Prince was trying to get his first deal, which he now admits he entered into naïvely, the majors – then CBS, Warner, RCA, Capitol-EMI, PolyGram and MCA – already had the industry in the bag. Their nationwide monopoly of distribution was in place, and they were already snapping up smaller labels: Motown, for example, was distributed by MCA, Virgin by WEA (the distribution arm standing for Warner/Elektra/Atlantic). By the 1990s, things were a little less complicated. The industry was even less diverse. The majors are now Sony (Epic, CBS, Columbia and S2); BMG (Arista, RCA, Def Jam); EMI (Parlophone, Chrysalis, Capitol and Virgin); PolyGram (Mercury, Polydor, A&M, Island and Motown); and, of course, Time–Warner (WEA, Warner Bros Records, East West and Atlantic). The newest contender is the aforementioned Dreamworks SKG Music, marketed by Geffen Records, part of MCA Inc. (renamed Universal Studios Inc. in December 1996), which is in turn owned by Seagram, the global beverage and entertainment company.

The result of all this merging is simple: artists looking for a deal have nowhere near as many labels to choose from, and lawyers orchestrating the deals don't want to alienate one label for fear they might jeopardise a deal for their next client. 'Lawyers and managers never forget their power is tenuous,' wrote Frederic Dannen in his 1991 book, *Hit Men*. 'Artists may fire them or fall from the charts. Record labels are happy to exploit this insecurity. The result is a much too cosy relationship between labels and artists' representatives.'

Indulgence, experimentation and risk-taking are far less common today. The dropping of a new act before it has even completed its first album is more and more common. 'At a major you have to sell several million albums to experience profit because of the way the deal is structured,' says J. R. Reynolds, R&B editor of *Billboard* magazine. 'In the US, an artist has to go platinum [1 million units], whereas an independent could sell 300,000 and make a profit. MC Hammer, back in the old days, was selling records out of the trunk of his car and making all kinds of money. When he went to a major, he experienced a decline, a lot of it attributed to waste.' In 1991, the American business magazine *Forbes* listed Hammer's income at $33 million. By 1996 he had filed for bankruptcy.

'The crime they get away with legally in the music business wouldn't be stood for anywhere else,' says Greg Tate. 'Somebody loans you $250,000 and you make them a million.'

This is how an advance works: the record company pays a sum to the artist, and then keeps the artist's royalties until that sum is paid off. The key to understanding contracts is the word 'recoupable'. Manufacturing costs, studio time, packaging, travel, limousines, videos, are all recoupable – paid out of the artist's royalties, not gross receipts. Traditionally, promotion, advertising and marketing are non-recoupable. A record company can make a profit off an album while the artist's account is still in the red. And don't forget about cross-collateralisation, a useful device whereby if an artist is in the red for one album, but the second would have recouped his advance and then some, the profit on the second goes towards paying off the debt on the first.

'You're gonna have to do a lotta hard work to find out how much you're selling anyway, because the labels are always going to undercut it,' Tate continues. 'And if you're not the writer, you're not getting jack. Look at Sarah Vaughan, stuck with a 25-year contract. Look at George Michael. You can't beat the labels at this game, because they invented it.'

'When a new artist agrees to a deal, nobody tells them it's a loan,' says Charles Aaron of *Spin*. 'Take the Fugees, for example. They are well educated, have strong family members behind them, they own their own company, but it's difficult doing everything. Look at REM, now the richest band in the world. They are smart. You can bet they are putting away their Warner advance to put their kids through college. Poor Prince. He spent his money on making more music.'

When it came time for REM to renegotiate their Warner deal in August 1996, the by now beleaguered company offered them $80 million for five albums. But by October, newspaper headlines were screaming, 'REM flop rocks record moguls'. The much-hyped *New Adventures in Hi-Fi* hadn't sold as strongly as other releases.

'The great shame of deals like that given to REM,' says David Fricke, 'is it suggests that is the standard to which you must aspire. Artists get greedy. Why does every label feel you need to sell two, three, four million copies? A lot of acts were signed by ambulance-chasing A&R weasel-fest approaches in the wake of Nirvana and Pearl Jam and they got hosed, big-time. They put out a record, it does okay. The next one doesn't do okay. They end up looking for another deal, working in a car wash somewhere. I can't imagine another business with that kind of casual attention to people's careers. But anyone who enters a deal blindly in this day and age gets what they deserve.'

'It has been the case since the emancipation that black people were not allowed to enter the higher echelons of the industry,' says Rickey Vincent, who not only wrote *Funk*, but also teaches ethnic studies at San Francisco State University. 'In the 1960s and 1970s there was a sense of optimism at Motown, Stax, Philadelphia International. But by the late 1970s the industry had figured out there was a lot of money at stake and they needed to control every aspect of the music.'

'R&B artists have the more difficult time because they are perceived as a minority and usually the senior executives are not as familiar with that music and culture,' says J. R. Reynolds. 'The number of black music executives isn't commensurate with the contribution black music makes across the board.' In the week we spoke, 28 September 1996, black acts in the Hot 100 pop singles chart numbered forty-three. 'But even the most insensitive senior executive recognises that if an artist can make them money, then all of a sudden they become colour-blind. Prince's marketability has fallen off tremendously in recent years, whether because of his age, or because of the fact that record buyers are so young and trendy now.'

'A white kid in a grunge group is more likely to have an uncle who's a lawyer than, say, the rapper KRS-One, who was homeless on the streets of New York when he signed his deal,' said *Newsweek* magazine. 'Rap acts are routinely signed for half the advance the average new white alternative band can expect.'

Wendy Day of the Rap Coalition, an organisation based in Brooklyn, New York, that tries to organise and protect young black artists, has calculated that even if a record goes gold in the US – 500,000 copies – the artist could actually be earning $12 an hour. An artist on a royalty rate of 12 per cent gets about 96 cents on each CD sold. The label will recoup its advance from that 96 cents, as well as putting money aside from that 96 cents to cover any unsold units. Free TLC.

'Michael Jackson has put together a really strong management machine outside his label,' says J. R. Reynolds. 'In the case of Prince, it was a revolving door over at Paisley Park. He makes inexperienced people vice-president of his company. This is something black artists tend to do: they surround themselves with people who were with them from the beginning, but they are putting these people – family, friends – in a position in which they have no experience. By the time they have learned the job, they have already squandered millions of dollars.'

'Prince has not had the good sense to turn his business over to the right people since 1988, when he fired the managers, lawyers and accountants who had been with him since 1979,' commented Jon Bream.

Prince and Owen Husney parted company because he found they could no longer discuss business. It became harder and harder to get a decision of any kind from Prince. The manager who was able to stand up to him, and who became a close friend, was Steve Fargnoli, of Cavallo, Rufallo and Fargnoli (affectionately known as Spaghetti Inc.). Bob Cavallo and Joe Ruffalo were then two music business veterans in their forties, who had learned the ropes with the Lovin' Spoonful and Earth, Wind & Fire. They were joined in 1977 by Fargnoli, a 27-year-old history graduate turned booking agent. The firm took over Prince's career in 1979 and were with him during his most productive period, until right after the hugely successful *Lovesexy* tour. They made the Oscar-winning movie *Purple Rain* possible. It was Fargnoli who was able to convince Prince back in 1987 that Paisley Park Studios could not be used as a personal playground and must pay its way. The reasons for their parting company are still unclear, but Fargnoli would later claim Prince had failed to take their advice from as early as 1985, right after *Purple Rain* transformed the quirky, eccentric genius into a star with the clout to do exactly as he pleased.

Fargnoli declined to return my calls for this book. Part of the agreement when he split with Prince was that he would not have any involvement with any books about his former client. He is now based in London, the head of Pure Management, looking after the likes of Donna Lewis and World Party.

After the fall-out with Fargnoli, Prince turned to Albert Magnoli, the director and co-screenwriter of *Purple Rain*, who had never managed anyone before in his life. 'In 1987, after we had finished shooting the film of *Sign o' the Times*, I was asked to stick around and put together some documentary footage, behind-the-scenes stuff,' says Magnoli. 'We were working together a lot during '87 and '88, and Prince asked me if I would take over his personal and business affairs just to straighten things out. After thinking about it for a few months, I said yes.'

'Albert Magnoli is the biggest male chauvinist I've ever met in my entire life,' says Karen Krattinger, Prince's assistant at that time. 'Until the day I left, Magnoli had to call me to get to Prince, he never had Prince's number. The same with Cavallo, Ruffalo and Fargnoli – if they wanted to speak to Prince they had to call me. Magnoli couldn't stand me, he resented the fact I was closer to Prince than he was. When it came down it was New Year's Eve going into '89. Prince called me and asked me to have someone pick up some paperwork at the airport, so I sent a runner, said take this to Prince, wait, and bring it to me. Of course I wasn't letting anything go anywhere without seeing it and copying it and documenting it, and what it was, it was a draft that Magnoli had made to fire Cavallo, Ruffalo and Fargnoli, fire Lee Phillips, the attorney. I called Prince and said, "Is there something you want to tell me?" He said, "Oh, it's gonna be great. Magnoli understands me, it's gonna be wonderful." Magnoli wanted me out. Whatever he said to Prince, Prince didn't fight to keep me and I felt very betrayed.'

Krattinger was told by Magnoli not to bother coming into Paisley Park, but she went in to gather her belongings and say goodbye to her staff. Prince told her to write to him, and she did, two or three times, but he never replied. 'The shocking thing was being involved in every single aspect of his life – his family, the women, his career, his band, his home – for five years, and all of a sudden I was gone, completely cut off, like I was dead. I don't know why Prince does that. I've seen him twice in all these years.' She received numerous offers to buy her story, but she turned them all down. 'I got two months' severance, that was it. People said, you know all the dirt, you know about all the women, but I would never do that. Prince doesn't deserve that. He paid me to be there. I feel proud I didn't try to blackmail him.' She heard that, after Magnoli left, Prince wanted her back, but he didn't pick up the phone to ask her. She might have said yes then, but not now. She is married, living just outside Nashville city limits, and is a partner in a management company. She was replaced at Paisley by Therese Stoulil. 'Therese got thrown in more and more as things fell apart,' says Krattinger. 'She would phone me and say, "I sit here and think, what would Karen do?" She left in the autumn of '96, and I know she went through the same sort of hurt I did.' After leaving Prince, Krattinger went to work as tour manager for The The. 'We were in New Zealand, I was still feeling devastated. I turned on the TV and *Purple Rain* was on. I thought, how am I ever going to get him out of my life?'

Magnoli was meanwhile juggling Prince's increasingly complex financial affairs. Wasn't the decision to manage Prince rather strange for someone with no experience in that area? 'Our relationship had developed past the professional point – we were very close friends,' says Magnoli by way of explanation. 'It was a natural inclination on his part to just say, hey, would you like to get involved in this and stick with me for a while? We agreed it would be for a short period of time. We had a long-term dream of being able, with Mark Canton of Warner, to develop a Broadway programme, whereby Prince could write music for the stage. We wanted to renegotiate the record deal, so that it was more realistic and would give Prince a little more artistic leverage. And we wanted to create a film company that would allow us to continue making musicals. We did the videos, we were on our way to negotiating these things, when I was offered to go and direct *Tango and Cash* for Mark and Jon Peters.'

It was an offer too good to refuse. Prince was temporarily left to his own devices. His next film project, without Magnoli, would turn out to be *Graffiti Bridge*. Magnoli has continued to direct films; his latest, which finished shooting in January 1997, was a low-budget sci-fi adventure starring Michael York. 'When I met Prince, I was taken by his tremendous vulnerability. His artistry doesn't come out of strength or arrogance or aggression, it comes out of a profound vulnerability. When we saw each other for the first time, that's when I thought all was right with the world, because I said, we're gonna do okay. We enjoyed each other's company, we talked about a lot of things. Prince has gone through a lot of transitions in the last few years. I would love to work with him again. Actually, we do have something up our sleeves. We have a project that we've talked about and that is still relevant. Another movie. A big movie.'

He was succeeded, after a year and a half at the helm, by Randy Phillips and Arnold Stiefel. Then, on 20 December 1990, Prince made the first of a series of ill-advised decisions. His contract with Phillips and Stiefel was only for twelve months, and when that expired he decided to manage himself. Jill Willis, who previously handled his publicity at the New York PR firm Rogers & Cowan, and Gilbert Davison, his friend and former head of security, would act as executive vice-president and president, respectively, of Paisley Park Enterprises.

The first year that Prince was effectively his own manager, with Willis and Davison running day-to-day business, was a year of cancelled concerts, controversy and endless lawsuits. The cracks between Prince and Warner were beginning to show. They were finding it increasingly difficult, without a management team, to communicate with him. In February, Fargnoli's firm sued Prince, saying he released records in competition with one another. They claimed he had failed to pay what had been agreed in the severance deal. They sought publishing royalties from him for songs written while he was still managed by them. 'The settlement agreement included [the firm] being paid in the future on a percentage of royalties, including publishing,' said Jill Willis. Prince in turn sued his former lawyers over the settlement with Fargnoli. In December, Fargnoli would bring another lawsuit, claiming the song 'Jughead' on *Diamonds and Pearls* was about him, calling him a 'parasite'. The track mentions a manager who causes his client to 'die broke'. He claimed $5 million.

In January 1991, Prince walked off stage during his first appearance at the 'Rock in Rio' festival. The stage was pelted with objects, and jeering Guns 'N' Roses fans shouted 'Prince is a faggot!' when he came on in a black leotard. He played 'Kiss' and 'Purple Rain', the first few bars of which would melt the heart of even the most die-hard Axl Rose fan. His dancers were dripping sweat, but the superfit Prince didn't even look moist. At the end of his performance, he gave a little speech: 'Rio, there's a war going on. I don't know whassup but I think we'd all be better off living for love.' He bought the TV rights to his second performance and refused MTV permission to air the show.

In August he released 'Gett Off', much against Warner's advice – they felt it was far too raunchy. Indeed, the video, in which he sported his new Carmen Miranda look, was based on Bob Guccione's *Caligula* movie, and had to be excised of its bare breasts before MTV would air it. Warner wanted him to release 'Cream' as a single instead. Fans in Britain pushed 'Gett Off' to number four. Their reward? The cancellation of his only European date that year, at Blenheim Palace on 31 August.

Diamond Promotions, who had set up the concert, were new to the game. Because they weren't one of the seasoned promoters, they used the money they had earned staging raves and remortgaged their homes to pay Prince an advance of approximately £300,000. They allegedly cut some corners – factors contributing to the cancellation included failure to insure the workmen putting up the stage, and not hiring the expensive, but extra-safe, crash barriers Prince insisted on.

When Prince announced he was not going to appear – his statement said he pulled out owing to 'the promoter's continuing failure to fulfil critical obligations to vendors, suppliers and other production personnel and companies' – the ticket money that should have been held in an escrow account for that very eventuality had already been spent on the advance and costs. Some agencies gave fans a straight refund of their money; they wrongly believed they would be reimbursed, and many went out of business. No information on what ticket-holders should do was forthcoming; a month later, 48,000 were still awaiting refunds, and the fraud squad was called in (although no fraud was found to have taken place). Diamond Promotions accused Prince of holding on to the advance at the fans' expense. The only address fans were given for advice was the official fan club office in Croydon; it received tens of thousands of letters, which were all replied to, pushing the club into £38,000 of debt; Paisley later sent £8,000 towards administration costs. It was a mess. Not until that December did Jill Willis, by then running Paisley Park, fly to London for a press conference, announcing that Blenheim ticket-holders could exchange their tickets for the next year's tour. Prince was under no legal obligation to do this, and it cost him £800,000. In the end, 30,000 were given priority seats, an organisational feat performed by the experienced promoter Barry Clayman. Fan club members were eventually given their Blenheim tickets back as souvenirs.

Prince had cancelled British shows before, of course. His scheduled Wembley Stadium dates in June 1987, the *Sign o' the Times* tour, were scrapped ostensibly because 'Prince's whole set would be ruined if it was wet,' his label announced, and an alternative indoor venue couldn't be found (Earls Court was already booked). The real reason could have been problems with the promoter, or disappointing ticket sales. The European leg of the tour had been a success, and his decision to skip Britain and the US was, says Eric Leeds, 'the biggest mistake he ever made. He had momentum going with the record, but he said the concert film would fill in the gaps.' The fans obliged (at the press screening of the *Sign o' the Times* movie, critics clapped and sang along – unprecedented) and flocked to his next British tour, *Lovesexy*. This time round, though, after Blenheim, they were less inclined to be indulgent.

Prince was desperate to repolish his tarnished image. He contacted the BBC's *Omnibus* team and offered footage from the aborted Albert Magnoli documentary, and archive film that included a benefit concert at Paisley and rehearsals for the *Lovesexy* tour. As Bob Portway, the producer of the programme, recalls: 'He sent poor old Gilbert Davison to London to oversee the editing, and provided us with a list of changes he wanted. We really didn't have much artistic control. While we were at Paisley, shooting, we got bored and started filming the resident cat.

Immediately, one of his minions ran over shouting, "That's Paisley! You can't film him, he's Prince's cat.'"

In August 1992, Prince and Warner signed the deal that would reputedly earn the star $100 million. It would fund six albums, each with an advance of $10 million, and provide joint-venture funding for Paisley Park Records, another new label, and payment for Prince in the role of vice-president of A&R. Oh, and a suite of offices in the Warner building in Century City, California.

'I was one of the people who put that deal together,' says Jill Willis. 'At first, Prince was very happy with the deal. But he felt it gave them even greater control over him. I was with Prince for three years, heading up Paisley Park Enterprises during a very difficult time for him.' She left Prince in 1993, 'to have more of a life, slow down. I'd moved to Minneapolis, was constantly going on trips to LA. It looks exciting from the outside but it was hard work. I spoke to Prince every day but I can't say we had a personal relationship. Gilbert stayed a year or so after I left, then Prince decided to go completely on his own. He had learned a lot, but he couldn't possibly be involved with every detail – he hired people and they hired people.' Willis now runs her own company in Minneapolis – Renaissance, whose client roster is headed by Donny Osmond. She has a farm and horses. She doesn't ever bump into Prince around town.

So why did Prince suddenly announce to the world, on 27 April 1993, that he was to retire from studio recording? Mo Ostin and Lenny Waronker were told the bad news by Gilbert Davison. Prince would fulfil his contract with songs from his vault, which at that time numbered about five hundred. The statement said that after fifteen albums in fifteen years, he was turning his talents to other media. He was angry that his $\female$ album hadn't been a hit, and wanted Warner to release another album that summer. They refused. Compare Prince's output to Michael Jackson's: the pale one had released just five albums in the same fifteen-year period.

Although that $100 million made the headlines, many in the industry called it absurd. If Prince had been guaranteed that amount, it is unlikely Warner would make a penny. The figure was the very highest he could make at the very best levels of sales performance. At his royalty rate of 20 per cent, he would have to sell five million copies before Warner could recoup its advance. At best the label had a chance of breaking even, and they certainly wouldn't want him putting out album after album, not giving them a chance to recoup their money. Once the label had committed themselves to figures of that sort, they felt they would have more control over his output. They wanted to apply proven hit-making strategies: release one album a year; ensure it contains a string of potential singles, and put those out with a variety of mixes; ensure their artist adhered to the advice of in-house promotion and marketing departments. And Warner will have built in financial safeguards, perhaps stipulating that any unrecouped advance be taken out of his publishing income. Many in the industry believed Prince didn't have it in him to support such a deal.

On 7 June 1993, Prince's thirty-fifth birthday, he announced to the world that he was changing his name to ⚥ – a symbol representing both a man and a woman. Bob Merlis commented at the time: 'He said to people in our building you can call me anything you want.' An employee at Paisley Park said that Prince still answered to Prince. While he was in New York to make the announcement, an MTV reporter asked him how he would like to be called and he replied, 'Just call me darling.' The tabloid press, though, had a field day. They called him every name under the sun. That he merely wanted the freedom to put out more material under his new name went unnoticed.

Warner might have wanted Prince to put on the brakes, but he had other ideas. The man born Prince Roger Nelson later explained to *Vibe*'s Alan Light: 'I'm not the son of Nel. I don't know who that is, Nel's son, and that's my last name. I asked Gilbert [Davison] if he knew who David was, and he didn't know what I was talking about. I would wake up at nights thinking, "Who am I?" I don't mind if people are cynical or make jokes. You find out quickly who respects and who disrespects you. It took Muhammad Ali years before people stopped calling him Cassius Clay.'

That year, Warner released his greatest-hits package, which the now former Prince helpfully backed up with the announcement, 'Greatest-hits albums are for artists who are dead, physically and professionally.'

Warner didn't take the name-change well. They managed to send out floppy disks with the new typographical character to newspapers, and it was used with varying degrees of success (it was put into the system at the *Sunday Times* on a press night and corrupted the computer system for four hours. The disk wasn't used again). Warner's full-page announcement in *Billboard* was full of jokey squiggles and symbols presenting the change:

We here at 🛡 treat our artists with a

lot of ♡. It makes us ☺ when they

become ⭐⭐ . If our artists want to be

called ◎ or ☯ that's cool. We just

want to make a $ and have a good time.

So here's the new Prince album. But

don't call him Prince, call him . O. K.?

☮ W.B.

Prince was not amused. He took out an ad the next week that read:

We here at **NPG** treat our artists with *respect.* It makes us ☹ when they are ☹ . If they have new ♫ they want 2 give to their 📻s that's cool. We just want 2 bring u ♫ so u can have a good time. So here's the new album from ⚥ and friends. Just don't call him Prince. O.K.?

☮ and be Wild. N.P.G.

He played Wembley Stadium in August 1993 (thankfully, it didn't rain), as part of his ⚥ tour, and fans were treated to an amazing after-show gig at the Forum in north London. The show wasn't confirmed until 7 P.M. the same evening, after fans had already taken their seats in the stadium. The management wanted Eileen Murton to make an announcement on stage, asking fans to approach her after the main show for their party tickets. She told the management she thought the idea was ill-conceived: she would have been trampled by those entitled to tickets and lynched by those who weren't. Consequently, despite all the thrusting of tickets at fans leaving the show, the Forum was barely half-full. A shame. It was a great night.

Prince even attempted stage-diving, but unfortunately his fans were so in awe of him they parted and he fell to the floor. 'As I watched the spectacle from the balcony,' says Murton, 'he simply disappeared. A few fans did gingerly help him up and found him giggling. One girl stroked his bum. He gave her a huge smile.'

The party after his Wembley Arena show that September, at Bagley Studios, a shabby warehouse in King's Cross, north London, was an unmitigated disaster. Tickets handed in at the door were openly resold to those further back in the queue, and the numbers inside exceeded fire regulations many times over. Security and first aid were non-existent, and those overcome by the conditions found it hard to leave, their path blocked by locked doors. Many people, including Kylie Minogue and George Michael, gave up and went home before Prince came on stage. One fan fainted and was deposited in a puddle in the sawdust outside; she came to as Prince stepped out of his limousine, and wasn't pleased not to be looking her best. Prince himself looked extremely nervous, as he saw the crush in front of the stage and eyed the beer bottles in people's hands. He refused to go on until 3 A.M. Angry fans called in the police; there was one with a broken arm and many with cracked ribs. It would take more than a fawning *Omnibus* documentary to make up for *that* night.

Controversy, the official fan club and magazine, had started out as a photocopied fanzine in 1986, and went on to receive many accolades in its own right. After a couple of years, Murton was invited by Prince to run his official fan club, while being allowed to retain her independence – a situation completely unheard of throughout the fan-club world, where managements traditionally retain a strong grip. The club brought together Prince fans all over the world, organising the best and cheapest seats at his concerts as well as social gatherings and conventions. Prince enjoyed the magazine and was always keen to read his copy, and used it to try to explain his change of name (that took a very long letter from Mayte).

'I used to send Prince's copy of the magazine by special air-mail,' says Murton. 'I was told he used to walk around Paisley with it, and wouldn't put it down until he'd read it cover to cover. The *Batman* issue was one of his favourites. He had his PA phone me and I could hear him talking in the background – his voice was instantly recognisable – telling her to tell me what he liked. His office sent us photographs for each issue. Once he personally chose a master transparency to be sent with a note saying it was for the centre spread. It was of his bare torso, nothing else. The master copy gives superb reproduction and we treated it with kid gloves before returning it. The printer phoned me up and said, "I can't print this, it's pornographic, you can see his pubes!" Debatable, but we printed it anyway.'

Fans even clubbed together to pay for his star in the Hollywood Walk of Fame. Karen Lee, then working at Paisley Park, had already approached the committee that decides who receives this rather dubious honour – all you really have to do is be nominated, be selected, stump up $5,000 and turn up at the ceremony. She then approached Controversy and asked if fans would like to contribute to the cost; $2,000 was raised by the time of the club's closure, but that year Prince lost out to Duran Duran. After the closure, Paisley Park took over responsibility for the funds but never bothered to reapply.

Murton organised two Controversy conventions in Minneapolis, in 1991 and 1992, which seemed to cause Prince a great deal of amusement. He would do things such as place a skip outside Paisley Park and fill it with CDs – with security cameras videoing the fans as they dived headlong into it. Just as all the fans had got safely back on to the coaches, he would make sure a band member drove up, thus ensuring chaos. 'Prince found the security tapes hysterical, and watched them a number of times,' says Murton. His staff also organised some excellent entertainment during convention weeks. One such event was an album-listening party at Glam Slam which Prince's mother attended. A commemorative card, designed and printed at Paisley Park, was given to each party-goer. Band members were present to talk to or dance with.

The magazine was always very down to earth and put all the tabloid stories in their place – denying, for example, that Prince had a passion for collecting and reconditioning vacuum cleaners. He even invited Controversy members backstage at Wembley to ask him questions, and took a handful on board the tour bus during the *Lovesexy* tour.

'Alan Leeds called me at 11 P.M. one night,' says Murton. 'He said that Prince had had such a good time meeting the kids on the tour coach and at the airport, he wondered if they'd like to watch him rehearsing. I phoned people at home, but they were either asleep or had turned the phone off. The hardened fans were still camped outside Prince's hotel and uncontactable. I picked up one lad in Croydon and agreed to meet some others at the studio in King's Cross, but when we got to the studio, there were only a couple of fans who'd managed to find it. I don't think it occurred to Prince that getting people to the notoriously seedy area of King's Cross at midnight wasn't the easiest thing in the world. In any event, he looked great – relaxed, playing his guitar about two feet away from us alongside the rest of the band. It got to two or three in the morning, and I asked Steve Fargnoli whether Prince minded working this late. He said, "No, he's playing – this is how he relaxes."'

But by the autumn of 1983, the good relationship between Prince and his fan club was soured by the Wembley Arena concert on the night of the Bagley Studios débâcle. According to Murton, 'A tour crew member named Stefan, wearing an official-looking Controversy laminate as well as an official tour laminate pass, and one of Prince's personal bodyguards, Arthur, who was identified by all complainants from a photograph which appeared in the national press, recruited twenty-two young girls to collect names and addresses for them, purportedly for the fan club, before the concert. The girls were promised front-row seats (which was an impossible claim, as all tickets for Wembley were pre-sold), a T-shirt worth £20 and a ticket to the party at Bagley's later that evening for their efforts. When one girl queried the Controversy connection, she was assured by Arthur that they were indeed helping the fan club. The girls stood outside the concert hall as instructed until they were advised by Arthur to hurry along, as Prince was already on stage. No front-row tickets. They were told to collect the rest of their goodies after the show, but were finally ejected by Wembley security. What had for many of these girls been their first-ever concert turned into disappointment when they realised they'd been duped. Only five of the twenty-two wrote to Controversy. The scheme had nothing to do with the club – it was some sort of wheeze to obtain names for the database Paisley Park was building up for its retail outlet.

'When I heard what had gone on, and couldn't get anyone at Paisley Park to discuss what had been done, I felt personally deceived,' says Murton. 'I felt that that fan club members had been betrayed. No matter how much I liked the fans and the club, I was also running a business and couldn't foresee any future with Paisley staff acting as loose cannons – they could ruin the fan club's reputation. Despite their actions, I knew there was nothing malicious in what they'd done. By that time, the Park was having financial difficulties and the staff were worn to a frazzle. Nobody would have thought through the possible consequences, and that in itself could cause untold problems in the future.

'Sadly, the closure [of the club] had nothing to do with Prince or the fans, the two parties for whom the club existed. I don't think anyone denies that the Controversy crowd and Prince had a good thing going. However, it is with management teams that fan clubs deal, and I felt we couldn't continue.' After Murton told Paisley Park about her decision, she got a call from Duane Nelson, by then almost running Prince's affairs. He told her that Prince felt 'hurt and abandoned'.

All good things, they say, never last.

In February 1994, Prince received a blow from Warner, who announced they were terminating the Paisley Park Records label, a joint venture since 1992. Apart from Prince releases and a reunion album by his funky foils The Time in 1990, it hadn't come up with a hit. Albums by Eric Leeds, Mavis Staples, George Clinton and the NPG, as well as Carmen Electra's debut, had all failed to catch fire – although Prince, of course, blamed Warner. The plush offices in Century City, which he had never set foot in, were closed, its twelve staff laid off.

'Prince was fed up,' says Greg Tate. 'A senior Warner executive told Prince he didn't have it in him to make another hit record. The next day, Prince wrote "The Most Beautiful Girl In The World". It was his first British number one.'

Prince stumped up $2 million of his own money and put the record out on his NPG label, distributed through Bellmark Records (whose president, Al Bell, was also part of Stax Records in the 1960s). Warner didn't send out press copies or do any of the marketing or promotion. It was Britain's number one in April that year; in the US it reached number three on the *Billboard* Hot 100 pop chart. Prince, accompanied by Mayte, made a special video for *Top of the Pops*. It featured a rather shaky, obviously handmade logo of the programme's name propped up in the background. Is that what happens when you take away Warner's big-bucks marketing departments?

He had pulled a hit out of the bag before, of course. After the commercial failure of *Around the World in a Day*, widely considered to be his *Sgt Pepper*, he wrote 'Kiss', a huge smash. But 'Beautiful Girl' was especially satisfying for him. It not only proved he could top the charts; it would change the course of his career. He realised he didn't need a major label any more. He had just got a very big idea. There was only one obstacle: he had to get out of that deal with Warner.

Compare the way he delivered *The Gold Experience* to Warner with the way he handed over *Around the World in a Day*, on 21 February 1985. When that album was ready, a purple limousine pulled up outside the label's Burbank offices and Prince, wearing an antique purple kimono, his father, John L. Nelson, and Wendy Melvoin entered the building. 'I've seen Shaun Cassidy walk into this building,' said an excited employee, 'but nothing like this.' About 150 Warner staff and executives, including Mo Ostin, were crammed into the fourth-floor conference room. Apart from whispering to Ostin, Prince was silent. He sat on the floor with Melvoin and his father while the tape of the album blasted at full volume. 'Everyone stood up at the end and applauded. But he'd already left the building,' said the employee.

By the time the *Gold* album was ready, the industry's usually sober newspaper of record, *Billboard*, found the animosity between Prince and Warner something of a joke. The label had rescheduled the release twice because, they claimed, Prince failed to deliver the master. 'Their relationship has deteriorated to such a point that his new record may never come out,' it reported in October 1994. 'Maybe Warner executives just don't know how to ask for him by name when they call on the phone. He now feels his much-publicised $100 million deal may have been a way to lock him into institution-alised slavery. For $100 million we'd walk barefoot across hot coals singing "Raspberry Beret" in Swahili.'

This wasn't a good time to think of going it alone. The non-sellout *Gold* tour of 1995 pretty much scuppered his finances, which had been going from bad to worse. His autonomous, eccentric and pro-lific way of working was not synonymous with good business. 'Prince was used to keeping his recording studio open twenty-four hours a day, seven days a week, in case on a whim he wanted to make some music,' says a Warner director of publicity. 'You know how much a state-of-the-art studio costs to run? It's a shame. Once, when he wanted to make a video, he could make a video. He's not broke, but he can't make a video. Warner gave him $25 million to set up a label. You can't blame us. Look at what Madonna has managed to do with hers. Prince spent $2 million filming Carmen [Electra] in Egypt, but do you know anyone who bought her record?'

Things hadn't been going smoothly at Paisley Park for a while. In 1993, Prince changed his top executives three times. He continued to spend money, notably on an album, *Child of the Sun*, by Mayte, which largely remained in boxes in record warehouses. The Glam Slam club in his home town, co-owned by Gilbert Davison and a local busi-nesswoman, Ruth Whitney Bowe, had opened in 1990 with a per-formance by Rosie Gaines, but it was dogged by bad press (it was host to some great bands in its time – Oasis played there in 1995). Davison, always slick in a suit and a ponytail, was fond of giving guests a grand tour of the premises, the VIP room, the largest bar in the state, the merchandise shop he boasted was 'the only place in

America you can buy Prince's personal fan magazine from London, *Controversy'*. ('Not true,' says Eileen Murton. 'You could buy it in record stores.') In 1993 Bowe took Davison to court, claiming she was 'involuntarily separated' from her job as manager of the club. She claimed bartenders 'served alcohol to Prince's under-age girlfriend' and that Davison had threatened to throw her in the trunk of a car.

By January 1995, PPE was not paying its bills on time and the studios were beginning to look decidedly shabby. A local film production company was owed $450,000 and settled for 70 cents on the dollar (it later went bust). Davison had left Prince's employ in the summer of 1994, and so Prince's stepbrother, Duane, was running the shop, along with Therese Stoulil, Prince's loyal PA for over ten years, and Juli Knapp Winge, a former assistant at the old Paisley Park label. Rob Light, long-term LA booking agent, was fulfilling some duties. Prince was still paying off the contracts of some of the employees fired when the Century City offices closed.

In October 1995 the Glam Slam club closed its doors and re-opened with a new name, Quest, and no affiliation with Prince. It is still open for business. Its sole owner? Gilbert Davison. He had astutely ensured he had his name on the liquor licence. Local people began to think there was something seriously wrong over at Paisley.

Forbes, the American business magazine, ran a piece headlined 'Princely Pauper', stating that the star had been helped out of bankruptcy by a loan from Warner and owed them millions. He hadn't been in the top-forty earnings list of entertainers since 1993. According to Robert LaFranco, who compiles the top forty list, 'Prince probably still owes them money. He owed between $10 and $15 million two years ago. His records didn't sell and he was in the red. They probably take money out of his publishing royalties, which brings him in around $5 million a year. And his back catalogue will continue to be used to offset the loan.'

In February 1996, the Miami Glam Slam club closed, as did the NPG merchandise shop in the Uptown area of Minneapolis, selling such items as his fragrance, 'Get Wild' (he was sued by Joan Collins because it was too similar to hers). Paisley Park was closed as a studio for hire – it was already heavily mortgaged and cost millions of dollars a year just to keep up and running. In April, he laid off one of the employees who had been with him the longest, Mark 'Red' White. When asked to talk about the years he had worked with Prince, he replied, 'Those are ten years of my life I don't even want to think about.' By October, even Duane, Juli Knapp Winge, Therese Stoulil and in-house publicist Renee Watson were all history.

Stoulil declined to comment for this book. She said that she was worried about law suits flying around when other former members of staff had talked to the press. It seemed that the people who had been with Prince the longest, who had dedicated years of their lives to him, were feeling bitter, rejected, foolish.

Also in February, the NPG shop in Camden, north London, went into liquidation. Chris Poole, whose name was on the lease, told the *Evening Standard* its debts were not substantial, 'less than £20,000', and that his wife, Marie, who had run the shop, was taking 'a well-deserved rest after working seven days a week for two and a half years'. He failed to mention, though, the £250,000 Prince had put up to open it only two years before. Gone.

Poole and his London PR firm, Poole Edwards, found out their services were no longer needed after five years of working with Prince. 'I think Prince got through six publicists in the US – there is only one firm left in New York that he hasn't already used. His personal assistant, his valet, he just dumped them. It's unfair, he takes a valet and expects him to promote concerts, and when he fails, he'll blow him away. We didn't fall out. I think I had become so involved in his getting out of Warner and the slave thing that he wanted to do something fresh, publicity-wise. In the time I worked for him I showed him huge loyalty above and beyond the call of duty, and feel a little pissed off. But I've got lots of other clients. You get an emotional attachment to someone and we were close, but I've seen him reduce people to tears. He didn't even do me the favour of giving me a personal call and saying, hey, I hope you understand. Some minion called me and said, we don't want to use you any more.

'I know from running the shop an awful lot of the fans have become disillusioned. It's ironic, record companies are all evil, and then immediately after leaving Warner he is like a dog who rolls over. He still owes me money, by the way, so I hope his next album sells well.'

Warner's services were indeed no longer needed. The release of *Chaos and Disorder* put the nail in the coffin of their relationship. 'I was bitter before, but now I've washed my face,' Prince said in the cursory bit of promotion he was persuaded to do (two short press interviews worldwide). 'We feel if he's happier somewhere else, we don't have any beef with him,' said Bob Merlis, the relief evident in his voice.

Prince now had a record that had bombed spectacularly, and a baby on the way. Was his freedom from a major label about to become the artistic equivalent of sharecropping after the real emancipation?

'Bulk sales are the name of the game,' wrote Robert Sandall in the *Sunday Times* in 1988. 'Who knows, who cared, how many copies of *Sgt Pepper* the Beatles sold? Yet who has not heard that Michael Jackson's *Thriller* has shifted more than fifty million units?'

'The nature of celebrity has changed,' wrote David Toop in *The Face* in 1990. 'The extraordinary degree of fame, wealth and market penetration attained by celebrities has become a record-breaking pursuit, like sport; but the downfall is rapid and cruel.'

People weren't queuing up to sign Prince to a new deal, but he didn't have enough money to completely go it alone. Russell Simmons, the head of Def Jam Records, who has made a fortune out of judging exactly what young people want, said, 'I wouldn't pay a penny more than $400,000 for his contract.'

'He is breaking on Prince 'cause he's jealous of us,' said his dinner date that evening, Veronica Webb.

'Things over at Paisley Park are down to the bare bones,' said Alan Light in October 1996. 'They keep saying, it's okay, we're going to reopen the studio. It's painful to see it. He should be worrying about his music, with people around him to run the organisation. Even when I interviewed him three years ago, he had this universe around him where nothing touched him that he didn't want to. There was this wall. Does that make him a freak? Sure, but it's an amazing environment to establish as an artist. He could work any time he wanted.'

Come 1997, though, Madonna, who was born within a month of Prince, and whose Maverick label was funded by Warner, decided to step in. She had always had a great deal of respect for Prince. She spent a few days in Minneapolis prior to her appearance on Live Aid in 1985 – he helped out with the choreography for that performance. And in 1989, they duetted on the Prince-penned 'Love Song' on her *Like a Prayer* album, and he also mooted the idea of casting her in one of his movies. Madonna flew to Minneapolis and had a meeting with him at Paisley Park. Her idea, still unresolved, was a merger between Maverick and its roster of young talent, and NPG Records.

Warner Records were reeling from the aftershock of the previous year. In March 1997, between 70 and 100 staff were laid off. That streamlining followed redundancies of between 16 and 20 staff in their black music division. Despite having the best-selling album of 1996, Alanis Morissette's *Jagged Little Pill*, on the Maverick label, it had been a bad year. Not only had Warner lost their most high-profile act, they had experienced a 6 per cent decline in revenue. The company's worldwide music sales were down, to $3.95 billion from $4.19 billion the year before.

'The very vocal nature of Prince's battle gave the Sonys and the MCAs pause for thought,' says David Fricke. 'If Warner, the great artist-oriented label, can't handle him, how are the great Japanese corporate forefathers going to deal with his stuff? He's stymied. The business doesn't suit him and he doesn't suit the business, yet even when he screws up he's interesting. His dregs are better than most people's carefully calculated product.'

Will Prince ever make the cover of *Rolling Stone* again? 'The no-tape-recorders-allowed, no-notebook-allowed thing, that's boring,' continues Fricke. 'He did that with David Sinclair for *The Times* when he agreed to talk about *Chaos*, and Sinclair said the guy was dull and kinda useless. His manipulative instincts aren't as effective as he thinks they are. It's not funny any more.'

Prince no longer considered himself a slave. His next plan was to release *Emancipation*, a three-CD set 'about the Egyptians, the building of the pyramids'. There would be a cover of the Stylistics' 'Betcha By Golly Wow!', a sample of the heartbeat of his new baby (now there's a new slant on hip-hop) and 'I Can't Make You Love Me', the Bonnie Raitt song ('Ain't no more,' he grinned). He also had plans for a world tour in 1997, to include the US, where he hadn't toured since 1993.

'There isn't an artist who hasn't hit the wall where they are past their peak,' says Susan Rogers, his former engineer. 'Look at Stevie Wonder. Prince is highly intelligent, he'll be able to deal with it. He understands it's inevitable. He will evolve and start putting out vital work again.'

Alan Light: 'You just put out a record that fell off the charts. You haven't been able to sell a record for years. You can blame the record company all you want. You have to win your fans back and putting something out there that's going to cost $25 hardly seems the way to do that. Get on the road and just blow people's minds. You do it better than anybody else alive. I'm worried that people no longer think he's relevant. Remind us why it is we love you so much – make a great record.'

He was about to do just that.

10

Nø I ain't dead yet but what abøut U?

'He is the African folkloric trickster, but transmogrified into a skinny asthmatic with a punk's lurid sensibility.'

That is not a description of Prince, although it fits him perfectly. It describes another of pop's eccentric misfits, Tricky, out of Bristol via London, who feels he could be the British Prince. 'I'm a mongrel,' he says of his Welsh/African/Jamaican heritage, 'but they always say the mongrel is the cleverest animal in the litter.'

Tricky has a creative compulsion that is quickly building up a backlog to rival Prince's. He is also seen as the devil incarnate by black-music-loving purists and the hip-hop community alike: he wears make-up, wedding gowns, he has even dated white women (notably Björk). At New York's Irving Plaza, he gave a performance of 'When Doves Cry' that made the crowd of alternative white boys and hip-hop B-boys down their differences. (That song won't lie down: it's also in the 1997 film *Romeo and Juliet* and on the album by new Sony signing Ginuwine.)

Prince, like Michael Jackson, seemed to run from his blackness. Apart from Cathy Glover and Rosie Gaines, and briefly Nona Gaye, all the featured women in his live shows and videos have been white or Hispanic. 'The scene in *Under the Cherry Moon* where Prince, who has been getting it on with Francesca Annis and Kristin Scott Thomas, runs in terror from a dark-skinned black woman who might want his sexual services,' says Vernon Reid. 'I found that very disturbing.' During the sex scene with Scott Thomas in his car, Prince torments her about her white, repressed attitude to sex. 'You're real quiet at first, then you get loud, then you get black – Oh shit, Christ, oh shit!'

Spike Lee wrote a letter to Prince, challenging him on the women he chose to work with. 'Are there going to be any women of dark complexion in your music videos or your films?' he wrote. Prince wasn't bothered. He told Spike to look at all his work, not just his most successful pieces. 'I used to pull him up on why he didn't use more black women in his videos,' says Rosie Gaines. 'I suggested he ask Spike Lee to direct the video for "Money Don't Matter". I said, "Black people don't understand you any more, Prince. You got to get them back on board."'

'Prince has a huge popularity among black folks,' says Rickey Vincent. 'We all went along and accepted his favouring white women. I've never seen any artist who has had that much undeserving lustful affection from black folks even though he wasn't typical of a black sex symbol. If Teddy Pendergrass had turned up with a white woman in the 1970s, we'd have been really offended. But for some reason, we put up with Prince.'

He grew up in the 'jungle fever capital of America'. As *Village Voice* columnist Lisa Jones writes in her book *Bulletproof Diva*, 'In Prince's new digs, Glam Slam, you'd think black women were pre-historic mammals that didn't make it through the Stone Age. Just as fossils holding up the wall. You would think Afrocentricity never made it past Cleveland.'

'I grew up in a tough part of New York where it wasn't integrated at all,' says the writer Kevin Powell. 'America is not integrated. Until I saw Prince I didn't think integration existed. He was saying, what does it matter if my band is mixed-race? Today, it is out of the question for a hip-hop or R&B artist to have anyone white or Hispanic as a love interest or dancer in their video. But they're hypocritical –

most have white management, white video directors. Change the people behind the scenes as well.'

'I think we are naïve thinking that when people make a video they are making all the artistic choices,' says bell hooks. 'Prince wouldn't have been able to say, I'll have all black women behind me. He hasn't married white – Mayte's not like white white, right? Prince is the opposite of somebody who crossed over. He crossed over, with *Purple Rain*, and crossed back. That is exactly why he is not the rage he used to be. His journey is a lesson in what happens when a black artist crosses over and is rewarded by whites as not being black-identified, when in fact he was always black-identified, except they didn't know it. Look at the Fugees, relegated to the black music divisions until they are a success, then they are everybody's success.'

Greg Tate is clear about what side of the race fence Prince has been sitting on, even during his breakthrough *1999* period. 'He includes on the same album a song made to order for "Apartheid-Oriented Radio", "Little Red Corvette", and another that snidely instructs all the white people how to clap on the beat, "D.M.S.R.".'

There is a fine line between appealing to a broad audience and selling out your own race. 'To fully appreciate the sickness of [Michael] Jackson's savaging of his African physiognomy you have to recall that back when he wore the face he was born with, black folk thought he was the prettiest thing since sliced sushi,' Tate wrote in *Flyboy in the Buttermilk*. Prince still has the face he was born with, but his image has changed drastically over the years – the large Afro of the 1970s was relaxed and coloured, his naturally 'high yellow' complexion caked in pancake, which is out of kilter with what today's young record-buyers want.

At the beginning of the 1980s, the war on poverty was replaced by the war on drugs. By 1982, crack cocaine had swept the streets of every major US city. In the 1980s, black faces all but disappeared from television, even from dance movies (*Footloose* did not feature one black person). By 1982, black music had become narcissistic, hedonistic, reflected in Prince's *1999*, released that year. Black videos might have made their debut on MTV in this year (Michael Jackson's

'Beat It' and Prince's 'Little Red Corvette'), but only by masquerading as 'white' music. 'In 1985, there was only one message song on the R&B chart, "We Are The World". In 1975 there had been thirteen. Gone were the throaty divas, the Arethas and Chaka Khans. Instead came Vanity and Apollonia with all those nasty songs. Even little Janet Jackson had to get nasty to get attention,' wrote Nelson George in *The Death of Rhythm and Blues*. There wasn't any hope: that was the real difference between Prince and Sly and Jimi and Marvin.

In the late 1990s, can music really give hope to a community of people who are eight times more likely to be murdered than whites, where a third of black American males in their twenties are in jail, on parole or probation?

Black kids want someone who is blacker than they are; white kids want the real deal. Mary J. Blige is far cooler, with her raised-in-the-ghetto-princess blonde wig, than Mariah Carey, who in the early press releases issued by her record company was marketed as white, denying her mixed-race heritage. 'They came to see the nose,' wrote Lisa Jones in *Bulletproof Diva*. 'The nose never lies. Even the missing nose of Egypt's great Sphinx tells a story.' The nose in question was Carey's: Columbia/CBS (now Sony) had spent a fortune on promoting their new find – they would make a video, scrap it, and shoot a new one. Carey has pink skin, blonde-streaked hair. But on the CD cover photograph, a strand of that hair snakes strategically across her nose. That's why all these black journalists had come to the lunch. To see the real thing up close and personal. Carey set the record straight: 'My father is black and Venezuelan. My mother is Irish.' The statement made the *New York Post* the next day. Are record companies in the 1990s so out of touch that they really believe they have to pass their performers off as white? After that lunch, Carey's videos started to feature black bit-players, in an attempt to appeal to both sides.

'Imagine an entire generation of young males coming of age and modelling themselves on Dr Dre or Mike Tyson,' wrote Lisa Jones. 'Will they live forever as adolescents, sorta like Prince, stroking his way through "Lady Cab Driver": this is for the Middle Passage, umhh, this is for chattel slavery, umhh, this for Howard Beach, uhh, yeah, that's the one.'

But you can't count Prince out quite yet. *Emancipation* even ventures into techno on the third CD (happily, his attempt at ragga was confined to *Chaos and Disorder*). Hell, if David Bowie can record a jungle record at the age of fifty, who are we to complain? And, as Nelson George said, hip-hop has outlasted the Minneapolis sound as a recorded and cultural force, but 'Who would you rather see live?' Prince's music is also being seen as a return to real songwriting, real music.

'Prince is the link between the generation who are into hip-hop, and the tradition of black popular music,' says Greg Tate. 'He's an encyclopedia of black music, he's the way in, he embodies James Brown, Jimi, Duke Ellington. Modern R&B is moving away from the R Kelly school – which is really gangsta rap, except he's singing – to those who are drawing on the older traditions, Lauryn from the Fugees reinventing Roberta Flack, or D'Angelo and Maxwell reinventing Prince and Marvin Gaye. It's stuff we haven't heard for fifteen years.'

'Computers are as cold as the people are. That's what I went through with *The Black Album*. All this gangsta rap, I did that years ago,' says Prince. 'I have always done it kind of differently, half-sung, you know, like "Irresistible Bitch".' In the same way that funk bit the dust, the revolutionary music of the 1980s, hip-hop, has been discredited and depoliticised by gangsta rap. But it looks as though the late 1990s hip-hop soul of the likes of R Kelly and Jodeci is being overtaken by young men with guitars who write great, romantic love songs. Prince can be as rude as anyone ('I sincerely wanna fuck the taste out of your mouth,' he sang in 'Let's Pretend We're Married'), but at least if his tongue wasn't in his cheek, it was somewhere else. The ultra-macho, humourless hip-hop soul ('You remind me of my Jeep,' croons R Kelly, and that's about as imaginative as it gets) is more than ready for a re-think.

'I'm getting older, which I love,' says Prince. 'And I respect music even more now. I love hip-hop but I want something positive. They went through James's music, through George's music, now they're trying to go through mine. I just got a bunch of requests, but you know it starts out bitch this [he sticks his fingers in his ears]. Some of these acts I really dig, but I don't want my music used that way.'

In the early 1990s, one of the few soul bands playing real music was Tony Toni Toné, from the Bay Area in California. 'When we were growing up there was a musician on every block, we'd have guitar battles in our back yard playing Hendrix, Funkadelic,' says D'wayne Wiggins, guitarist. 'When people started calling our sound retro, I wasn't sure what they were talking about. We were just playing real music with real instruments.' Bay Area resident Sheila E was a big influence; drummer Timothy Christian Riley and singer Raphael Saadiq, whose falsetto owes more than a nod to Prince, started out in Sheila's band in 1984. 'She had to fire us when Prince decided he wanted her in Minneapolis,' says Riley.

By 1996, though, Prince could stop worrying about his legacy of live music and serious singing. D'Angelo is one of the young men playing all the (real) instruments and serenading in a faultless falsetto who are taking over the charts, along with the likes of Maxwell and Tony Rich. 'Prince came to see me play in Paris,' says Maxwell, who is half Caribbean and half Puerto Rican. He writes love songs and dresses his dates before they go out. 'It totally freaked me out, that he says he likes my music. His music is from the heart, full of emotion. That's real music – the definition isn't whether you use computers or not, it's whether you mean what you sing.'

Prince invited Tony Rich to jam with him over Christmas at Paisley Park, sat him on his lap and enquired, 'So what do you want for Christmas?'

'Prince's stuff is a collage of those who came before,' said D'Angelo at the launch party of *Emancipation*. 'He latches on to the music he loves, then does his own thing. I grew up listening to *Sign o' the Times, Parade*.'

Vibe magazine described D'Angelo as 'a hip-hop head who'd been soaked in a sound vault of Earth, Wind & Fire, soaked to capacity with the juice of strong little jazz struts, Marvin Gaye's godlike crooning and Prince's epic, climactic wails'. Prince was one of the stars who queued to see D'Angelo's first shows in New York and couldn't get in. D'Angelo popped out to fetch him.

Young female singer-songwriters are far from condemning Prince as a misogynist who disrespects black women. Laurneá, former Arrested Development member, cites Prince as an influence. Ambersunshower, whose debut album is quirky and poetic, spent her high-school days in Harlem listening to *For You*, *Dirty Mind*, *Sign o' the Times*, *Parade*. Me'shell Ndegéocello, whose new album features the work of Wendy Melvoin, is also a longtime fan. 'I am probably the biggest Prince fan in the world,' says the Warner artist who champions the rights of bisexual African-American women in her powerful songs. 'He's like my best friend, my mentor. I can always call him up and he'll help me out. Growing up, it never bothered me he had white people in his band, white women. Look at me, I'm now working with Wendy – we met at my local gym in LA. I was just into the music. As a musician he can work with anyone, as long as you come to the table offering creativity.'

'Music is my language,' says Prince. 'Me'shell? She's no talker, believe me. But when we played . . . Perfect understanding.'

Dallas Austin, a young record producer who has resuscitated the fortunes of Motown with Boyz II Men and who also developed TLC, worked with George Clinton at Paisley Park on Prince's *1-800-NEW-FUNK* album. 'When Prince first came out, he was writing every song, playing every instrument, didn't care what anybody thought about him. When I heard that, I knew what I wanted to be. When I was ten I was playing Funkadelic and Prince. I thought everybody listened to different kinds of music. Later on, people started saying to me, "You like that shit – that's white music."'

'Just think of all the new artists who have been influenced by Prince's one-man-studio thing,' says *Rolling Stone*'s David Fricke. 'Him being such a pain in the ass to his record company is inspiring in itself. We like to see those guys messed up!'

And, of course, there is Tricky, who freely admits he would not be making music were it not for the influence of Prince – not just his freaky clothes and make-up and devilish air, but his willingness to experiment. Jungle, not hip-hop, not soul, is the new jazz.

'Prince is a genius,' says Vernon Reid. 'He has amazing depth. He's aware of his larger-than-life aspect, but he really is that thing, he's not a pretender to the throne. He's also in a lot of pain. The degree to which he faces his own internal struggle is the degree to which he'll have real happiness. For the music he's given us he deserves happiness. The music he does at that point will be in another place.'

Prince was still trying to get those young fans on board at Christmas, trying to play the cool Santa. As part of his 'Love 4 One Another' charity, he invited two hundred Midwestern high-school students from Chicago, Detroit and the Twin Cities who had achieved good grades or done good deeds to a concert at Paisley Park. They not only got a seventy-minute show, but were allowed to ask Prince and Mayte questions. And they were each given a parka with ⚤ emblazoned on the back. 'Are we gonna get CDs?' one brave little boy yelled. 'You can get them at the record store,' Prince replied. He was booed roundly.

Prince performed two half-hour sets on Paisley's cavernous sound stage, broadcast live around the world by MTV and critically shredded around the world the next day. The *Los Angeles Times*'s Robert Hilburn, a critic who had championed Prince for much of his career, gleefully informed readers the next day that he hadn't even bothered to stay up late enough to catch the performance of tracks from *Emancipation* at the launch party in November 1996. Prince and his band, it transpired, had mimed to a backing tape: it had become blatantly obvious when one of the guitarists started singing just like Rosie Gaines – no easy task. 'It's cheating,' Prince had said in 1994 when forced to lip-synch to 'The Most Beautiful Girl In The World' at the World Music Awards. 'See, if I would lip-synch, I'd be doing backflips, hanging from the rafters, but to cheat *and* be tired.' Maybe tonight, understandably, he was just plain tired. 'In the old days, whenever we did television, Prince would always insist on playing it live,' commented saxophonist Eric Leeds. 'The weird thing about the Paisley Park event was that he had total control, and he chose not to do it.' Not everyone was about to give Prince some space.

His new label, EMI, meanwhile, were pulling out all the stops. They had got Chris Evans on board, who trumpeted on his Radio 1 breakfast show the fact he was going to interview Prince. When Prince changed his mind – anyone who has met him knows the irreverent approach Evans adopts on his *TFI Friday* TV show would be a disaster – he can't have realised the embarrassment the empty seat on the private jet would cause EMI, or the on-air venom that would ensue. Evans told his listeners not to buy the new record. The response in the *Daily Mirror*, which was also excluded from the party, was similar. EMI flew Ric Blaxill, executive producer of *Top of the Pops*, and his team over on Concorde. They wanted to film an unplugged version of the single for that week's show, but it was by now 4 A.M. Even superstars have their limits. *Top of the Pops* had rashly trailered a 'live, exclusive, secret' performance from Paisley Park. They came away with a copy of the video.

EMI had managed to coerce Prince into confirming an appearance, his only date in Britain that year, at the Smash Hits Awards show in December, televised by the BBC. But those wondering how he would fit in among the Peter Andrés and Ants & Decs of this world would never have the chance to find out. He was unhappy with the performance of his new band. Morris Hayes and Kirk Johnson were old Prince hands; Rhonda Smith and Kathleen Dyson, both from Montreal, had been recommended by Sheila E. They are both more than competent guitar players (Dyson was taking flamenco guitar lessons in town from a local musician-cum-cab driver who, he insists, used to live in the same apartment building as Prince), but they were unimpressive that night. Prince would make an addition to the line-up in December of guitarist Mike Scott, formerly with Sounds of Blackness. The Artist told EMI that he simply wanted to prepare more, particularly if he was to tour the world, as planned. He cancelled with two days' notice, but the official line fed to the press was that he was grieving for his son and couldn't leave Mayte. That didn't go down well with the fans, already confused about the way he was dealing with his private life. How come he was able to fulfil all those other commitments – the party, the interview, the videos – so soon after what must have been the most traumatic event in his life?

I asked Prince at the party how much music he can have left inside him, given that he has 1,000 unreleased songs already stashed away in his vaults. 'A new song every day, for the rest of my life,' he said. Music, he went on, was 'my best friend and my worst friend'. In a way it was a curse. His music went on even if everything around him was breaking into little pieces.

Despite everything, and because *Emancipation* was an exceptional return to form, the album reached number eleven on the *Billboard* pop album chart and number six on the R&B chart. The first single reached number eleven in Britain; the album peaked at number eighteen. The second single, the double A-side of 'The Holy River' and 'Somebody's Somebody', entered the UK Top 40 at number nineteen. The video for 'Somebody's Somebody' was a patchwork of shots of him in a New York hotel room and live performance footage – it looked cheap and can't have helped the mediocre sales. He was still wearing the anorak from the 'Betcha By Golly Wow!' video, and the woollen outfit seen in numerous publicity photos. The seldom-seen video for 'The Holy River' was better, featuring The Artist diving into a waterfall, then getting out a flannel and having a wash. Prince, though, seemed unconcerned about sales. 'It's an expensive package, so I'm not surprised it has dropped down the charts, but there are at least eighteen singles on it, so it will go up again,' he said. 'I've made my money off of it already. We're going to do a lot of benefit concerts to promote it.'

By March, it was clear the album wasn't doing as well as he, and EMI, had hoped. He threw a party at Paisley Park, and another at the New York club Life, to celebrate the fact that it had gone double platinum, or had passed the two-million mark. Platinum and gold discs are a dubious honour bestowed by the Record Industry Association of America (RIAA). Dubious, because the RIAA takes its figures from the number of albums shipped to record stores, not albums sold. Prince had indeed shipped 700,000 copies to stores in America. But that figure would only have got him one gold album; because *Emancipation* is a triple album, that figure is automatically tripled – hence the double platinum status. But of the 700,000 sent out to stores, by the end of March he had sold precisely 448,000. In the UK, the Chart Information Network listed sales at 81,000. Still, it wasn't all bad news. Because of the independent nature of the release, he did indeed make money. Under his old contract, he would have had to sell 500,000 just to break even. On his percentage of the price of the album in the shops, he had already made an estimated $5 million. The gamble, financially at least, had paid off.

At the *Emancipation* launch party, Charles Koppelman, the 56-year-old chairman of EMI-Capitol Records Group North America, who had brought Prince on board, was telling everyone how happy he was to be working with The Artist after all these years. So great was his respect, his fat cigar remained resolutely unlit. But in May 1997, Koppelman was dismissed by the parent company, EMI Music, who were unhappy they were still only the fifth biggest player in the US. Koppelman was one of thirty-five senior executives fired by EMI as part of the streamlining of its North American business. In June 1997, EMI Records was closed down. The label was lagging behind its stable-mates Virgin, who had had a huge success with the Spice Girls, and Capitol. The fate of the label's roster of artists, who included not only Prince but also Sinéad O'Connor and D'Angelo, was uncertain at the time of going to press, but most were likely to be absorbed into the company's other labels.

As Jim Walsh says, 'The record is too daunting for people to pick up right out of the gate – this is a two-year project and it will sell steadily. Especially if he tours. I went over to Paisley for a concert the Saturday after Christmas and there is still no one who can touch this guy live. He can lay on his back and play twenty minutes of blues guitar. He was gritty, lean and nasty. Forget all the personal stuff. Listen to the music.'

After Christmas 1996, Prince did eight small shows in the US – the Roseland Ballroom in New York, The Roxy in Boston – all the proceeds going to charity. He also cancelled seven shows, the official reason given that tickets had been bought by touts and hadn't reached the fans. Prince rescheduled the dates and was joined on stage by his hero, Carlos Santana, at San José University. Prince was almost bursting with pride to be playing alongside Santana – the introverted teenager who had been too shy to say much on their first meeting was, for the moment, well and truly exorcised.

He did at last bring his new band to Britain, to perform at the Brits on 24 February. The night before his all-day rehearsal at Earls Court for the televised awards ceremony, he turned up late at the party given by designer Miuccia Prada after her first catwalk show in London during fashion week. It was held at the In and Out club on Piccadilly, with absolutely no press or cameras allowed inside. The atmosphere was very relaxed, with stars in town for the Brits and the fashion shows – Björk, Damien Hirst, Vivienne Westwood, Laurence Fishburne – sitting outside under rugs in the courtyard, or roaming from table to table in the restaurant, and food courtesy of Quo Vadis. Naomi Campbell arrived with her new love Joaquín Cortés. Prince arrived with his bodyguards. He stayed a couple of hours, very unusual for him, and chatted, ate, chilled.

Things weren't quite so relaxed the next evening at the Brits. Prince was nowhere near the top of the bill, and he didn't win anything. The show opened with the Spice Girls (who all said they wanted to meet Prince) and was closed by the Bee Gees, the anti-funks whose anaemic career had bugged Prince for going on twenty years. Prince and his band performed 'Emancipation', and he looked good in a black and white flowing jacket and loose pants. But he was nervous (he needn't have been; neither Liam Gallagher nor Jarvis Cocker was in the vicinity) and the head mike only smacked of Madonna or Janet Jackson pretending they weren't really lip-synching. He even kept his gloves on to play the guitar. And at the press conference backstage, he refused to say a word, despite the press corps calling out all of his appellations and then some, and the fact that the press call was being broadcast on radio. Prince and his band all wore the white anoraks seen in the videos, which you can buy from

Prince's retail outlet on the Web with all major credit cards. (They were on sale for $400 each; only eleven have so far been sold to the public.) When Prince is being silent, you need a Sheila or a Cat to lighten things up. But the band all stood around like dummies. The press prefer a Noel or a Damon swigging lager and chatting up blondes to someone making like a misery-guts. Among the young, mainly British, pop stars who all turned up wearing what they had happened to wake up in, the ever-pristine Prince seemed hopelessly out of date. But he was still the one star everybody wanted to see close up. During his performance, however lacklustre, Jay Kay of Jamiroquai, Lauryn Hill and Noel Gallagher all craned their necks to see him, absolutely transfixed.

Prince told EMI that he wanted to do a show while he was in Britain – in a club or small theatre, maybe. They told him that no venue could be found at such short notice. Band members said that Prince was surprised; Warner would have turfed out the Spice Girls if they'd had to. His only other performance that week was live in the studio for *Top of the Pops* (on the day the Grammys were being handed out in New York to the likes of Toni Braxton, the Fugees, Celine Dion and the Beatles – Prince hasn't won one since 'Kiss'). This time he sang 'The Holy River' (just for good measure, the CD single included a remix of 'The Most Beautiful Girl In The World' and a blatant ad for Prince merchandise). He was wedged in between those great British exports the Spice Girls and Bush, and could have out-performed both of them if he chose. But he seemed petulant – how he always looks when he's nervous. The anoraks were out in full force. And he was wearing impenetrable black sunglasses when we wanted to see his eyes. He did take his gloves off, though. The band were okay, supplemented by pre-recorded tapes. He didn't instil a great deal of confidence by announcing later that he felt his all-time favourite band would consist of Wendy Melvoin and Lisa Coleman, whom he had fired from The Revolution a decade before, Sheila E on percussion, former NPG drummer Michael Bland, and only bassist Rhonda Smith from the current line-up.

'I think there's a great record in there, and it's phenomenal he has the output he has,' says Wendy. 'There is a mad genius to it, which is nice and all, but sometimes there's a golden egg and sometimes there's a turd. I would prefer it if he put out eleven brilliant tracks instead of every time you put it on you go, that one's good, that one's not so good.'

'If you isolate yourself from other people's opinions or adversity, there's no growth,' says Lisa. 'Maybe his band and the people around him are brilliant and he just doesn't listen to them, maybe they don't know how to talk to him. We were really young when we were with him.'

'And fearless,' adds Wendy.

Far better than his appearance on *Top of the Pops* was his set at the VH-1 honours concert on 10 April at the Universal Amphitheater in Los Angeles. Even though he was in the company of Stevie Wonder, James Taylor and Celine Dion, for whom he wrote the beautiful ballad 'With This Tear', he got the biggest cheers of the evening. As well as 'The Holy River', he performed snatches of 'Take Me With U' and 'Raspberry Beret'. He sang live, and looked happier than he had in a long time. He was wearing a pink devoré velvet blouse and flares, and Mayte had tattooed his hands with henna. Tabloid reports the next day mentioned that he had travelled to LA without his wife, and had turned up with a 'mystery woman'. They published a photograph of him with said woman, whose identity was no mystery at all. It was his bass-player, Rhonda.

The positive reviews for *Emancipation* in the press far outweighed the negative ones. 'An artist refreshed and not just a pop star concentrating that little bit harder to prove a point to his old record company,' said Laura Lee Davies in *Time Out*.

'There are stunning moments, as on "Slave", where he harnesses a murky drumbeat to a 1990s-style cottonfield chant of "They just keep trying to break my heart" . . . Songs that offer an honest reflection of events in his life, instead of the usual voyeuristic fantasies': David Sinclair, *The Times*.

The notable exception was Andrew Smith in the *Sunday Times*'s 'Culture' section: 'Oh how the alarm bells must have been ringing at

EMI when Prince strolled in with a big grin and *Emancipation* tucked under his arm . . . Prince still takes a childlike delight in music. Concomitant to that is the need for someone to change his nappy and send him to bed without his supper once in a while.'

Rather more perceptive was Ekow Eshun, writing in *The Face*. 'I find listening to it an unsatisfying experience. It is too polished, too pristine, stripped clean of the filth and the funk that characterised his earlier work. In the same way that I found talking to him frustrating, it is equally disappointing to listen to his latest work, because where there was once honesty, abandon, exposure, there is now surface and silence in place of a beating, vital heart.'

'I heard "Betcha By Golly Wow!", and I thought, just stop for a minute and listen to that vocal,' says Susan Rogers. 'The guy is thirty-eight years old and listen to his falsetto, it's amazing – he's one of the great vocalists in the history of R&B. When people look back at Sam Cooke and Al Green, Otis, they praise them to the skies, but we have someone like that right now in our midst.'

Prince, though, is pleased with the reaction. 'People seem to like it. The critics haven't always been kind in the past, but reviews for this have been better. I don't like people who criticise music when they're not musicians.' He once called critics 'mamma jammas' and 'sidewinders'. Back in 1990, commentators hadn't been quite so appreciative of his soundtrack to *Graffiti Bridge*. 'I hate reading about what some guy sitting at a desk thinks about me,' he moaned to *Rolling Stone*. 'You know, "He's back and he's black." Whew! No one's mentioning the lyrics.' Even though *The Times* trashed *Graffiti Bridge*'s lyrics, 'That's okay. They're paying attention.' In 1991, defending *Diamonds and Pearls*, he said: 'We should stop arguing and stop attacking each other. The first time I heard Yoko Ono sing, I went, "Hey, you got to quit that – today!" But I had to stop myself. How can I say she shouldn't sing?'

Prince has explained the lyrics of his new work as 'about the pyramids, how they are lined up with the constellation'. He also told me the album was 'a celebration of things that led up to this point. Faith in God got me to this point.' Mostly, though, and with the odd old

Prince touch, like 'Can U get me excited / Till my love is long', the songs are about falling in love, fidelity, marriage. The album contains some of his most beautiful ballads to date: 'Soul Sanctuary'; 'Friend, Lover, Sister, Mother, Wife', the song he composed for his wedding day; and the incredibly seductive 'One Kiss At A Time'. Wow. We missed you, Prince.

When it came time to clear permission for any Prince lyrics reproduced in this book, I approached Warner Chappell for all the songs recorded before the split. For the lyrics on *Emancipation*, I contacted the New York office of Prince's attorney, L. Londell McMillan. The person on the other end of the phone said, 'Try Warner Chappell.' No, he is no longer associated with Warner. I was put on to somebody else. 'Try Warner Chappell.' I phoned Paisley Park. The man on reception said that nobody is assisting Prince in matters like these, and I should fax him the request on his personal number. I did. 'Dear Sir,' I wrote, 'can I please have your permission to reproduce the following lyrics from *Emancipation*.' No response. While clearing all the pre-*Emancipation* lyrics with Warner Chappell, I casually asked whether they knew who I needed to approach for Prince's new recordings. 'Oh, *Emancipation*, that's Warner Chappell.' The text they confirmed to me in writing is as follows: 'Reprinted by kind permission of Warner Chappell Music Publishing Limited.' Prince's freedom from his Warner obligations, it would appear, is not as absolute as we had been led to believe. Warner, it transpires, still share publishing rights, and royalties, with their former artist. Free at last?

January 1998. Prince had just finished his Jam of the Year tour, which took in seventy-one cities across the United States. He and the band went on the road without a record deal, without even a promoter, and he still managed to come sixth in Pollstar's chart of top US tours for 1997. Prince earned over $24.6 million, playing to people who hadn't seen him in a stadium since Lovesexy in 1988. 'Most artists tour when a new album is released,' noted *Variety*.

'Prince didn't start until eight months after *Emancipation,* and a month after his record label went out of business....Once again, Prince is doing things his own way.'

Prince even sold out in his home town, and, wrote Jon Bream of the concerts at the Target Center: 'Prince is simply the best. He has reasserted himself as the best one-man performer in the business. It was just the man, his moves, and his instruments. He slid across the stage on the heels of his boots. He played bass with his left leg over the instrument's neck.' Indeed, he lolled atop his piano, did several splits and had so many poses, it was hard to believe he would soon be forty. He later jammed for almost another two hours at Paisley Park, singing Jackie Wilson and Temptations numbers, and even performed a drum and bass version of Sly Stone's 'Thank You (Falettinme Be Mice Elf Again)'. Prince was supported for much of the tour by Graham Central Station, led by Sly Stone's former bassist, Larry Graham, who, along with Prince's old pinup, Chaka Khan, were to be found working in the new year at the studio at Paisley Park on their own projects.

The tour, surprisingly, included very few songs from *Emancipation* – instead there were mostly old hits, such as 'Kiss', 'The Cross', 'Do Me, Baby', 'The Beautiful Ones', 'When Doves Cry' – hell, most of *Purple Rain*. He was joined onstage by some old friends too, including Rosie Gaines and Sheila E, and by his new homie, D'Angelo, in New York. During one show he sat at the piano and doodled with the first few bars of 'Darling Nikki' and wandered into another tune. The crowd booed until he went back and did it justice. 'Prince, Comeback of the Year,' screamed February's *Vibe* magazine, and the critics were pretty much unanimous in their praise. 'He epitomises sexuality in its rawest, most poetic form,' said the *Dallas Morning News*.

Mayte made a brief appearance on stage at an after-show performance at Glam Slam in Miami. But she was busy doing her own thing. She too went on the road with her twenty-one-member dance troupe, the NPG Dance Company, and a production called Around the World in a Day, all set to Prince music, including 'Kamasutra'. 'His music has Arabic, it has ballet, it has hip-hop,' she told a Minneapolis TV station. 'I've been dancing to it for years!' She and Prince had a farewell dinner in a small restaurant in September. They ate outside but were bothered by bees. Prince quipped that this was because of his wife's nickname for him, 'Honey'.

Around the World in a Day premiered at the Detroit Music Hall, with choreography by Mayte and Dwight Rhoden, formerly with Alvin Ailey American Dance Theater. The show mixed ballet and hip-hop with jazz, and was very well received by critics and audiences. Prince was visibly moved when Mayte took her bow. They were joined in an after-show dinner by Stevie Wonder. They formed an impromptu supergroup, with Prince on drums, Tony Rich on keys, Larry Graham on bass and Stevie on keys and vocals, performing 'Superstition' and an original they made up on the spot.

The downside, come the beginning of 1998, was that we hadn't had a Prince release since 1996 – and considering that one of the reasons Prince wanted to go it alone was to release more music, we were all getting a little impatient. But his new releases would turn out to be well worth waiting for.

Because of the way his deal with EMI was structured, Prince reportedly made more money from *Emancipation* than he did from *Purple Rain*. He would stand to make even more money from sales of his 1998 offerings – the long-awaited triple CD *Crystal Ball*, and a twelve-track, mostly acoustic album, *The Truth*. The albums could only be ordered via his Web site (*www.love4oneanother.com*) or on his phone line, 1-800-NEW-FUNK, at a cost of $50, plus $20 postage for those outside the US. He stated that he would only press the CDs after 80,000 preorders. A possible distribution deal at the end of January 1998, with the Best Buy chain of record stores, seemed only to hold up the release – a date still unconfirmed at the time of going to press.

The first two tracks of *The Truth* make your hair stand on end – no mean feat as this album is only released as an accompaniment to three CDs of material that is mostly from Prince's vintage period, 1986 to 1991. The title track has just Prince's voice, a lazy guitar, and a hand that occasionally leans across and strokes a keyboard. And who needs anything else when the voice is like this: lazy, hurt, down, full of regret and longing. There are still the eccentric Prince touches – a loud ticking clock on 'The Truth', a rooster crowing on the whimsical ballad 'Dionne' – and on the title track, when Prince breaks into a tortured scream, you realise that he is at last singing the blues. The second track, 'Don't Play Me', is a highly personal song, sparse save for snatches of a woman's voice through what sounds like a megaphone and a spooky keyboard. It's his (hopefully final) dig at the music industry, his risque image, and the ridiculous notion of Ebonics. 'I'm over thirty and I don't smoke weed/I put my ass away and the music I play/I ain't the type of stereo you're trying to feed/I use proper English, and I'm straight.' He hasn't lost his sense of humour, though: 'Don't play me, I already do in my car.'

The album contains soulful ballads: 'Circle of Amour', a tribute to four friends from high school, and 'The Other Side of the Pillow'.'Dionne', with its slide guitar and sweet falsetto, is reminiscent of 'Starfish and Coffee' or 'The Ballad of Dorothy Parker'.'Animal Kingdom' starts off sounding like John Lennon and explains why Prince now doesn't even eat blue cheese – dolphins are sampled, and they must be a particular love of Prince's. Remember 'If I came back as a dolphin/would you cut off my fins', from the *Gold* album? There is only one real dance track, the flamenco-based 'Fascination', which has a pop at Michael Jackson: 'Singing from the telly, making more bucks than sense/So-called king gives birth to so-called Prince'.

The last track, 'Welcome 2 the Dawn', opines that 'Every choice you make is karma, so be careful what you do.' As Jim Walsh wrote in the *St Paul Pioneer Press:* 'This is an even more overtly spiritual work than *Emancipation*...A roadmap to the lessons he has learned and the person he has become. That person is, to put it crudely, an adult.'

And what of the long-awaited Crystal Ball? The precise track listing was still unconfirmed at time of going to press. We can

expect thirty tracks on this triple CD – but *Emancipation* it is not, more Prince's greatest bootleg hits, the tracks the record companies did not want you to hear, plus tracks not in circulation, such as 'Cloreen Baconskin' (Morris Day circa 1983?), and new ones such as 'Poom Poom', 'Make Yo Mamma Happy' and 'Da Bang'. Take the title track. It lasts close to nine minutes – no wonder Warner vetoed its appearance on *Sign o' the Times*. Prince has that helium, cartoonish voice from 'Girlfriend' or 'Feel U Up'. It changes tack about halfway through – you can hear Wendy singing her heart out – and presages *Around the World in a Day*'s experimentation with different instruments (it also has soaring strings worthy of a James Bond soundtrack). That can only be Sheila working up a sweat on the drums. This track alone is worth the cost of the album. It is Prince drunk on his own genius.

Perhaps the most keenly awaited track apart from 'Crystal Ball' and 'Dream Factory', both pre-SOTT and heavily influenced by Wendy, Lisa and Susannah, is 'Days of Wild', familiar from live performances and from *The Beautiful Experience* video. Why it was left off the *Gold* album is hard to fathom: it is eccentric, profane, very funny. Mayte raps, 'Hold on to your wig', Prince drawls effortlessly. He again returns to his theme of not being violent towards women; if he was accused of ever hitting a woman, he says: 'If a woman ever said I did, she's motherfucking lying I'm a set-up kid.' Sometimes his rhyming is just so sweet.

Also here are songs from the *Parade* era: 'An Honest Man', formerly an achingly beautiful instrumental from *Under the Cherry Moon*, and 'Sexual Suicide', which is so *Parade*, an album with a style that didn't seem to bleed into anything he has done since. 'Suicide', like *Parade*, is stripped down to the bones, leaving you wanting more. 'Last Heart' is about a woman who keeps breaking his heart, with a sax interlude and the slightly hurried pace of his first two albums.

'Crucial' is a jazzy track circa 1986 or 1987, with Eric Leeds getting a chance to improvise. It is a little reminiscent of 'Adore': he isn't ever ashamed to beg. It's a great track, with Prince's falsetto at its best, his singing style very similar to that on 'Betcha by Golly'.

'Acknowledge Me' has been aired before on *Soul Train*, and was recorded by the NPG for their album *Exodus*, but left off. Prince's guttural throaty 'Whoah whoah yeah' makes you laugh out loud. 'The Ride' is familiar from *The Beautiful Experience*; 'Good Love' is from the *Bright Lights, Big City* soundtrack. 'Ripopgodzippa' (it's about stripping, not God) was in the movie *Showgirls* (oh dear) and also was left off the *Gold* album and the film's soundtrack.

'Love Sign' is a duet with Nona Gaye from the 1-800-NEW-FUNK compilation; this version includes a sample from DMSR.

'Hide the Bone' (you can guess what that means) is also from the *Gold* period, and was played live in 1994. '2Morrow' includes a sample of the 'Most Beautiful Girl in the World'. 'P Control' is a remix of the track on the *Gold* album, and although this song shocked audiences rather when he first played it live, its heart is in the right place: women should never be slaves to men, and women always hold the power.

The song '18 and Over' (is it referring to Mayte finally coming of age?) has the lyrics '18 and over, I wanna phone ya', or could it be 'I wanna bone ya'? Hard to tell, but knowing Prince it's probably the second option. It's another *Gold* period song, with a funky drumbeat, and he played it live in after shows, when he added a lazy rap, 'Now that I've got your attention, there's a couple of new positions that I wanna mention' (the one that makes his baby go Oww!) from *Feel Good*. And little bits of *Come*.

'What's My Name' and 'Strays of the World' are from the Glam Slam Ulysses project: 'Strays' is a ballad, with a bit of the pomp of 'Purple Rain', or perhaps 'Graffiti Bridge', with Prince putting on a funny voice. It's a bit of a mishmash, really.

'So Dark' is reportedly the same track as 'Dark' on *Come* but it could be an earlier version, with different instrumentation. A beautiful, sexy ballad, slightly slowed down here. 'Took my money, took all my self-esteem...How could ya, baby?' He's right. It really does seem as if someone has turned out all the lights. He has that deep sexy voice, you know the one from *TMBGITW*, and a high-pitched scream. 'Calhoun Square' sounds as if it is from the same period as 'Peach':

sparse, with a wah-wah guitar. Prince sings as if he is being strangled.

Those praying that included somewhere will be Prince's duet with Mavis Staples, 'God Is Alive', a bootleg version of her album track from 1988, could be disappointed. Shame. It is awesome.

The signs are good that the new music, when we get it, will put Prince back at the top of the charts where he belongs. But at the beginning of 1998, solely on the back of his most successful American tour in ten years, and fifteen years after Prince sat down and wrote it, *Purple Rain* was back in the Billboard top 50 albums chart. Somebody at Warner Bros. must be smiling.

Epilogue

In 1996, Prince and Mayte had been so excited about becoming parents, just like any other couple, and their enthusiasm had been made very public. *Emancipation* includes tracks called 'Let's Have A Baby' and 'Curious Child'; while pregnant, Mayte wore a short black dress with the word 'baby' in white lettering across her chest and an arrow pointing to her stomach. They had also been planning to release a multimedia package of children's stories in time for Christmas: a read-along cassette, book and CD, with versions in English, Spanish and German, all featuring multi-racial characters. The sleeve notes for *Emancipation* even contain a photograph of her bare, pregnant stomach. Prince would talk of little else: 'I can't wait for my baby to look up and see Mayte's eyes. Look at those eyes. That's the first thing this baby is going to see in the world.'

One of the world's most famous bachelors wanted everyone to know he had settled down and was ready to be part of a real family – something he hadn't really known since he was seven, when his parents split up. Now that the baby had been born with serious health problems, he just wanted for him and his wife to be able to deal with the situation quietly, and in their own way.

In the days after the baby was born, Prince flew to Japan for two days to promote *Emancipation*; he chatted about his new music, was witty, relaxed, and enthusiastic about the record in a way he hadn't been for years. He even made his own television ad: 'Okay, so I'm now a used-car salesman.' That same week he directed the video for the first single, 'Betcha By Golly Wow!', featuring smiling infants and Mayte beaming on a hospital bed. (It was the first time he had released a cover version, though he does have his spin on Madonna's 'Like A Prayer' locked in his vaults.) He flew to Chicago to record the Oprah Winfrey show. He spoke to the newspapers *USA Today* and the *International Herald Tribune*. When Oprah, one of the best interviewers in the business and a woman who could probably get the Pope to confess to being a Protestant, asked about the situation with the baby, he replied, 'It's all good.' He told a press conference (his first) at Paisley Park that Mayte wouldn't be joining him on stage for the foreseeable future, as it was 'Mom time for her right now', and that he was 'enjoying being a father'. But the baby was already dead.

'Prince and Mayte are entitled to grieve however they choose, but people are astounded they were able to go on *Oprah* and *The Today Show* and seem so normal,' says Cheryl Johnson. 'It tells you they're not normal, and Mayte will get tired of being adored and worshipped and controlled and told to rein in her emotions. On *Oprah*, Prince was sitting so close to Mayte she was like a dummy on a ventriloquist's lap. And when Oprah asked the question about the baby, her head swivelled just like Charlie McCarthy's; she immediately deferred to Prince . . . Mayte is young and fit. She is a beautiful specimen of a human being. Who could have predicted they would have this much trouble?'

On Friday, 28 February 1997, two of Prince's former employees were talking to Minneapolis homicide detectives. The employees were the twin sisters Erlene and Arlene Mojica, who had been fired by Paisley Park Enterprises on 23 December. Nobody knows for certain the circumstances surrounding their dismissal – neither they nor their lawyer, Larry Altman, would comment, although there were rumours that they had tried to sell their story to a British newspaper. The sisters had undoubtedly been particularly close to Mayte – they were Puerto Rican, Spanish-speaking, of about the same age as her, and had helped her through her pregnancy, the birth and the tragedy of the baby's illness and death. One of the two women is even listed on the baby's death certificate as the person with the power of attorney to give authorities information about the death.

The baby had been listed on the birth certificate with no first name but with the last name Garcia, born to Mayte Garcia-Nelson on 16 October. The mother 'refused information' pertaining to the father's identity, according to the certificate. The death certificate, filed in Hennepin County on 4 November, lists the child's name as Boy, and the last name as Gregory. It lists the mother's name as Mia Gregory and leaves blank the boxes for the child's father. The cause of death is listed as 'complications caused by Pfeiffer's Syndrome'. For weeks after the filing of that certificate, county officials asked Abbotts Northwestern Hospital in central Minneapolis, where the child was born, for a matching birth certificate. A month later, a birth certificate listing a boy with only the last name of Garcia was filed.

Larry Altman stated that he was looking into the circumstances of their being fired and into other details, including 'medical matters [concerning] Prince's family'. It is unclear what information the women offered authorities. Dr John Fangman, listed as the baby's doctor, attributed Boy Gregory's death to natural causes. Authorities did not perform an autopsy, and as the body was cremated on the day he died, there is no possibility of further examination. Medical reports were obtained. Pat Diamond, the deputy Hennepin County attorney, said, 'We have been assisting the Minneapolis Police Department and the Hennepin County medical examiner concerning a review of the circumstances surrounding this death.' He also added that there was no case pending at that time concerning the death of Boy Gregory.

Whatever the Mojica sisters had to say to the local homicide department, there were strange anomalies in documents that should have been perfectly straightforward. Why had Mayte not listed Prince as the father? The baby had not been a secret, and the name Nelson had not proved troublesome on their wedding certificate. And why then call the baby, undoubtedly the same child, Boy Gregory? And why sack the two women? Was it because they had become too close to Mayte? Do these events explain Prince's strange behaviour in public during the promotion of his new album? A sad event the couple had wanted to put behind them now looked likely to drag on for months.

The sisters did indeed sell their story, to the *News of the World*, who ran it on 9 March. Erlene, employed as a nanny by the couple in July 1996, described how she had been called by Prince and told that they had to convince Mayte that enough was enough; the baby should be taken off his life-support machine and allowed to die. The baby had already been operated on twice in his first week of life. The sisters said he stopped breathing at 8:45 A.M. on 23 October. Arlene, a body-builder employed since the summer of 1995 as Mayte's assistant and bodyguard, rang Prince, who didn't want to be present, to tell him it was all over. The body was cremated later that day. They said also that Mayte had discovered she was pregnant after using a home kit from a chemist; for the first two and a half months, the sisters say, Prince forbade his wife from seeing a doctor. When she did persuade him that she needed an ultrasound, he insisted on a woman doctor. A second scan, showing the baby's deformities, was published in the *News of the World*, along with the prints the parents took of their baby's tiny feet. The name on the scan was Arlene Mojica – the *News of the World* story claimed Mayte didn't want Prince to find out she had had another test.

Leslee Jaeger, the doctor at North Memorial Hospital in Robbinsdale, where Mayte had received antenatal care, explained the options. Jaeger recommended a full chromosome test to find out the nature of the problem, but also said Mayte could either have a termination or go ahead and have the baby. In late September, Mayte was admitted in severe pain. Prince was summoned but, according to the sisters, refused to allow his wife to stay. Prince and the sisters then took Mayte in his limo to Abbotts Northwestern. The sisters took her inside while Prince waited in the car. Mayte was admitted under the name Marlene Gong, which was changed to Mia Gregory the next day, after her accompanying pet Yorkshire terrier. Hospital staff, though, immediately recognised her. She was given injections to stop her miscarrying. A month later, the baby was delivered by Caesarean section and transferred to the nearby Children's Health Care Hospital. The child was in pain and unlikely to survive. It became clear that the reason the sisters spoke to the authorities was that they had been instructed by Prince to turn off the baby's life-support machine.

The sisters also claimed they had once had to rush Prince to an emergency room when he had overdosed on drink and pills. He has, from the very start of his career, been very publicly opposed to alcohol and drugs – he likes to be in control, and sees them as a weakness. He banned the sale of alcohol at his concerts long ago, and even at the launch party for *Emancipation* the choice of beverage was sparkling apple or pear juice. Everyone around him when he was a teenager and in his early twenties – his manager, personal assistant, band members – confirm that his clean-living image was not a façade. His only interests were music and sex, and he had a strict policy of sacking any employee caught taking drugs. But that policy is almost impossible to enforce in the music business. Indeed, band members, his stepbrother Duane, and former girlfriends Vanity and Kim Basinger all admit to drug-taking. Whether Prince was unaware of their habits, or merely tolerant, is impossible to know. As he has got older, his ability to work hard on little sleep has done little to dispel the rumours, so this latest revelation can't have pleased him.

The sisters said they had received no compensation when they were dismissed. They also maintained that Prince was unhappy that his wife had failed to regain her figure after the birth. He had indeed announced that Mayte would no longer appear on stage in his band – but would her career be put permanently on hold? Was she expected to sit alone in that pink and blue house in the middle of nowhere?

On the Monday morning after the story appeared in the *News of the World*, Prince and his attorney, Bob Weinstine, went to court to seek a temporary restraining order preventing the women from talking to the media. A hearing was set for 27 March at the Carver County

Courthouse. Larry Altman said Prince would probably sue the women over their statements to the media. He also said that the sisters claimed their names were forged on confidentiality agreements.

That Thursday, Carver County Court was packed with the world's press. Prince's lawyer, Joe Friedberg, asked the judge to keep the case secret. 'This is a case about a contract to keep things private,' he told the court. The Mojicas' lawyer disagreed. 'Money and power should not dictate that the proceedings in this matter or in any other matter be held behind closed doors,' said Altman. The court did eventually decide, however, that the contract dispute was a private matter and ruled in favour of a gag order.

The dispute centred around whether the sisters, who told the authorities that they believed Prince's decision to turn off the baby's life-support was premature, should be bound to the confidentiality agreement Prince claims they signed. They claim they were sacked because they refused to sign anything, and that their signatures were subsequently forged. They gave a videotaped interview to a freelance journalist, Tom Gasparoli, who effectively became their agent, insisting they take the story to the authorities and the press. In the interview, given before the gag order, they stated they wanted to speak out because of their guilt and anger. But medical staff at the hospital felt that a parent's rights to privacy had been violated. Dr Robert Gorlin, a University of Minnesota professor who has written a book on Pfeiffer's Syndrome, said that the baby would have been unlikely to live very long. The medical examiner's office finally ruled in June 1997 that the baby had died from natural causes. A decision that is made privately and with great difficulty every day in hospital wards had been made very public, and much more difficult to handle.

Appendix
All the critics love U

For You

Prince, the one-name 18-year-old Minneapolitan with obvious chutzpah to spare, has produced an album that, if nothing else, is a technical marvel and a curiosity piece. A one-man band (with vocalist), Prince plays all the various guitar, keyboard and percussion instruments (I counted 18, many of them exotic) and sings lead and backup for the album's nine songs, all of which he composed and arranged. Somebody named C. Moon collaborated on the lyrics to one tune; otherwise this album is all Prince's – and two recording studios.

The album was recorded at the Record Plant in Sausalito, California, and remixed at Sound Labs in Los Angeles. Ordinarily, I wouldn't plug recording studios, but in this case, it's necessary, because this LP is mostly a product of studio wizardry.

The music is all soul-tinged, but it's not that easily categorised. In my notes, I used names like Stevie Wonder, George Benson, the Stylistics, Diana Ross, the Mills Brothers and Ink Spots, Billy Cobham and Carlos Santana, in making comparisons.

The album's sound is dominated by synthesizers and tenor to falsetto vocals, and pity the listener who doesn't care for either. There are a number of ballads, a couple of funky dance numbers, and even a heavy metal piece.

The title tune, 'For You', finds Prince doing multiple voices *a capella*, sounding almost barbershop-quartet-ish, and tipping off how he would use the studio for the rest of the album.

'In Love' features funky rhythms (the album is far stronger rhythmically than melodically or harmonically), a strong synthesizer sound and vocal blend remindful of Stevie Wonder's work. 'Soft And Wet' sounds much like the previous cut, except that it's very difficult to make out the lyrics and no lyric sheet is provided. 'Just As Long As We're Together' has a too-busy background, but a solid danceable beat, and one of the most important among the exotic instruments Prince plays on this track is the Handclapsandfingasnaps. You figure it out. 'Crazy You' has Prince playing a George Benson-like electric guitar lead, backed by a nice acoustic rhythm guitar in support of his solo vocal. The drip drip of the water drums is gimmicky.

On what Prince calls The Other Side, 'Baby' is either a put-on of 1950s tear-jerker, teeny-bopper love songs or an indication of Prince's youth. She's pregnant and he's asking whether they should go on living together or get married and wondering how this happened to someone as careful as he is. Musically there's a lot of doo-wah, doo-wah and the vocal blend sounds a bit like the Stylistics. 'My Love Is Forever' is a hard funk tune with woodblocks contributing to the solid rhythm. There are some brief Santana-like electric guitar riffs, too. 'So Blue' features an excellent falsetto vocal on an easygoing ballad about lost love. There's a strumming acoustic guitar background that sounds like one might hear behind the Mills Brothers or Ink Spots. This tune also shows why Prince felt he didn't need any female singers for the album. 'I'm Yours' is the hard rocker with brief, screaming guitar passages, some Billy Cobham-like synchronized drum rolls, and multiple voice tracks.

There's nothing musically startling here. Prince has down pat all the current soul-pop-funk basics on a number of instruments and he has combined them into something that is interesting, all right, but more because one man did it than because of the music itself. There are no solos, so one cannot measure the extent of Prince's ability on any of the instruments. That he can sing, however, is very clear. And his composing and arranging abilities are impressive.

So if he'd use those abilities, hire himself a band (preferably with at least one horn), and go from there, he'd have a very promising career ahead of him.

PUBLICATION: *St Paul Dispatch*
DATE: 1 June 1978
WRITER: Bob Protzman

Prince

Prince is one of those do-it-all artists we're seeing more of lately. He wrote, produced and arranged the music here, and played all the instruments and sung all the vocals. An egocentric guy to be sure, but his instincts are generally sound.

At 19, Prince possesses many of the same qualities that have made the public so excited about Stevie Wonder. His music, which employs funk/rock techniques, is completely accessible without screaming 'commercial'.

Prince knows how to construct songs that are packed with enticing lyrics and hooks. The emphasis is always on young lust, and he sings about it with the highest-pitched pipes this side of Michael Jackson. 'I Wanna Be Your Lover' is the strongest attention-grabber, but Prince's album isn't overloaded with other songs in that same party vein. Equally effective are the ballads ('When We're Dancing Close And Slow', 'With You'), which have a dreamy, almost classical quality. Prince's music can't be pigeonholed into one category, and that's to his credit.

Horns weren't utilised on this album, but the 27-plus instruments he plays – including drums, guitars, pianos and multitracked synthesizers – give the effect of a full orchestra. It's tempting to describe someone like Prince by offering comparisons to other artists in the same mould. Fortunately, Prince is too much of an original to fit into a mould.

PUBLICATION: *Los Angeles Times*
DATE: 17 February 1980
WRITER: Connie Johnson

Dirty Mind

Prince's third album for Warner Bros continues his safari through the jungle of teenage lust and heavy breathing.

The 20-year-old Minneapolitan's lyrics are even more provocative this time around, as provocative as the jacket photos. On the front Prince is wearing what is now his standard concert garb, a mini-brief, and on the back, the star recumbent in bed and looking impatient. Clearly someone is late. Of course, he could be waiting for room service.

In the title tune a young man pants for his girlfriend ('I just wanna lay you down in my daddy's car . . .'), while in 'When You Were Mine' a *ménage à trois* dissolves. She goes off with the other guy, leaving Prince recumbent in bed and waiting for room service – an especially ungrateful thing to do, since he used to let her wear his clothes. In 'Sister', a 16-year-old male is seduced by his older sister, and in the notorious 'Head', which Prince and his band performed during their date at the Orpheum Theater last winter, the two characters (Lisa Coleman sharing the vocal) behave as nature and Alfred Kinsey intended.

Much of this is seedy and vulgar, not because it is explicit sexually but because it is presented in the most sensationalist terms. The implication is always that sex is naughty and proceeds in a manner fraught with guilt and unhappiness. The essence, in sum, of a Dirty Mind.

The 'packaging' of Prince, whether it be his own idea or something dreamed up in the board rooms at Warners, seems less bold and daring, less demeaning. Prince obviously has talent. Once again, he maintains clearly all the production credits on the album: arrangements, compositions and performances.

While none of the songs on *Dirty Mind* seem hit-bound to the degree of 'Sexy Dancer' and 'I Wanna Be Your Lover', the songs here are catchy and danceable. Prince has developed his own unique instrumental sound, a disco-funk mode that is quite recognisable as his, and even though the falsetto vocal style he affects is not the ultimate in flexibility – he sounds positively scratchy, in fact, in 'When You Were Mine' – that sound is, at least, unusual. Unusual counts for a lot in pop music.

My guess is that Prince will be working in a three-piece suit in a year or two.

PUBLICATION: *Minneapolis Tribune*
DATE: 7 November 1980
WRITER: Michael Anthony

Controversy

Prince is a neo-hippy. Similar to Lennon a decade ago, he imagines a personal Shangri-la where there are no rules, no racial distinctions, no clothes, no money . . . but lotsa sex. But while the original hippies' Eden was a rural one, Prince's is urban. On *Dirty Mind*, he called it Uptown: 'Where I come from / We don't let society, tell us what to be.' (He sure wasn't talking about Uptown, folks.) On his latest and fourth record, *Controversy*, he calls its inhabitants 'the new breed' – individuals who believe more in Eros than Agape, more in anarchy than communalism. His noble savage – unbent by what Dylan once called 'society's pliers' – is an urchin of the asphalt.

Crazy-quilt pop politics from the likes of Jefferson Airplane many years ago had the advantage of context and novelty. At first, Prince's social and political outrageousness seemed forced, borrowed and overly narcissistic (not surprising, considering he's a child of the 1970s). Prince concluded *Dirty Mind* – a record that up to that point was obsessed only with incest, fellatio, priapism and the like – with the chant, 'You're gonna have to fight your own damn war / Cuz we don't wanna fight no more.' One had to wonder, What war? What fighting?

Turns out that brazen little mantra was a hint of things to come. Prince's *Controversy* is a much more mature work than *Dirty Mind*, which doesn't necessarily mean it's better – it isn't. But it does give fascinating expression to the young man's expanding political consciousness, which still remains a bit naive. (At one point in 'Sexuality' he calls for his minions to organise – this after his long track record of wild-in-the-streetism.)

Controversy also displays Prince's spiralling egoism – and I don't mean that in a pejorative sense. He is preoccupied with how the world perceives him ('Controversy') and how the world will treat his celebrity status ('Annie Christian'). Therefore, his egoism is a very healthy and positive kind, as he ponders how he and his image are fitting into the world.

Since Prince's Bambi prettiness makes him appear extremely androgynous, and his lineage makes him appear as mixed-blood, it's inevitable that we speak of him as the perfect, composite American pop star for the 1980s. And his ambitions are that lofty, thank God. With *Controversy*, one gets the feeling that Prince knows he stands on the verge of superstardom. He explores its hazards in 'Annie Christian' (a sort of emblematic, all-purpose character seen by Prince in a Manichaean light as the embodiment of all that is evil or sick in America and the ubiquitous perpetrator of our recent heinous crimes – the Lennon assassination, the Reagan attempt, the Atlanta homicides): 'Until you're crucified / I'll live my life in taxi cabs.'

So while the New Conservatives build up a head of steam, and the arms race escalates to dizzyingly ridiculous heights, Prince will become more and more relevant: a context of antinomies is catching up to him, giving his outrageousness resonance, as millions of Americans become alienated when they find themselves outside the tight circle circumscribed by the smug, white-bread haves. And his millenarianism is more appropriate now, as brinkmanship increasingly becomes a global tactic again.

I once said that if rock 'n' roll were a newspaper, the Clash would be the front page and the Ramones would be the funny papers. Well, a couple of years have passed, and I might be tempted to amend that to say that the Clash would be the op/ed page. But anyway, to extend the conceit, Prince, up until this album, would have been the personals. But not anymore, totally. He's beginning to compete with Strummer & Company for hard news.

The big problem Prince faces as an artist is how to square the funky-punky cheesecake with serious statements on the state of the world and the American culture. It is precisely this schizophrenia that threatens to pull *Controversy* apart at the seams. 'Annie Christian' is an eerie brood-piece on the dark side of the American dream: the dues of success. It's set in a modified chant context, with Prince singspeaking in his normal voice over menacing guitar snarls that are tucked midway into the mix and a metronomic rhythm punched up by distant handclaps. 'Annie Christian' is a new musical form for Prince, one that he would do well to pursue. Too bad it's followed by one of his crude, stock-in-trade sex dissertations, 'Jack U Off'. The music is uninteresting – it sounds like break music – and the song's placement almost sabotages the effect of 'Annie Christian'. 'Let's Work' is not as lame, but its music is a Prince cliché.

The sequencing of *Controversy* is often atrocious. There almost should have been a serious side and a sex side. Which would have made everything nice and cosy if the penis weren't a political tool in Prince's world view: 'Sexuality is all we'll ever need'; 'I'm not gonna stop [fucking] till the war is over'. Prince perceives himself as on a mission (from God? – his religious inclinations are even murkier; I don't think his recitative of the Lord's Prayer is blasphemous at all, especially considering God got another nod in the liner notes) to torpedo our collective Puritan superego. (Seems Uncle Hef didn't do such a good job. Remember how many of us rock crits have been saying the 1980s might be like the 1950s? So Ike had Presley and Ronnie's got Prince.) He doesn't believe in original sin; kids are poisoned by culture ('atmosphere' in Prince's nomenclature). The moral pendulum is swinging back to the right, so what better way to scare the bejesus out of Falwell's legions than to celebrate the runaway id?

But hell, even Rolling Stones fans find him threatening – and certainly they've seen enough strangeness from Mick and the boys. Maybe it's Prince's cockiness, or that he dares to be prissy and still call himself a man. For me, it's precisely that quality of brashness that makes Prince – and his local cohorts in The Time – so appealing. They're so sure they're gonna make it that they're gonna seize the time. There's nothing tentative about them – their dress, or their address to rock 'n' roll.

Nor is there anything tentative about their music. It's aggressive and daring: they're willing to integrate anything. *Controversy* has more music than *Dirty Mind* (both contain eight songs, but the former logs in at 36:24, the latter 28:37) and perhaps a wider range of it. For instance, the double synthesizer assault is toned down some, and Prince's delicate falsetto is only one end of a number of vocal guises used here.

Prince's slow-burn orgasm on vinyl, 'Do Me, Baby', is a command bedroom performance and should become a classic in the genre. 'Ronnie, Talk To Russia' has a smidgen of heavy metal guitar, but the goofy song comes off sounding more like Dave Edmunds with something to say. 'Private Joy', like 'Uptown' on *Dirty Mind*, is the sure-fire dance jam: it contains the line, 'If anybody asks, you belong to Prince'. And while 'Controversy' is a great single in a wonderfully simple kind of way (musically), 'Sexuality' is really Prince's manifesto and the key to solving the record's apparent double-mindedness. Certainly it's symptomatic of his future directions. The next LP should be a fully formed delineation of Prince's vision. *Controversy* is one step along the way.

PUBLICATION: *Sweet Potato* (which became *City Pages*)
DATE: November 1981
WRITER: R. Anderson

1999

Whether Prince has ditched the ideals that made his previous four albums so provocative for the lucrative lure of compromise, or whether, despite what the sales figures say, his influence has infiltrated mainstream pop to the point where his imitations go virtually unnoticed, the plain fact is that much of *1999* sounds disappointingly familiar.

Perhaps plagiarists like The Time and Vanity 6 have forced his hand, perhaps the danger of self-parody called for a dramatic shift of emphasis but, whatever the motivation, *1999* sounds like a collection of crudely calculated manoeuvres towards popular ingratiation. Gone is the essentially wide-eyed *naif* eulogising the joys of sexual self-discovery; the Prince of *1999* is a stud without balls, paranoically obsessed with his position as first minister of sexual politics, strutting mucho macho bravado and sacrificing tender intimacy to boasting prowess.

Whereas, say, the breathtakingly explicit 'Do Me, Baby' from last year's *Controversy* album unashamedly celebrated carnal ecstasy and, in context with 'Ronnie, Talk To Russia', proposed love as an alternative to man's self-destruction, much of *1999* is hackneyed, bop-against-the-bomb, outrage-for-outrage's sake. The imagery has grown self-consciously horny, the automobile-humping equation of 'Little Red Corvette', the jet-setting clichés of 'International Lover' and 'Bucks Fizz' nudge-nudge, wink-wink innuendo of 'Let's Pretend We're Married' uncharacteristically touting for cheap thrills and self-aggrandisement.

I suppose, in all honesty, it was commercially inevitable that Prince would become a cartoon of his former sensitivities, betraying previous insistence that any act of love is natural for an antithetical freak appeal. But when the fourth side of this, his first double album, boasts climaxes like the preposterously sensuous 'Lady Cab Driver' and the wickedly self-deflating 'All The Critics Love U In New York', I can't help but wish that the rest of the album's public exposures had remained his private indiscretions.

PUBLICATION: *Melody Maker*
DATE: 13 November 1982
WRITER: Steve Sutherland

Purple Rain

Beware of soundtrack albums, even one from as brilliant a pop-rock strategist as Prince. Pop artists' visions usually end up tarnished as other considerations take precedence in the film project.

In the case of *Purple Rain*, however, the discipline and demands involved in the movie have added a surprising and valuable new approachability to Prince's music.

Aware that he has to reach beyond his hard-core following if the film is to succeed, Prince has toned down the extreme aspects of his pop game-plan. Instead of the X-rated lyrics and sexual bravado that have been at the heart of his maverick persona, he leans toward more conventional language.

Things still get steamy during 'Darling Nikki', but most of the lyrics are no more out of radio bounds than Marvin Gaye's 'Sexual Healing'. Prince's music, too, has shed some of its quirky, experimental edges. Rather than play all the instruments himself, Prince records with a band (The Revolution) for the first time, gaining added rock punch. He also has moved confidently into richer pop orchestrations.

The impressive thing is that Prince – one of the half-dozen most arresting figures in modern pop/rock – has made these adjustments without diluting the essence of his music. One reason is the sculptured, impassioned vocals, which range from the bedroom whispers of 'The Beautiful Ones' to a touch of the primal-scream force of John Lennon's *Plastic Ono Band* LP.

Equally important are the richly crafted songs, which touch on ambition and desire on various levels: social, spiritual and sensual. The opening 'Let's Go Crazy' is a lively restatement of the party-as-salvation doctrine that underlies Prince's Church of Erotic Pop. The song, which kicks off with a church-organ backdrop, is a good-natured social pep talk: 'If the elevator tries to bring you down / Go crazy / Punch a higher floor'.

'When Doves Cry', the first of what should be at least three hit singles from the album, is an affecting look at alienation and romantic tension – with gripping lyrics that are both bluntly personal and gracefully theatrical. The LP's centrepiece, however, is the title track: a haunting pop landscape whose vocal suggests both a Lennon-like vulnerability and a Hendrix-ish robustness.

Purple Rain may not have the bold social/psychological reach of Prince's previous three albums, but its clear ambitious tones stamp it as his most consistent and fully defined collection. With the expected film and video exposure, the album could double or triple the 2.3 million sales registered by 1982's *1999*. Rather than cheapen his vision, Prince has simply made it possible for more people to share it. This is a work of enormous pop imagination and appeal.

PUBLICATION: *Los Angeles Times*
DATE: 24 June 1984
WRITER: Robert Hilburn

Around the World in a Day

What a long, strange trip this one is. *Around the World in a Day* isn't at all shy about making its intentions known. The cover, gatefold, naturally, introduces Prince's vision of Paisley Park, the American twin of our very own Itchycoo. A mess of violent colour assaults the senses and the clues keep on coming; heavy-handed symbolism rules the day, gaudy displays of childish Summer Of Love typography reveal lyrics that veer from awesome naivety to terminal fetishism, and then there's those titles: 'Paisley Park' itself, 'Raspberry Beret', 'Tamborine' . . . getting the picture?

It's true – Prince has been standing in the purple rain so long it's gone to his head. Welcome to psychedelia part 69.

Can this really be what the world needs now? Todd Rundgren has done it all before. Frank Zappa has sent the whole thing up before. We've even had our own little revival here before – so just what is the point? Perhaps in the secret world of Prince there doesn't have to be one. When you're that far out maybe it's impossible to come down to the level of us poor mortals.

Since the magnificent pop funk of *1999* Prince has slipped away into the arcane garden of opiate atmospheres and sexual delights, and with *Around the World* he's finally realised his own personal Xanadu. A haven of Technicolor bliss wherein our fragile hero can contemplate his navel until the grass turns blue.

The opening and title track sets the scene: tinkling finger-cymbals and synthetic Pan pipes usher in this flimsy menagerie of corn-fed fantasy. A rosy look back at the 'rosy' Sixties – a time that was really so much more than flowers in the hair. In this performance there are no Asian wars, no mass protests, no Black Panthers, no Angry Brigade, no Yippies, no Altamont, no Kent State massacres, no dark drugs.

'Around The World' is as lightweight as the balloon it suggests. A triumph for that whimsical studio trickery Prince has become master of maybe, but no more. 'Paisley Park' follows . . . 'There aren't any rules in Paisley Park,' drools the mad boy. How quaint. There's even backwards guitars here too.

'Condition Of The Heart' is more of the same, before 'Raspberry Beret' (the titles do have a measure of unintentional humour) allows a hint of pop to creep in with a string section soaked in period style.

'Tamborine' finishes side one on an uncharacteristically minimal note with a funk bass, handclaps and Prince's increasingly strangled vocals.

'America', colour-coded in white and blue in case you're too deranged by now to get the message, is an offensive tirade of tacky, drum-banging Reaganism. 'Communism is just a word, but if the Government turns over, it'll be the only word that's heard', according to this paranoid casualty of fame. 'Keep the children free', he adds to this cutting analysis of contemporary Babylon. Free to zap those commie gooks down Nicaragua way.

'Pop Life' is the one concession to out and out hedonism while 'Temptation', a massive sludgy blues slop, tries desperately to reconcile Prince's fascination with satin-covered flesh with his new age of 'enlightenment'. The big one comes sandwiched between the two: 'The Ladder' concerns itself with the eternal search for the lost chord and if this was the Seventies we'd say it was the key to a heavy concept album . . . man.

In fact it's more lame-brain indulgence. The kind of ramble you might have expected from those unfortunate enough to have taken the bad acid at Woodstock. Imagine Prince filtered through the most laborious Van Morrison dirge and you'd be close to the misery of 'The Ladder'.

Just why Prince has deserted what he does best, the irresistible teen trash epic, remains a mystery, but by the wild look in his eyes of late he appears to be suffering from a bad case of the Howard Hughes syndrome. Yet as a full-blown neurotic recluse one would still expect him to come up with more than this cartoon re-run of psychedelia's most trivial conceits. That he expects us to join him in this ludicrous diversion says much about his state of mind.

To paraphrase the booming voice of God from 'Around The World In A Day', 'come in Prince, your time is up!'

PUBLICATION: *Melody Maker*
DATE: 4 May 1985
WRITER: Ian Pye

☥

Parade

They used to say the genius of Hendrix was that his guitar acted as an extension of his total being, that he agonised and fantasised through that axe. Well, the same applies to Prince – everything he treats has a Midas touch, a litmus feel for the most effective groove, an intuitive thrust at the erogenous zones where the physical and spiritual collide in orgasm.

No one plays the clarinet the way you play my heart, swoons the precocious one over a beauteous, humping beat and the equation between music and emotion is sealed with a 'Kiss'. This LP, ladies and gentlemen, is alive.

I believe Prince is currently pop's greatest operator, a wizard, a true star. He is calculating and innocent – one eye tearful, coy, expressing hurt, the other cocked, laughing, coquettish, showing off. And, of course, sex is his sacred plaything. He's Freudian beyond fault and fabrication and there's a shocking intelligence working us up into a lather inside these songs, hand-jobs yet the pure effusions of a man-child wide-eyed and naked with wonder.

They're amoral in that lust and love, pleasure and pain, are indistinguishable, immoral in that he's aware of the dandy outrage of it all, and boldly hedonistic in that Prince advocates all experience enriches life. As he screams in ecstasy here: 'I want to live life to the ultimate high.'

So *Parade* is a soft-porn paradise, a sensual sacrament, supposedly the soundtrack to our doe-eyed hero's next exhibition of narcissism on film. The first side's well weird, nursery-rhyme songs subjected to sensory overload. Prince luxuriates in submitting himself to his senses, whether he's evoking *Sgt Pepper* in the symphonic collage of 'Christopher Tracy's Parade', trying on machismo in the cocky 'New Position', crooning like a camp Valentino in the gorgeously melodramatic 'Under The Cherry Moon' or turning tricks through the psychedelic funk circus riot of 'Life Can Be So Nice'.

And side two, if anything, is more illicit, more abandoned to delight. 'Kiss', of course, is perfection – Bo Diddley, Curtis Mayfield, Marc Bolan and Jayne Mansfield licking off their fingers after something good and dirty. 'Mountains'/'Do U Lie?' is delightfully daft cosmic vaudeville, wigged and powdered and rustling in velvets. And then there's the finale, this LP's 'Purple Rain', 'Sometimes It Snows In April', an acrobatic ballad that employs the simple sentimentality of country music to express deep loss so poetically, so personally – it's indecent when his vocal spirals into luscious grief, celebrating the sadness to the very last sob.

I've heard tell that, while I've been under this spell, lesser mortals have been saying dull things about revivalism and Beatles fetish. Such cold fish don't deserve the privilege of your time because, when all's said and done, when you're panting on the pillow, when the incense has cleared and you're catching your first sweet breath from this glorious vertigo, you'll realise *Parade* eclipses everything else you've heard this year.

Seriously, Godlike.

PUBLICATION: *Melody Maker*
DATE: 12 April 1986
WRITER: Steve Sutherland

Sign o' the Times

Before he became Prime Minister and got wrapped up in the sludge of Suez, Eden spread his lush and florid waistcoat over barren scenery and beauty and called it home. 200 million years of evolution and what are we left with? The aerosol air freshener. No wonder love and beauty hitched a ride to Woodstock and died of exposure. That is almost died . . .

Deep in the swamp of Minneapolis Prince had discovered the inspiration to re-create Eden – a land where people tend their begonias in peace, where dissonance is hurled into harmony, where a serpent's kiss won't give you herpes, and where the sun always shines . . . except when it's raining. It's a fecund soil that's innocent but never childish. Prince yearns for experience not ignorance.

The Revolution may be over but the solo Paisley Prince keeps the Parade marching towards Utopia. He doesn't just re-write musical history, he translates it into an intuitive Esperanto: less a who's who and more a what's what. Who else could turn Sun banners into sleek-thighed victory rolls ('Sign O' The Times')? Who else could bring flares back out of camphor coffins? Who else could touch gospel and release Go Go ('Play In The Sunshine') or squeeze rap out of rhythm 'n' purples ('Housequake')? *Sign o' the Times* (the album) doesn't just shake the rafters – the party is swept off its foundations, landing somewhere between the Yellow Brick Road and the passage of wet dreams. Nothing you'll hear this year will eclipse this French kiss. Really.

It gnarls at its conventional tethers driven crazy by the stupored scent of sex on its tail. 'I'm gonna do it cos it's so divine.' It is. No Aids, no condoms, no Norman Fowler icebergs, it's all so divine, almost perfect symmetry. Almost . . .

Thirteen songs, four sides, all known dance steps at sixes and sevens and just one fatal flaw. Why does the inner sleeve present him with those ridiculous glasses? Why the skyward gaze? They're not even rose-tinted. Second sight perhaps? A gold crucifix dangles above his Krishna kimono, but his glistens in the sun – pure and simple.

Like Madonna, Prince has faith. Unlike Madonna, who has a devout belief in herself, Prince believes in his genius, in his creation. Alarm clocks carousel around crosstown traffic, Stravinsky violins, and Minnie Mouse serenades and Prince just knows it will all fit. He knows he is right – except when he's wrong (*Under the Cherry Moon*).

The unworldly muses of hallucination twizzle in their milk bar stools waiting for the next shake of funk, the next wink of Mae West, the next thrust of Prince's peace. Not long now. 'Hot Thing' (thang) struts and shimmers sparse across the risible marshmallow flock of 'Starfish And Coffee' with its hysterical 'butterscotch clouds' and 'a tangerine' as a lone sax snakes around a signature left in Coltrane's cobwebbed legacy. Prince's shrieks of delight are as compulsive as his hedonism. My bunions are swept under the carpet, left in the midst of the sins of abandon.

Prince, however, doesn't succumb to such frailty (he has such petite feet). There are hints of the Temptations, slices of Isaac Hayes, traces of Sly Stone, even footprints of Robert Palmer, but Prince triumphs over the clutch of stray crotchets – and love triumphs over all. It has to. Prince's only competition is with Prince, with 'Little Red Corvette', with 'Dirty Mind', with 'Kiss'. His dove could so easily have become an albatross in natty disguise. But then 'U Got The Look' jack-knifes expectation and smothers all reservations. Now even the Sioux have back their Eden. It shivers with effortless panache and seething motion leaving the flaccid 'Ballad Of Dorothy Parker' and the Ruby turn-off smooch of 'Adore' to wallow in still water.

Prince's quest for Valhalla is insatiable, his aspirations unpredictable. Why duet with Sheena Easton? Was he wearing those glasses at the time? Perhaps he thought Sheena was someone else? She must have thought so too, for she sounds incredible: out of control, out on a limb, and well out of sensual bounds. And that's Prince's real genius. La di da di da, stimulation without a care in the world – this world anyway. The question of how much further Prince can go over the top without disappearing becomes irrelevant. He dedicates the album to the glory of God, but it's Christopher Columbus that also deserves his praise be's. The world is round, Eden is a perfect sphere, and therefore there is nowhere Prince can't travel. Every twist of production oozes with intrigue as beginnings and endings collide with arbitrary occasion. A bar of the bridal suite, an orchestra tuning up, a careless 'bullshit' from the bandleader, it all makes no odds. The start and stop are merely a three-minute time lapse. Stop. MMMMM – STOMP!!

The pastiche vaudeville of 'Strange Relationship' battens down the hatches, cutting through the baroque comedy of Camille's low-sprung purring during 'If I Was Your Girlfriend' ('Is it really necessary for me to leave the room when you take your clothes off . . . You don't have to make babies to make love . . .'). Yet comedy and tragedy are fused in the orbit of fascination. 'I Could Never Take The Place Of Your Man' shaves the stubble off sorrow and romance with Prince removing his Diana Dors frock and donning his Valentino bow. He gives the time: 'It was 10:32 on a lonely Friday night . . .' He gives the place: 'She was standing by the bar'. He even almost gives her a voice: 'She said all she wanted was a good man'. Then Prince gives a guitar solo and the film detonates into a thousand fragments of dancing tinsel. There was no time, no place. None that is real anyway.

'The Cross' reveals all. Almost. Ghettos to my left, flowers to my right and paradox, sorry paradise straight ahead. Who gave Eden his waistcoat? God, that's who. Who gave Prince his Paisley Park? The same who. 'The Cross' is hideously melodramatic – entering with a lonely acoustic guitar, building a tower of babble, before cascading into a crescendo of metal. It's also sanctimonious crap. It's mawkish God-rock. Worst of all . . . it works! There's a peculiar sense of fulfilment, of desire momentarily quenched by galloping through virgin pastures . . . without a horse! Even the live track 'It's Gonna Be A Beautiful Night' effuses completion, a totality of sound and instinct. I'm full now. Full of dreams, full of fire.

I'd always wondered what God did after his tea-break on the Eighth Day.

Truly this man is a genius.

PUBLICATION: *Melody Maker*
DATE: 4 April 1987
WRITER: Ted Mico

The Black Album

There are basically two schools of Prince fans. There's those that believe he's a genius and genius-is-as-genius-does, so we should worship every pout and squeak this other-worldly immortal puts out.

Then there's those, like myself, who think he's a genius sporadically; his best work ranking with anything from Marvin or Van or Bruce or Presley but who just as often mars his talent with questionable indulgences, tiresome narcissism and dubious taste. A guy who needs to be kept in line.

There is one salient, unarguable fact about Prince. He loves to play and record, play and record; it is his life force. Not for him the painstaking and fraught three-year album construction of Jacko, he just keeps banging them out. His idea of relaxation after a monster three- or four-hour show is to get a hall, invite some celebs along and play for another hour. It could be he needs another interest (apart from the one in his bedroom).

The Black Album, the Prince album, with no official release shares its title with a legendary Beatles bootleg from their final days. Maybe it's Nelson Roger's bid for similar immortality. Maybe the Washington Wives had a hand in stopping it (though I doubt it, there's nothing really gross or explicit here, certainly nothing as lowdown dirty as Marvin Sease's 'Candy Licker', which has spent 37 weeks on the black American charts. But, hey, I'm not going to underestimate the hang-up and influence of powerful loonies like the WWs). The other possibility is perhaps the most reassuring. Whether there are newer rudimentary workouts or out-takes from *Sign o' the Times*, the wildly uneven double album (originally planned as a triple), they may never see the light of day because an astute A&R department has persuaded the peach prodigy that it is work well below his habitual standard.

The Black Album sounds like a warm-up therapy session for His Royal Selfishness. This is the biggest indulgence of all but not necessarily a bad thing. When his mentor Sly Stone did something similar he pulled off some of his greatest work, the astonishing *There's a Riot Going On* LP, the definitive example of a star's support system caving in as he came to terms with the outside world. Prince gave us and himself a peak of that world with *Sign o' the Times*, but *The Black Album* is strictly smalltime shillyshallying.

There's 'Cindy C', a song about (yawn) making it with a French model. OK, OK, so he gets laid more often with an infinitely more lavish and voluptuous parade of dollies than we mere mortals but this severe midget over-compensation crisis does have its limitations. 'I just hate to see an erection go to waste,' he sings on 'Hard Rock [*sic*] In A Funky Place'. Well I'm sure you know what to do boyo – drain the bag and let's hear about something else.

He does change tack for 'Dead On It', castigating the rappers from NYC, saying that they're not a patch on the Minneapolis gallery of starchildren. This is even more depressing, being puerile petty bitchiness. The guy should be secure enough with his own formidable talent not to get bogged down in this sort of thing. It would be like the *NME* replying to criticism from a smalltime rag with half its circulation. Bruce Springsteen sniping at the Weather Prophets, Elvis coming back to 'have a word' with Shakin' Stevens.

Musically it's much the same – half-assed ideas, smart jams, clinks of electro and tape varispeed but nothing that comes together with the same wizardry as 'If I Was Your Girlfriend', nothing that connects or takes stock of past, present and future like '1999' or 'Pop Life'. 'Superfunkicalifragisexy' has promise, with its intimations of a secret sex rite involving squirrel meat (he may be a fruitcake but at least he's no vegetarian). The dance porridge is lifted with dervishing spins, yells, shrieks and pants. On the right track, but not quite the Full Havana. '2 Nigs United 4 West Compton' has a title that wouldn't be out of place on an early Fall album but it's a severely bungled heavy acid horrorshow.

The Black Album is Prince getting rid of the detritus, a man juggling with ideas and directions. Naturally I'd rather listen to it than anything else released this week but it's not worthy of the guy, having neither the depth nor the quality he should be attaining. Maybe those guardians of artistic licence have a point when they say the public doesn't have an inalienable right to everything a musician records. From this Black Album, I don't get the enlightening, personal-universe-turned-into-communal-experience vibe that good Prince stuff gives out. Now consigned to the collectors and fanatics grapevine, it just makes me feel like a voyeur.

PUBLICATION: *New Musical Express*
DATE: 23 January 1988
WRITER: Gavin Martin

Lovesexy

Prince's albums stopped making artistic sense a long time ago.

There never seems to be any logical connection between one LP and the next. The only constant seems to be his approach. Shock the listeners in such a way that they will be riveted to the record.

The big shock of *Lovesexy* (Paisley Park), which arrives in record stores this week, is that it doesn't shock. There is nothing on it that his faithful or even casual pop-music followers would not have come to expect from Prince – from the nude cover photo (with his legs strategically placed), to the coyly suggestive lyrics, to the irresistible funk, to the stunning poetic ballads, to the stylised rapping, to the evocative guitar solos, to the obsessiveness with the spiritual. Together, it all works. *Lovesexy* is a solid and ultimately rewarding record.

The nine-song album is Prince's most consistent and cohesive effort since the landmark *Purple Rain* in 1984. The songs make sense together. Moreover, many of them can be linked either in theme or style to selections on previous Prince albums. Maybe this provocative Minneapolis visionary is starting to make artistic sense.

If any themes have run through all six of his albums since 1980's *Dirty Mind*, his first visionary expression, it has been the struggle between sin and salvation, and society's inability to confront destructive forces.

In three of the songs on this album, Prince manages to intertwine his principal themes by repeating the phrases 'new power' (generation), which is vague but suggests a positive connotation, and 'lovesexy', which is not vague. The concepts crop up in the first two selections on the record. The opening 'Eye No' acknowledges a heaven and a hell, and then discusses the challenges the devil poses and the strengths that the Lord offers. Musically, the tune presages things to come on this record because the song goes all over the place from a spacey introduction to a quirky funk with jagged saxophones to a bombastic ending during which cocktail conversation is juxtaposed with a booming preacher's voice urging prayer. 'Eye No' is a bold beginning.

Next stop is 'Alphabet St', a place of sin for a stud on the prowl. Actually, the tune takes a Jimmy Swaggart-like turn as the protagonist says he would rather watch than participate. An inside-out guitar funk, 'Alphabet St' is Prince's first single from this album. (The radio version does not include the sassy rap section uttered by Cat, a singer-dancer in Prince's band.) Although the music is, at first, vaguely reminiscent of 'Kiss', Prince's 1986 smash, this one probably won't scale to the top of the charts.

The protagonist scores on the ensuing 'Glam Slam'. The chorus – 'glam slam, thank u ma'am, u really make my day' – sums up the trivial content, but the musical arrangement intrigues. Perhaps the thickest number Prince has ever put together, 'Glam Slam' initially comes across like one of Todd Rundgren's multilayered pop-rock opuses before it melds extended jungle rhythms underneath orchestral melodies. Eventually it builds to orchestral rock 'n' roll before finishing with a dark, heavy code of orchestral strings.

The ending of 'Glam Slam' may be designed to contrast with the beginning of 'Anna Stesia', which could be viewed as the album's centrepiece. It's another of Prince's powerful, emotional confrontations between sex and salvation but this time he clearly proclaims his faith. The song contains his most pained guitar solo since 'Purple Rain' and a rap rendered in a British accent. Near the end, the singer gets lost in the song when voices representing the sinner and his inner, spiritual being grapple with each other. Musically, 'Anna Stesia' is an airy, exquisite answer to the noisy rock 'n' roll rave-up of the spiritual 'The Cross' on last year's *Sign o' the Times*.

Side 2 opens with 'Dance On', a 1988 trash-can funk update of the 1982 song '1999'. 'Dance On' may have been a more obvious choice for a first single, even though it echoes the theme of 'Sign O' The

Times', the initial single from Prince's last album. This one has a good dance beat and enough musical eccentricities, such as the rock star singing in his upper, middle and lower registers, to be alluring in the strange and wondrous way that Prince is.

He continues with the dance beat on 'Lovesexy', a dense rock-funk workout with a syncopated rap, wild-rock guitar and a nasty closing rap filled with slick street euphemisms for bedroom acts. Then the licentious libertine gets romantic on 'When 2 R In Love', a pretty, poetic ballad that was originally recorded for last year's much-publicised *Black Album* that was never released. On *Lovesexy*, this ballad sounds like Prince emulating Joni Mitchell – whom he has long admired – with elegant, cascading sounds, reminiscent of his very first album, set to the hip rhythms of his recent work.

The next number, 'I Wish U Heaven', is a throwaway musically (except for a jazzy guitar break) but serves as a necessary purgatory before the resurrection of Prince's favourite themes. 'Positivity', the album's finale, details how the devil can turn people into a wayward life of crime, so it calls for love, honesty, peace and harmony to turn the world around. This spare funk excursion's repetitive quality works in a brain-washing kind of way. Again, Prince, backed by the same band he used on 'Sign O' The Times', goes all over the place musically with rocking guitar (which is buried too softly in the sound mix), a ghetto rap, weird jazzy horn solos, Beatlesque sounds recall-ing their Ravi Shankar days, and flowing water at the end to purify things, followed by heavenly orchestral strings.

Somehow it all makes sense. Whether *Lovesexy* will make big dol-lars and cents for Prince remains to be seen. Unlike most of his other albums, this one does not contain any can't-miss candidates for hits. 'Dance On' would be the most logical, and 'Positivity' has possibili-ties; both will likely find favour with dance-club disc jockeys but may strike out with radio programmers.

Perhaps Prince is finally due to break through with a ballad. 'Anna Stesia' is eccentric but exquisite. 'When 2 R In Love' will probably be a favourite on black-music radio stations as were 'Slow Love' and 'Forever In My Life' from *Sign o' the Times*, even though neither was released and promoted as a single. If the verse with the sexually aggressive imagery were edited out of 'When 2 R In Love', the tune could be well received by programmers at various kinds of radio formats.

Of course, predicting the fate of a Prince LP upon its release is risky. His albums invariably improve with age (this one takes a half-dozen listenings before it begins to sink in), even though the prolific recording artist gets impatient with each record and often outgrows it before people have a chance to embrace it. He never allowed last year's *Sign o' the Times*, an often brilliant 18-song double-disc, to take hold with record buyers (it was the overwhelming choice for album of the year in a nationwide poll of more than 200 critics conducted by New York's *Village Voice* magazine), he quashed the project's momentum by releasing an esoteric second single, 'If I Was Your Girlfriend', after the LP's title track had zoomed up to number 1, and by opting to promote the music via a concert film with limited distribution instead of an extensive concert tour of the United States (he did a limited European tour).

Lovesexy is a dense record whose layered and often complex sound (get out the headphones or buy the compact disc) as well as its preoccupation with the spiritual will invite comparisons to *Around the World in a Day*, Prince's follow-up to *Purple Rain*. *Around the World* yielded a couple of sizeable hit singles but was ultimately artistically unsatisfying. *Lovesexy* may not produce any major hits but it is a worthy follow up to *Sign o' the Times*.

PUBLICATION: *Minneapolis Star Tribune*
DATE: 5 September 1988
WRITER: Jon Bream

Batman

Those who know about these things say that *Batman* will be the biggest movie of the year. In America, where it opens on Friday, people have apparently been queuing just to see the 90-second trailer.

Far from being the camp figure of fun portrayed by Adam West in the television series, the new-look caped crusader is a character of an altogether more sinister and ambiguous nature. A semi-psychotic midnight rambler, lurking on rooftops and in shadowy doorways, he preys without mercy on the criminal element of a Gotham City turned into a fantastically nightmarish urban sprawl.

Unfortunately there is little of this stark dramatic quality detectable in Prince's *Batman* soundtrack album which, apart from the single 'Batdance' and the 'guest presence' of the actors' voices on a few of the tracks, actually seems on first listening to have precious little to do with *Batman*, the movie.

Of the nine new compositions which comprise the album, five are eminently serviceable, four-on-the-floor funk grooves of a type which Prince has long since proved himself able to run off in his sleep. 'Partyman', introduced by the voice of Jack Nicholson (as The Joker) saying, 'Gentlemen, let's broaden our minds,' has an appropriately jokey, scampering feel. 'Trust' is a light, up-tempo belter, 'Lemon Crush' an excuse for a murky, sexy rap and 'The Future' a sparse, tough romp, with a skittish cowbell and moody atmospherics towards the end. Whatever else may be happening in the shadows, the mean streets of Gotham City are certainly rocking to an all-night party beat.

But despite some imaginative scratching and sampling on 'Batdance' – the first time that Prince has seriously turned his hand to such techniques – there is a distinctly throwaway quality to much of this material, particularly the heavy rock riffing of 'Electric Chair'. Certainly there is nothing here to match either the instinctive, chilling version of urban blight put across so brilliantly on 'Sign O' The Times', or the cute pop dandyism of 'Alphabet St'.

There is plenty of sex, however, including a drearily kitsch duet with Sheena Easton ('Arms Of Orion'), and a dreadfully overwrought ballad called 'Scandalous', which was co-written by Prince's father, John L. Nelson. This is not the sort of song I would end up writing with my dad. It begins with a soothing Radio 2-style string section, against which Prince pitches his voice in a squeaky, salacious falsetto, teetering on the edge of hysteria. 'I want to wrap my legs around you girl,' he pleads, having by now worked himself into a fearful lather.

This is undoubtedly an album in the right place at the right time and it will presumably earn the little fellow a mint. Perhaps it will click when we get a chance to see the movie ourselves (it opens in London on August 11), but simply heard cold the collection is something of a disappointment.

PUBLICATION: *The Times*
DATE: 17 June 1989
WRITER: David Sinclair

Graffiti Bridge

Prince's latest journey in mind and funk starts with a confessional letter. 'Dear Dad,' he intones in a low voice, 'things didn't turn out like I wanted them to. Sometimes I feel like I'm going to explode.' Whereupon a menacing boom segues into the backbeat-happy 'Can't Stop This Feeling I Got'. Thing is, this Prince album sounds less like it is going to explode than most. At his best over the last decade, Prince has been the reigning funk auteur, exploring areas of genre-smashing, gender-bashing, R&B, rock/pop where Sly Stone, Jimi Hendrix, and George Clinton have gone before.

Prince has mastered a brand of explosive intimacy, sketching out on the themes of lust and spiritual inquest. Musically, too, Prince works the studio in refreshing ways, piling texture upon texture, altering fashion by, say, simply leaving out the bass or stripping away any reverb. *Graffiti Bridge* is the aural companion to his third film project and it remains to be seen how the kinesthetic whole works. The sound aspect fails to excite the sense of risk and even revelation we've come to expect from him in the past.

Still, Prince rules his own court, and includes in this sampling such extra-Prince operations as sassy rap-sodies from The Time, the green-horn Tevin Campbell ('Round And Round'), gospel fortitude from Mavis Staples, and a slinkfunky *tête à tête* with George Clinton on 'We Can Funk'. Funk and controversy change their faces every few years, and – stacked up to the hip-hopping shuffle feels rampant now – this year's Prince project sounds like a sparkling thing of a slightly outmoded yesteryear.

PUBLICATION: *Downbeat*
DATE: January 1991
WRITER: Josef Woodard

Diamonds and Pearls

I fell off *Graffiti Bridge*. Just couldn't get across it, no matter how hard I tried. It was a wobbly Bridge; built on things borrowed (the best cuts featured Tevin Campbell and Mavis Staples on lead vocals) and things received (the other two good cuts were Prince-only jams – 'Joy In Repetition' and 'Thieves In The Temple'). It was a Bridge in need of serious repair. Maybe Prince was too busy writing and directing and acting and not busy enough composing.

Diamonds and Pearls, Prince's new LP with the New Power Generation, picks up the slack by being purely and unabashedly tuneful, revelling in its scattered attention to multi-leveled mingling of musical forms. The record is crammed to the rafters with styles: poppy glam-rock ('Cream'), rousing gospel ('Willing And Able'), hip-hop ('Jughead'), smooth-talkin' jazz ('Strollin"), and gliding retro-soul balladry ('Insatiable'). The cohesion is in the sheer forceful thrust of the band's musicianship – or as the liner notes read: '4 those of you who are wondering – a family is born and God bless us cuz we fonky'.

And detailed. Earlier recordings with The Revolution suffered from oftentimes wayward mixes; it was hard to decipher the exact strengths of the players and how they contributed to the songs. Check out 'Money Don't Matter 2Night' here: Levi Seacer's smooth, loping rhythm guitar twangs away, leading Michael B's pop-jazz drum flourishes and the multi-tracked vocal slides into a colourful Steely Dan-ish groove. Or the funk attack of 'Daddy Pop': Rosie Gaines's dazzlingly co-ordinated hoots, riffs and organ acrobatics force Prince into one of his finest vocal moments, a Sly Stone-ish grumble that positively purrs up next to the curvaceous, cut-and-mix beats.

Lyrically, Prince again reaches for relevancy, citing the Gulf War in a few cuts and adding rapped segments about greedy record-biz folk. But on *Diamonds and Pearls*, the words work best when they seem to come out of nowhere. 'Cream''s short guitar sling is introduced with 'Look up in the air. It's your guitar'. The chorus? 'Cream . . . sh-boogie-bop.'

Not as committedly focused as Prince's best work (*Dirty Mind*, *Parade*, *Lovesexy*) or as gallantly erratic as the worst (*Controversy*, *Around the World in a Day*, *Graffiti Bridge*), *Diamonds and Pearls* is a sultry, groovy, inventively jittery jewel box of diverse nuggets.

PUBLICATION: *Spin*
DATE: November 1991
WRITER: Scott Poulson-Bryant

Though he often acts like his existence depends on it, Prince probably couldn't shock anybody if he duded up in full drag and blew fish-kisses to Warner Bros chairman Mo Ostin. His days of controversy are over, unless he's willing to, say, off a pig in a rap song: the 'Sexy MF' video is simply Prince playing catch-up with Madonna's 'Justify My Love' and hundreds of pimpin'-ain't-easy hip-hop clips. But the song itself is a cuddly monster of a groove, his first party-tape must-have since 'Housequake' from 1987's *Sign o' the Times*. And most of the rest of ♀ cream sh-boogie-bops with aggressive aplomb as if our little purple buddy had never driven off *Graffiti Bridge*.

Unlike Bruce 'Entertainment Tonight' Springsteen – fidgeting sincerely with the common folk after hiding away all those years in his model-laden castle – Prince has revived himself musically by humping and stumping for the product. He worked 1991's *Diamonds and Pearls* like a 9 to 5. And though US sales stalled at double platinum somewhere behind Color Me Badd and Reba McEntire, it was his cockiest, most trend-savvy album in years. And that was always the coolest thing about Prince – he was the trendiest. At one time, he seemed to have the entire history of pop on floppy disks that he flipped through mid-solo. But hip-hop eluded him. A hostile, unfunny B-boy parody on 1988's *The Black Album* didn't help. Finally, with *Diamonds and Pearls*, more than ten years after hip-hop elder DJ Kool Herc left the building, he acknowledged the music's aesthetic (and economic) dominance and decided that scratching wasn't the enemy. On ♀ he's even hired a full-time sidekick – the loutish, tongue-twisting Tony M – and fully appropriated hip-hop's cut, paste, and steal production scheme.

'My Name Is Prince' is his umpteenth re-introduction, but here, the self-definition has a rumbling drum track work repeating – accented by screeches, turntable squiggles, burbling bass, and samples of squealing from Prince past – and a nasty edge of Michael-envy (you know, the King of Pop) that gets me all goose-pimply. While the funk jerks him along, Prince growls: 'I don't wanna be king / Cuz I've seen top / And it's just a dream.' Fancy clothes and such 'will save your face but it won't save your soul'. Face? Ouch! Then Tony M bellows: 'U must become a Prince before U're a king anyway.' Psych! The closest footnote might be LL Cool J's comeback throwdown: 'Mama Said Knock You Out', but LL never ended a chorus by imploring, 'Hurt Me!'

This is also some of Prince's buggiest doo-doo in years. After the tinkly, quiet-storm ballad 'Damn U' (which Babyface would blush for) there's a tripped-out send-up of his legendary interview wariness, starring Scientology diva and *Cheers* vet Kirstie Alley. Alley asks

Prince what he believes in. 'God,' he replies. 'Who is your God?' she follows up. 'You,' Prince whispers, laughing. But she doesn't get it, so he kick-starts 'Arrogance', a phuncky-phusiony real one in which we discover that if Prince is ever going to get over as a rapper, it'll be doing Louis Jordan, not Ice-T. Later, posing as a 320-year-old classical composer, he has phone sex with a playfully perturbed Alley on the intro to 'The Sacrifice Of Victor', a chaotically funky workout that has something to do with school busing and Prince's tormented personal Jesus. The lyrics, quite loonily affecting at times, would've cut deeper if they'd been sung more like Cameo's Larry Blackmon and less like silky smoothie Ralph Tresvant.

But why quibble? More often than not, this stuff is silly and crafty genius, and his Royal Weirdness seems perfectly comfy playing the harmlessly eccentric pop businessman (if $108 million and a Warner Bros office are thrown in, of course). Let Michael be the Rocky Horror Picture Show of pop. Because Prince may be the funkiest corporate vice-president in the history of rock 'n' roll, so just get off his dick, I mean desk, and shut up already.

PUBLICATION: *Spin*
DATE: November 1992
WRITER: Charles Aaron

The Hits / The B-Sides

He came from the Twin Cities, a precocious, pseudonymous figure plying the R&B trade with an androgynous squeal of a voice, an auteur's self-reliance, and a forceful will to bend the rules. It wasn't that Prince wanted to break the rules off at the source, and thus lose the music's nourishing rootedness. Instead, he found his spot in the evolutionary chain of the music by persistently pushing the R&B envelope – like James Brown, Sly Stone, George Clinton, and others before him.

After fifteen years in the spotlight and in his studio-bound hermitage, Prince has built up an impressive body of work – almost dizzying, really. When heard in a retrospective package, *The Hits/The B-Sides*, Prince's generous cultural imprint is plain to hear: it's in the house and in your face. (The package is also available in smaller, affordable chunks, as separate single *Hits* CDs, minus the third *B-Sides* disc in the three-CD set.) The album's arrival also signifies a departure. With fourteen albums under the belt, Prince is reportedly hanging up his purple robe – and studio life – altogether.

Whether or not the retirement news turns out to be a crafty ploy or a genuine transition, this package comes just in time. Of late, the Purple One seemed to be slipping off of his cutting edge, rendered slightly mouldy by the radical style shifts swirling around him under the hip-hop banner. His efforts to join the new rap/funkstream have been less than triumphant. Sonics and standards of acceptability in sexuality in black music have gone through enormous changes since Prince first holed himself up in the plush, Minneapolis pleasuredome of his home studio in the early 1980s.

On this three-hour-plus tour, Prince goes from the down-the-middle R&B of his early work, such as 'I Wanna Be Your Lover' or his tame version of 'I Feel For You' – later brought vividly to life by Chaka Khan – to the unreleased hip-hop plaything, 'Pope'. Here, Prince raps around studio paste-ups and the wryly self-revealing, anthemic refrain: 'You can be the president, I'd rather be the pope / You can be the side effect, I'd rather be the dope.'

Wisely, the comprehensive, non-chronologically ordered three-CD set kicks off with Prince's crowning achievement, 'When Doves Cry'. His shining hour, in terms of commercially viable artistic statement, 'When Doves Cry' indulges in poetic euphemism instead of titillation. Prince knew better than most that sex and sedition are key ingredients in pushing R&B conventions to new expressive levels, but his litanies of navel- and crotch-gazing get old.

History repeats and reinvents itself on this sprawling package – both Prince's own telescoped history and growth, and also his free-wheeling appropriation of R&B traditions, tailored to his own purposes. Dance-happy ditties like 'Let's Go Crazy', 'Delirious', and even '1999' stoke the timeless soul train, but cleverly take the fatalistic view of life on the dance floor as an ecstatic, non-rational refuge from the chill of life in the rational, real world.

Never content to abide by conventional wisdoms in the studio, Prince always shuffled the deck of possibilities. He often seemed to run away from anti-generated expectations – until we came to expect the unexpected. What made the post-James Brown lighten-up-ish hit, 'Kiss', so striking was the stark dryness of the tracks, *sans* any reverb to lubricate the texture. Similarly, 'When Doves Cry' bent rules and lured ears via its daring – but somehow logical – lack of a bass.

Given his whirlwind career thus far, it's easy to get lost in a purple haze when considering Prince's role in pop culture. But, despite the inventive genre-bending, his restless carnality and media image obsessiveness, Prince never waned when it came to the potency of his groove imperative.

It doesn't really matter that he's begging patience by dispensing with his name altogether, replacing it with a symbol that resembles a vulgar infraction of the treble clef – just as Michael Jackson once insisted on being referred to as King of Pop (trying to one-up Prince on the totem pole of royalty). What matters is that Prince stayed on his toes, creatively, where it counts. Long live.

PUBLICATION: *Downbeat*
DATE: January 1994
WRITER: Josef Woodard

Come

Hmm . . . let's see. Tombstone on the cover proclaiming 1993 as the year of Prince's death. A dramatic recollection from an abused child, complete with a scarifying warning: 'Don't abuse children, or else they'll turn out like me.' Vague talk about change, cosmic and other-wise. Could this be the major career announcement that has been pending since Prince, with a wave of his press agent's wand, became ♀?

Not so fast. Turns out that not much has changed except the name. The former Prince is still playing Artist Knows Best: when Warner Bros shut down Paisley Park Records and cautioned him about flooding the market, what did this royal pain do? He set up another label, arranged independent distribution for his overflow goods and promptly scored a told-you-so hit with the puzzlingly Princelike 'The Most Beautiful Girl In The World'. Then announced that he would fulfil his contract with Warner Bros by issuing mater-ial from the countless reels of studio tape he made as Prince. *Come*, whose songs carry a 1994 publishing registration, is the first such archive collection. Naturally this 'old' material is not to be con-fused with the music and worldview of the new, unpronounceable ♀.

Whatever you do, appreciate these latest moves as part of what has become the most spectacular slow-motion career derailment in the history of popular music. Ordinary artists just make duds; this guy specialises in public relations catastrophes that confuse his loyal fol-lowing and erode his stature as the major genre-busting innovator of the last decade. Ordinary artists tear up albums and start again, he's tearing up his entire identity and starting again.

So far, however, this grand makeover-in-progress feels like another layer of pancake plastered on to the face of a tired actor. ♀ might not be Prince anymore, but he still has the same toolbox. There's nothing on the uneven *Come* or the *1-800-NEW-FUNK* compilation, which was written and produced entirely by ♀, that will change anybody's impression of this artist. He's still horny. Still adventurous. He can't escape his sonic signatures, which derive not only from his Jekyll-and-Hyde voice and its gymnastic falsetto but also from his rhythmic exactitude, ability to imply different harmonies and rare gift for insinuating melody. Nobody builds a vamp the way he does. No other guitar crackles with that, dry, tart tang.

In the past, as he balanced these elements with the agility of a master orchestrator, Prince never left his imagination behind. He recognised that the interpretation had to sell the goods: he could give the raunchiest idea a sense of righteous grandeur and make a high-minded spiritual quest sound like an illicit affair. Not this time. *Come* features the most blatant soft-porn pillow talk Prince has ever released. At one point the lazy pulse of the title track becomes a forum for Prince to discourse on his (surprisingly ordinary) oral-sex techniques, and the closing 'Orgasm' comes off as a you-are-there live remote recording of a sexual encounter.

Following a pattern established albums ago, Prince all but abandons the convoluted spiritual concerns he voiced on '7' and other tracks from ♀ (1992). He's back to earth – talking Slylike and direct about 'Race', moaning about being done wrong in the taut gospel ballad 'Dark', returning to the relatively innocent seduction strategies of 'Soft And Wet' on the blazing, funky chant 'Pheromone'.

But that stuff always was easy for Prince. Indeed, portions of *Come*, including 'Space' and 'Loose', exhibit so little creativity you wonder whether they were born during studio catnaps. Ever since 'Alphabet St', his challenge has been to broaden the music and allow it to address real issues, to move away from the cartoon image that dogged him after *Purple Rain* and *Under the Cherry Moon*. It's possible to interpret the gospel-tinged 'The Sacrifice Of Victor', from ♀, as part of that campaign – an account of Prince's childhood that was, for an artist who is obsessively secretive, a major step.

With the graphically violent 'Papa', which chronicles the disciplining of a four-year-old, Prince elaborates on the hints in 'Victor' that he has been abused. 'Papa' probably won't make the box set, but its code is a fiery eruption worthy of the subject matter, and its candour is clear evidence that Prince wishes to be less restrained.

The same sense of forthright introspection marks the sauntering strut 'Letitgo', which many will read as an apologia for the excesses of the Prince era. In a regretful tone, it offers a past-tense acknowledgement that Prince, that notorious workaholic, wasn't always the most pleasant creature. An indictment of his self-absorption, the song suggests that whatever comes next will represent a change in attitude, 'Lover here, lover there / Who cried, who cared / Foolish pride / Never was a good seat at any of this man's shows / Until now, all I wanted 2 do was / Do do do what I do . . .But now I've got 2 let it go.'

That admonishment aside, *Come* documents Prince at a surprisingly mediocre point – still able to pop out thumping, genuinely new grooves but unwilling to leave them alone, cluttering them with banal lyrics and overwritten horn parts and missing wildly with indulgent experiments like 'Solo', one adventure in reverb best left in the vault.

PUBLICATION: *Rolling Stone*
DATE: 8 September 1994
WRITER: Tom Moon

The Gold Experience

With this LP, our former Prince turns in his most effortlessly eclectic set since 1987's *Sign o' the Times*. As his fourth album since rock's most quixotic auteur baptised himself with a name only dolphins and extraterrestrials can pronounce, *The Gold Experience* is surprisingly retro in sound and attitude. Longtime fans will recognise signature riffs from 'Purple Rain', '1999' and 'Controversy', as well as customised appropriations from glitter rock, the Ohio Players, art rock and the kind of quirky narrative poems Prince perfected upon the release of *Graffiti Bridge*.

Guiding the listener from track to track is the multilingual clatter of a feminine cyborg first deployed on the ex-Prince's interactive CD-ROM from last year. One of her first declarations – in Spanish – is that Prince has 'died' so that the New Power Generation may live. But who are the NPG, really? Although *The Gold Experience* enjoys the services of some very tight, skilful musicians (not the least of whom are the folks who compose the horn section from the old Paisley Park act Madhouse), all you really hear is the heart, soul and mind of our once and future Prince.

In case you're wondering, all his classic contradictions are still firmly in place. On the poppy political broadside 'We March', he cautions men not to call women bitches, then a few tracks later breaks his own commandment in the anti-love ditty 'Billy Jack Bitch'. On 'Eye Hate U', the soulful first single, he sings, 'I hate you . . . 'cause I love you, girl,' which sums up the Princely persona in a nutshell. He loves his women and his colleagues, but he can't allow them a dominant role in his life or his work. He loves the perks of stardom but has gone out of his way to reduce his own public profile to that of a virtual unknown. Add to all this a long-standing fascination with paradox, irony and subtle parody, and you get *The Gold Experience* in all its contrarian glory.

Like Michael Jackson, our erstwhile Prince has plenty to scream about, but he's nowhere near as dour about it as Elvis Presley's son-in-law. Instead he tries to have as much fun as possible while following his own schizoid genius as it dances along the precarious divide between the sacred and the profane.

As usual, the attempts at rap come off as part satire and part celebration of the form. The gutter feminism of 'Pussy Control' is earnestly phrased in the goofy syntax of the butt-loving Sir Mix-a-Lot, while the rabble-rousing lyrics of 'Now' are delivered in the twangy drawl of Arrested Development's Speech. But the most powerful revelation among this grab bag of edgy rhythms and melodies comes during the deceptively gentle 'Shy'. Its rhythm track recalls the imaginative noodling of 'Kiss' leavened with the melodic idiosyncrasies of a Joni Mitchell ballad but leaves a more indelible impression than either. The male protagonist of 'Shy' lands alone in Los Angeles and starts wandering the town in search of, well, poetry in motion.

This scenario was played out before in songs like 'Head' and 'Uptown', but, oh, what a difference a decade or so makes! Back in the *Dirty Mind* era, the main thing on a Princely woman's mind was sex. But the virginal Los Angeles riot grrrl encountered in 'Shy' is more inclined to brag about the men she killed than about the men she bedded – yet one more apocalyptic sign of the times we live in.

PUBLICATION: *Rolling Stone*
DATE: 2 November 1995
WRITER: Carol Cooper

Girl 6

The soundtrack for *Girl 6*, Spike Lee's paean to the phone sex industry, could easily be mistaken for another Prince greatest-hits set. With the exception of three new tunes, the album collects some of the royal one's most romantic – and kinky – old songs. Compiled under this sensual theme, his earlier jams seem to have new bite.

The butt-smacking drum-machine beats of 1984's 'Erotic City', featuring his old band, The Revolution, sound as good as they ever did. 'You're a sinner / I don't care / I just want your creamy thighs,' is the urge to freak someone on a dance floor.

The New Power Generation help Prince with the title track. Its lazy, funky groove contains snippets of ringing phones, 1987's 'Housequake', and 1985's 'Raspberry Beret', and features *Girl 6* star Theresa Randle speaking erotically. The album's only disappointment is the new ballad 'Don't Talk 2 Strangers', which has a cornball factor almost as high as 1991's 'Diamonds and Pearls'. (All thanks 2 God, 'D and P' is not included here.)

Even if you've never cared about the former Artist Formerly Known As Prince, the soundtrack for *Girl 6* is a perfect dance-and-slow-jam introduction to his esteemed, sexy body of work.

PUBLICATION: *Vibe*
DATE: June/July 1996
WRITER: Omoronke Idowu

Chaos and Disorder

On the back of the CD booklet is a disclaimer by The Artist Formerly Known As Prince: 'Originally intended 4 private use only, this compilation serves as the last original material recorded by 4 Warner Brothers Records.' His ongoing war of protest and whining against his record label is also reflected in the photos adorning the pages of the *Chaos and Disorder* booklet: a syringe with a dollar bill rolled up inside, a toilet with a heart floating in the water, and the master-tape vault inside Paisley Park Studios, framed by gold records. Before you hear a single note, you're prepped for a halfhearted transaction from a self-pitying celebrity.

The whole album – its vibe, purpose and effect – is summarised in the self-aggrandising 'I Rock Therefore I Am'. Elements from the proverbial kitchen sink – blaring horns, funky, stuttering drums, police sirens, rap-cum-reggae-style toasting – bracket defiant lyrics that flash hints of social commentary to mask what is essentially 's taunting of his record company. The lyrics gracelessly confuse the personal with the political.

Chaos and Disorder is distinguished by its confusion; even the title admits that the album's fractured parts never resolve into a thematic whole. At its best, the record sounds like a collection of polished demos. More often, though, it seems like the work of a Prince impersonator – someone who has closely studied the star's moves and mannerisms but has nothing new or substantial of his own to say. It's a drag act that becomes a drag real quickly.

 sings the delicate 'Dinner With Delores' in a high register, his lead vocals backed by a breezy, softly cooed chorus. Yet the result is still a less attractive twin of *Sign o' the Times*'s 'The Ballad Of Dorothy Parker'. The title track has a searing organ, Rosie Gaines's fiery backing vocals and wild drumming that suits 's manic blasts of lead guitar. It's wildly energetic – but also completely generic.

Whether he's just distracted by his record-company battles or has truly shot his wad, it's been a while since ⚥ has really had anything important to say in his music. It doesn't matter what The Artist Formerly Known As Prince calls himself, *Chaos and Disorder* is the sound of the man repeating himself badly.

PUBLICATION: *Rolling Stone*
DATE: 22 August 1996
WRITER: Ernest Hardy

⚥

Emancipation

He may be the most prolific superstar in the history of pop, but as Prince enters a new phase of his career with his first record for EMI, his stock is at a low ebb. His previous album, *Chaos and Disorder*, a desultory kiss-off to his former record company, has sold fewer than 40,000 copies in Britain, a dismal result for an artist of his stature.

As public interest has waned, so the media has tired of pandering to the little man's identity crises and crass promotional ploys. Not the best moment then, you would think, to chance his arm with a grandiose triple CD, ominously titled *Emancipation* and promising 'three hours of love, sex and liberty'. Frankly, it looks as if he's been given enough rope to hang himself, with slack to spare.

But, against the odds, slack is one thing this album is not. Gone for the most part is the empty braggadocio and slapdash production that have marred his output in recent years. Instead, along with the complex horn parts, barbershop soul harmonies and multiple layers of percussive activity, there is a return to the inventive vitality that used to be taken for granted.

There are sultry, pleading ballads, such as 'Soul Sanctuary' and 'Saviour'; uptempo dance tracks, notably a sensational electro-funk groove called 'New World'; affectionate cover versions of hits by the Stylistics ('Betcha By Golly Wow!'), the Delfonics ('La, La, La Means

I Love U') and Joan Osborne ('One Of Us'), and a handful of badass rap tracks, the heaviest being 'Face Down'.

While musically there is little he has not tackled before, there are some stunning moments, as on 'Slave', where he harnesses a murky drumbeat to a 1990s-style cottonfield chant of 'They just keep trying to break my heart'. And there are signs of a growing maturity in his lyrics. 'Let's Have A Baby' marks the first time he has looked beyond the mechanics to the consequences of sex, and, despite the self-pitying tone of 'White Mansion' and 'Damned If Eye Do', they are two of several songs that offer an honest reflection of the usual voyeuristic fantasies.

Although it is a lot to swallow, *Emancipation* is anything but the self-indulgent mess we might have expected. Never mind the quantity, enjoy the depth.

PUBLICATION: *The Times*
DATE: 22 November 1996
WRITER: David Sinclair

Year	Songs by & credited to Prince	Credited to pseudonym	Co-writer	Written for / recorded by	Album – title	Single	Notes
1977					Minneapolis Genius		P – session musician
1978	For You			Prince	For You		
	In Love			Prince	For You		
	Soft And Wet		Chris Moon	Prince	For You		
	Crazy You			Prince	For You		
	Just As Long As We're Together			Prince	For You		
	Baby			Prince	For You		
	My Love Is Forever			Prince	For You		
	So Blue			Prince	For You		
	I'm Yours			Prince	For You		
	So Blue			Prince		Single B-side	
1979	I Wanna Be Your Lover			Prince	Prince		
	Why You Wanna Treat Me So Bad?			Prince	Prince		
	Sexy Dancer			Prince	Prince		
	When We're Dancing Close And Slow			Prince	Prince		
	With You			Prince	Prince		
	Bambi			Prince	Prince		
	Still Waiting			Prince	Prince		
	I Feel For You			Prince	Prince		
1980	Dirty Mind			Prince	Dirty Mind		
	When You Were Mine			Prince	Dirty Mind		
	Do It All Night			Prince	Dirty Mind		
	Gotta Broken Heart Again			Prince	Dirty Mind		
	Uptown			Prince	Dirty Mind		
	Head			Prince	Dirty Mind		
	Sister			Prince	Dirty Mind		

Year	Songs by & credited to Prince	Credited to pseudonym	Co-writer	Written for/ recorded by	Album – title	Single	Notes
	FIRST TOUR: March 1980 through '81						
1981	Gotta Stop (Messin' About)			Prince		B-side	
	Controversy			Prince	Controversy		
	Sexuality			Prince	Controversy		
	Do Me, Baby			Prince	Controversy		
	Private Joy			Prince	Controversy		
	Ronnie, Talk To Russia			Prince	Controversy		
	Let's Work			Prince	Controversy		
	Annie Christian			Prince	Controversy		
	Jack U Off			Prince	Controversy		
	Just Another Sucker		Pepe Willie	94 East	94 East		
	Cool		Dez Dickerson	The Time	The Time		
	Get It Up			The Time	The Time		
	Girl			The Time	The Time		
	Oh, Baby			The Time	The Time		
	The Stick			The Time	The Time		
	I Don't Wanna Stop			Ren Woods	Azz Izz		Track pulled
	TOUR: DIRTY MIND TOUR, USA, Dec. '81 to March '82						
1982	How Come You Don't Call Me Anymore?			Prince		B-side	
	1999			Prince	1999		
	Little Red Corvette			Prince	1999		
	Delirious			Prince	1999		
	Let's Pretend We're Married			Prince	1999		
	D.M.S.R.			Prince	1999		
	Automatic			Prince	1999		
	Something In The Water (Does Not Compute)			Prince	1999		

Year	Title	Credit	Collaborator	Artist	Album	B-side
	Free	Jamie Starr		Prince	1999	
	Lady Cab Driver	Jamie Starr		Prince	1999	
	All The Critics Love U In New York			Prince	1999	
	International Lover			Prince	1999	
	Bite The Beat	Jamie Starr	Jesse Johnson	Vanity 6	Vanity 6	
	Drive Me Wild	Jamie Starr		Vanity 6	Vanity 6	
	Gigolos Get Lonely Too	Jamie Starr		The Time	What Time Is It?	B-side
	Grace	Jamie Starr		The Time	What Time Is It?	
	I Don't Wanna Leave You	Jamie Starr		The Time	What Time Is It?	
	If A Girl Answers (Don't Hang Up)	Jamie Starr	Terry Lewis	Vanity 6	Vanity 6	
	Make Up	Jamie Starr		Vanity 6	Vanity 6	
	Nasty Girl	Jamie Starr		Vanity 6	Vanity 6	
	Oneday I'mgonnabesomebody	Jamie Starr		The Time	What Time Is It?	
	777-9311	Jamie Starr		The Time	What Time Is It?	
	3 x 2 = 6	Jamie Starr		Vanity 6	Vanity 6	
	The Walk	Jamie Starr		The Time	What Time Is It?	
	Wet Dream	Jamie Starr		Vanity 6	Vanity 6	
	Wild And Loose	Jamie Starr	Dez Dickerson	The Time	What Time Is It?	
	TOUR: 1999 TOUR, USA, Dec. '81 to April '83					
1983	Horny Toad			Prince		B-side
	Irresistible Bitch			Prince		B-side
	Stand Back		Stevie Nicks	Stevie Nicks	The Wild Heart	
1984	17 Days			Prince		B-side
	Erotic City			Prince		B-side
	God			Prince		B-side
	Another Lonely Christmas			Prince		B-side
	Let's Go Crazy			Prince	Purple Rain	
	Take Me With U			Prince	Purple Rain	

Year	Songs by & credited to Prince	Credited to pseudonym	Co-writer	Written for/ recorded by	Album – title	Single	Notes
1984	The Beautiful Ones			Prince	Purple Rain		
	Computer Blue		LC,WM,MF,JLN*	Prince	Purple Rain		
	Darling Nikki			Prince	Purple Rain		
	When Doves Cry			Prince	Purple Rain		
	I Would Die 4 U			Prince	Purple Rain		
	Baby I'm A Star			Prince	Purple Rain		
	Purple Rain			Prince	Purple Rain		
	A Million Miles (I Love You)	Jamie Starr	Lisa Coleman	Apollonia 6	Apollonia 6		
	The Belle Of St. Mark	Jamie Starr		Sheila E.	The Glamorous Life		
	The Bird	Jamie Starr	MD,JJ*	The Time	Ice Cream Castle		
	Blue Limousine	Jamie Starr		Apollonia 6	Apollonia 6		
	Chili Sauce	Jamie Starr	MD,PP*	The Time	Ice Cream Castle		
	The Glamorous Life	Jamie Starr		Sheila E.	The Glamorous Life		
	Happy Birthday, Mr. Christian	Jamie Starr		Apollonia 6	Apollonia 6		
	Ice Cream Castles	Jamie Starr	MD,JJ*	The Time	Ice Cream Castle		
	If The Kid Can't Make You Come	Jamie Starr	MD,JJ*	The Time	Ice Cream Castle		
	In A Spanish Villa	Jamie Starr		Apollonia 6	Apollonia 6		
	Jungle Love	Jamie Starr	Morris Day	The Time	Ice Cream Castle		
	My Drawers	Jamie Starr	MD,JJ*	The Time	Ice Cream Castle		
	Next Time Wipe The Lipstick Off						
	Your Collar	Jamie Starr		Sheila E.	The Glamorous Life		
	Noon Rendezvous	Jamie Starr	Sheila E.	Sheila E.	The Glamorous Life		
	Oliver's House	Jamie Starr		Sheila E.	The Glamorous Life		
	Ooo She She Wa Wa	Jamie Starr		Apollonia 6	Apollonia 6		
	Sex Shooter	Jamie Starr		Apollonia 6	Apollonia 6		
	Strawberry Shortcake	Jamie Starr		Sheila E.	The Glamorous Life		
	Some Kind Of Lover	Jamie Starr	Brenda Bennett	Apollonia 6	Apollonia 6		
	Tricky	Jamie Starr		The Time	Ice Cream Castle	B-side	

Song	Alias	Musicians	Performer	Album	Notes
Sugar Walls	Alexander Nevermind		Sheena Easton	A Private Heaven	

1985

TOUR: PURPLE RAIN TOUR, USA, Nov. '84 to March '85

Song	Alias	Musicians	Performer	Album	Notes
4 The Tears In Your Eyes**			Prince		USA for Africa Album Contribution
She's Always In My Hair			Prince		B-side
Hello			Prince		B-side
Girl			Prince		B-side
Around The World In A Day		DC,JLN*	Prince	Around the World in a Day	('ATWIAD')
Paisley Park			Prince	ATWIAD	
Condition Of The Heart			Prince	ATWIAD	
Raspberry Beret			Prince	ATWIAD	
Tamborine			Prince	ATWIAD	
America		LC,WM,MF,BM,BZ*	Prince	ATWIAD	
Pop Life			Prince	ATWIAD	
The Ladder		JLN*	Prince	ATWIAD	
Temptation			Prince	ATWIAD	
Aquadella		EL,LS,SE*	Eric Leeds	Times Squared	
A Love Bizarre		Sheila E.	Sheila E.	Romance 1600	
The Dance Electric			Andre Cymone	AC	
Nothing Compares 2 U**			The Family	The Family	
Desire	Jamie Starr		The Family	The Family	
High Fashion	Jamie Starr		The Family	The Family	
Mutiny	Jamie Starr		The Family	The Family	
The Screams Of Passion	Jamie Starr		The Family	The Family	
Susannah's Pajamas	Jamie Starr	Eric Leeds	The Family	The Family	
Yes	Jamie Starr	Eric Leeds	The Family	The Family	

FILM: Purple Rain

Year	Songs by & credited to Prince	Credited to pseudonym	Co-writer	Written for/ recorded by	Album – title	Single	Notes
1986	Love Or $			Prince		B-side	
	Alexa De Paris			Prince		B-side	
	Christopher Tracy's Parade		JLN*	Prince	Parade		
	New Position			Prince	Parade		
	I Wonder U			Prince	Parade		
	Under The Cherry Moon		JLN*	Prince	Parade		
	Girls And Boys			Prince	Parade		
	Life Can Be So Nice			Prince	Parade		
	Venus De Milo			Prince	Parade		
	Mountains		LC, WM*	Prince	Parade		
	Do U Lie?			Prince	Parade		
	Kiss			Prince	Parade		
	Anotherloverholenyohead			Prince	Parade		
	Sometimes It Snows In April		LC, WM*	Prince	Parade		
	100 MPH			Mazarati	Mazarati		
	Manic Monday	Christopher Tracy		Bangles	Different Light		
	TOUR: PARADE TOUR, EUROPE & JAPAN, Aug. to Sept.						
1987	La La La, He He Hee			Prince		B-side	
	Sign O' The Times			Prince	Sign o' the Times		(SOTT)
	Play In The Sunshine			Prince	SOTT		
	Housequake			Prince	SOTT		
	The Ballad Of Dorothy Parker			Prince	SOTT		
	It			Prince	SOTT		
	Starfish And Coffee		Susannah Melvoin	Prince	SOTT		
	Slow Love		Carole Davis	Prince	SOTT		
	Hot Thing			Prince	SOTT		
	Forever In My Life			Prince	SOTT		

U Got The Look			Prince/Sheena Easton	SOTT	
If I Was Your Girlfriend			Prince	SOTT	
Strange Relationship			Prince	SOTT	
I Could Never Take The Place Of Your Man			Prince	SOTT	
The Cross			Prince	SOTT	
It's Gonna Be A Beautiful Night		EL,MF*	Prince	SOTT	
Adore			Prince	SOTT	
All Day, All Night			Jill Jones	Jill Jones	
Boy's Club		Sheila E.	Sheila E.	Sheila E.	
Eternity			Sheena Easton	No Sound But A Heart	
For Love			Jill Jones	Jill Jones	
G-Spot			Jill Jones	Jill Jones	
If I Could Get Your Attention			Taja Sevelle	Taja Sevelle	
Koo Koo		Sheila E.	Sheila E.	Sheila E.	
Love On A Blue Train		Sheila E.	Sheila E.	Sheila E.	
Mia Bocca			Jill Jones	Jill Jones	
One Day (I'm Gonna Make You Mine)	Sheila E.		Sheila E.	Sheila E.	
Pride And The Passion		Sheila E.	Sheila E.	Sheila E.	
Ten And 1/2		EL,LS,SE*	Madhouse		B-side
Thirteen And 1/4		EL,LS,SE*	Madhouse		B-side
With You			Jill Jones	Jill Jones	
Wouldn't You Love To Love Me?			Taja Sevelle	Taja Sevelle	
One	Madhouse		Madhouse	8	
Two	Madhouse		Madhouse	8	
Three	Madhouse		Madhouse	8	
Four	Madhouse		Madhouse	8	
Five	Madhouse		Madhouse	8	
Six	Madhouse		Madhouse	8	
Seven	Madhouse		Madhouse	8	

Year	Songs by & credited to Prince	Credited to pseudonym	Co-writer	Written for/ recorded by	Album – title	Single	Notes
1987	Eight	Madhouse		Madhouse	8		
	Nine	Madhouse		Madhouse	16		
	Ten	Madhouse	EL, LS, SE*	Madhouse	16		
	Eleven	Madhouse	EL, LS, SE*	Madhouse	16		
	Twelve	Madhouse		Madhouse	16		
	Thirteen	Madhouse		Madhouse	16		
	Fourteen	Madhouse		Madhouse	16		
	Fifteen	Madhouse	EL, LS, SE*	Madhouse	16		
	Sixteen	Madhouse	Eric Leeds	Madhouse	16		
	Baby Go-Go	Joey Coco		Nona Hendryx	Female Trouble		
	Baby, You're A Trip	Joey Coco		Jill Jones	Jill Jones		
	My Man	Joey Coco		Jill Jones	Jill Jones		
	Telepathy	Joey Coco		Deborah Allen	Telepathy		
	Violet Blue	Joey Coco		Jill Jones	Jill Jones		
	You're My Love	Joey Coco		Kenny Rogers	They Don't Make Them Like They Used To		

TOUR: SIGN O' THE TIMES TOUR, EUROPE & USA, CUT SHORT – Played beg. May to end June

FILM: Sign O' The Times

Year	Songs by & credited to Prince	Credited to pseudonym	Co-writer	Written for/ recorded by	Album – title	Single	Notes
1988	Good Love			Prince	Bright Lights, Big City		Soundtrack
	Escape			Prince		B-side	
	Scarlet Pussy			Prince		B-side	
	Eye No			Prince	Lovesexy		
	Alphabet St			Prince	Lovesexy		
	Glam Slam			Prince	Lovesexy		
	Anna Stesia			Prince	Lovesexy		
	Dance On			Prince	Lovesexy		
	Lovesexy			Prince	Lovesexy		

When 2 R In Love		Prince	Lovesexy	
I Wish U Heaven		Prince	Lovesexy	
So Strong		Dale	Riot In English	
Sticky Wicked		Chaka Khan	CK	
Cool Love	Joey Coco	Sheena Easton	The Lover In Me	
Neon Telephone	Joey Coco	Three O' Clock	Vermillion	
101	Joey Coco	Sheena Easton	The Lover In Me	

TOUR: LOVESEXY TOUR, WORLD, July '88 to Feb. '89

1989

200 Balloons		Prince		B-side
Feel U Up		Prince		B-side
I Luv U In Me		Prince		B-side
Scandalous Sex Suite		Prince		Maxi-single
The Future		Prince	Batman Motion Picture	Soundtrack
Electric Chair	Sheena Easton	Prince	Batman	
The Arms Of Orion		Prince/Sheena Easton	Batman	
Partyman		Prince	Batman	
Vicki Waiting		Prince	Batman	
Trust		Prince	Batman	
Lemon Crush		Prince	Batman	
Scandalous	JLN*	Prince	Batman	
Batdance		Prince	Batman	
Bliss	Levi Seacer	Kahoru Kohiruimaki	Time The Motion	
Come Home		Mavis Staples	Time Waits For No One	
I Guess I'm Crazy		Mavis Staples	Time Waits For No One	
Interesting		Mavis Staples	Time Waits For No One	
Jaguar	Sheena Easton	Mavis Staples	Time Waits For No One	
Love '89		Patti LaBelle	Be Yourself	
Love Song	Madonna	Madonna	Like A Prayer	
Mind Bells	Levi Seacer	Kahoru Kohiruimaki	Time The Motion	
Shall We Dance		Brown Mark	Good Feeling	

Year	Songs by & credited to Prince	Credited to pseudonym	Co-writer	Written for/ recorded by	Album – title	Single	Notes
1989	Time Waits For No One		Mavis Staples	Mavis Staples	Time Waits For No One		
	Train			Mavis Staples	Time Waits For No One		
	Yo Mistr r			Patti LaBelle	Be Yourself		
1990	The Lubricated Lady			Prince/NPG		Maxi-single	
	Loveleft, Loveright			Prince		Maxi-single	
	Can't Stop This Feeling I Got			Prince	Graffiti Bridge		
	New Power Generation			Prince	Graffiti Bridge		
	The Question Of U			Prince	Graffiti Bridge		
	Elephants And Flowers			Prince	Graffiti Bridge		
	Joy In Repetition			Prince	Graffiti Bridge		
	Tick, Tick, Bang			Prince	Graffiti Bridge		
	Thieves In The Temple			Prince	Graffiti Bridge		
	The Latest Fashion			Prince	Graffiti Bridge		
	Still Would Stand All Time			Prince	Graffiti Bridge		
	Graffiti Bridge			Prince	Graffiti Bridge		
	New Power Generation, Pt. II			Prince	Graffiti Bridge		
	Brother With A Purpose		Tony Moseley	Tony Moseley			Prince Maxi-single Track
	I Am		DZ,LS,EF*	Elisa Fiorillo	I Am		
	The Latest Fashion			Prince/The Time	[Prince] Graffiti Bridge		
	Love Machine		MD,LS*	The Time/Elisa Fiorillo	[Prince] Graffiti Bridge		
	Love's No Fun			Elisa Fiorillo	I Am		
	Melody Cool			Mavis Staples	[Prince] Graffiti Bridge		
	On The Way Up		DZ,LS,EF*	Elisa Fiorillo	I Am		
	Ooh This I Need			Elisa Fiorillo	I Am		
	Playgirl			Elisa Fiorillo	I Am		
	Release It		MD,LS*	The Time	[Prince] Graffiti Bridge		

Round And Round			Tevin Campbell	[Prince] Graffiti Bridge	
The Sex Of It			Kid Creole & Coconuts	Private Waters In The Great Divide	
					Prince Maxi-single Track
Shake!	T.C. Ellis	Morris Day	The Time	[Prince] Graffiti Bridge	
T.C.'s Rap	T.C. Ellis	T.C. Ellis			
We Can Funk		George Clinton	George Clinton	[Prince] Graffiti Bridge	
Chocolate	Jamie Starr		The Time	Pandemonium	
Data Bank	Jamie Starr		The Time	Pandemonium	
Donald Trump (Black Version)	Jamie Starr		The Time	Pandemonium	
Jerk Out	Jamie Starr	MD,JJ,TL*	The Time	Pandemonium	
My Summertime Thang	Jamie Starr		The Time	Pandemonium	

TOUR: NUDE TOUR, EUROPE & JAPAN, June to Sept.
FILM: Graffiti Bridge

1991

Horny Pony			Prince		B-side
Things Have Gotta Change			Prince/NPG		Maxi-single
2 The Wire			Prince/NPG		Maxi-single
Gangster Glam			Prince/NPG		Maxi-single
Clockin' The Jizz			Prince/NPG		Maxi-single
Q In Doubt			Prince/NPG		Maxi-single
Do Your Dance			Prince/NPG		Maxi-single
Thunder			Prince	Diamonds & Pearls	
Daddy Pop			Prince	Diamonds & Pearls	
Diamonds & Pearls			Prince	Diamonds & Pearls	
Cream			Prince	Diamonds & Pearls	
Strollin'			Prince	Diamonds & Pearls	
Willing And Able		LS,TM*	Prince	Diamonds & Pearls	
Gett Off			Prince	Diamonds & Pearls	
Walk Don't Walk			Prince	Diamonds & Pearls	
Jughead		TM,KJ*	NPG	[Prince] Diamonds & Pearls	
Money Don't Matter 2Night			Prince	Diamonds & Pearls	

Year	Songs by & credited to Prince	Credited to pseudonym	Co-writer	Written for/ recorded by	Album – title	Single	Notes
1991							
	Push			Prince	Diamonds & Pearls		
	Insatiable			Prince	Diamonds & Pearls		
	Live 4 Love		TM,KJ*	Prince	Diamonds & Pearls		
	Andorra		EL,LS,SE*	Eric Leeds	Times Squared		
	Bambi (Rap)			T.C. Ellis	True Confessions		
	Cape Horn			Eric Leeds	Times Squared		
	Don't Say U Love Me		Martika	Martika	Martika's Kitchen		
	The Dopamine Rush			Eric Leeds	Times Squared		
	Easy Does It		Eric Leeds	Eric Leeds	Times Squared		
	Five Women			Joe Cocker	Night Calls		
	Girl O' My Dreams			T.C. Ellis	True Confessions		
	If I Love U 2Nite			Mica Paris	Contribution		
	Little Rock		Eric Leeds	Eric Leeds	Times Squared		
	Love...Thy Will Be Done		Martika	Martika	Martika's Kitchen		
	Martika's Kitchen			Martika	Martika's Kitchen		
	Miss Thang			T.C. Ellis	True Confessions		
	Night Owl		EL,LS,SE*	Eric Leeds	Times Squared		
	Once Upon A Time		Eric Leeds	Eric Leeds	Times Squared		
	Overnight, Every Night		EL,LS,SE*	Eric Leeds	Times Squared		
	Spirit		LS,M,FB*	Martika	Martika's Kitchen		
	Times Squared		Eric Leeds	Eric Leeds	Times Squared		
	Elephant Box	Paisley Park	Ingrid Chavez	Ingrid Chavez	May 19 1992		
	Heaven Must Be Near	Paisley Park	LS,IC*	Ingrid Chavez	May 19 1992		
	I Hear Your Voice	Paisley Park	RG,FJ*	Patti LaBelle	Burnin'		
	Jadestone	Paisley Park	Ingrid Chavez	Ingrid Chavez	May 19 1992		
	Slappy Dappy	Paisley Park	Ingrid Chavez	Ingrid Chavez	May 19 1992		
	U	Paisley Park		Paula Abdul	Spellbound		
	Whispering Dandelions	Paisley Park	Ingrid Chavez	Ingrid Chavez	May 19 1992		

1992					
Call The Law		Prince			B-side
Thunder		Prince			Single
Violet The Organ Grinder		Prince			B-side
2 Whom It May Concern		Prince			B-side
My Name Is Prince	Tony M.	♓	♓		
Sexy MF	LS,TM*	♓	♓		
Love 2 The 9's		♓	♓		
The Morning Papers		♓	♓		
The Max		♓	♓		
Blue Light		♓	♓		
Eye Wanna Melt With U		♓	♓		
Sweet Baby		♓	♓		
The Continental		♓	♓		
Damn U		♓	♓		
Arrogance		♓	♓		
The Flow	Tony M.	♓	♓		
7	LF,JM*	♓	♓		
And God Created Woman		♓	♓		
3 Chains O' Gold		♓	♓		
The Sacrifice Of Victor		♓	♓		
Qualified	Kirk Johnson	Lois Lane		Precious	
With This Tear		Celine Dion		Celine Dion	
Tip O' My Tongue	Kirk Johnson	El DeBarge		In The Storm	
Born 2 B.R.E.E.D.	LS,ML*	Monie Love		In A Word Or 2	
In A Word Or 2	LS,ML*	Monie Love		In A Word Or 2	
Sunday Afternoon		Candy Dulfer		Sax-A-Go-Go	
Paris 1798430		Tevin Campbell		I'm Ready	
Shhh**		Tevin Campbell		I'm Ready	
The Halls Of Desire		Tevin Campbell		I'm Ready	
Uncle Sam		Tevin Campbell		I'm Ready	

Year	Songs by & credited to Prince	Credited to pseudonym	Co-writer	Written for/ recorded by	Album – title	Single	Notes
1992	Superhero**			Earth, Wind & Fire	Millennium		
	Hold Me			Jevetta Steele	Here It Is		
	The Voice		RG,FJ*	Mavis Staples	The Voice		
	House In Order			Mavis Staples	The Voice		
	Blood Is Thicker Than Time			Mavis Staples	The Voice		
	You Will Be Moved			Mavis Staples	The Voice		
	The Undertaker			Mavis Staples	The Voice		
	A Man Called Jesus			Mavis Staples	The Voice		
	Positivity			Mavis Staples	The Voice		
	Well Done			The Steeles	Heaven Help Us All		
	TOUR: DIAMONDS & PEARLS TOUR, AUSTRALIA, EUROPE, JAPAN, April to July						
1993	3-CD Compilation featuring the following new tracks recorded by Prince:						
	Nothing Compares 2 U			Prince	Greatest Hits		Live with Rosie Gaines
	Pink Cashmere			Prince	Greatest Hits		
	Peach			Prince	Greatest Hits		
	Pope			Prince	Greatest Hits		
	Power Fantastic			Prince	Greatest Hits		
	All That		Carmen	Carmen Electra	Carmen Electra		
	Fantasia		Carmen	Carmen Electra	Carmen Electra		
	Fun		Carmen	Carmen Electra	Carmen Electra		
	Go-Go-Dancer			Carmen Electra	Carmen Electra		
	Just A Little Lovin'		NPG, Tony M	Carmen Electra	Carmen Electra		
	Step To The Mic		NPG, Tony M, Carmen	Carmen Electra	Carmen Electra		
	Sunday Afternoon			Candy Dulfer	Sax-A-Go-Go		
	Allegiance			Howard Hewett	Allegiance		
	Aquadilla	Paisley Park		Eric Leeds	Things Left Unsaid		
	The Big Pump			George Clinton	Hey Man . . . Smell My Finger		

Get Blue	Louie Louie	Let's Get Started – Dance To The Rhythm
Why Should I Love You	Kate Bush	The Red Shoes
My Name Is Bart	Bart Simpson	Parody on MNIP for Simpsons cartoon

ULYSSES – An interactive musical theatrical production featured 13 of Prince's songs (some of which were later released by Prince/⚥) which premiered at Glam Slam West on 21 August 1993. Most of the songs were later released on Prince/⚥ albums. The songs featured were:
Strays Of The World, Dolphin, Interactive, Pheromone, Dark, Loose, Space, What's My Name, Endorphinmachine, Race, Come, Pope.

THE JOFFREY BALLET's "Billboards" performed to the following Prince songs, specially adapted by Prince for the Ballet:

Billboard 1: Sometimes It Snows In April – Sometimes It Snows In April; Trust; Baby I'm A Star.
Billboard 2: Thunder/Purple Rain – Thunder; Purple Rain.
Billboard 3: Slide – Computer Blue; The Beautiful Ones; Release It.
Billboard 4: Willing And Able – For You; It; Willing And Able.
TOUR: ⚥ TOUR ('ACT II'), AUSTRALIA, EUROPE, JAPAN

1994

Come	Come
Space	Come
Pheromone	Come
Loose	Come
Papa	Come
Race	Come
Dark	Come
Solo	Come
Letitgo	Come
Race	Come
LeGrind	The Black Album
Cindy C	The Black Album
Dead On It	The Black Album
When 2 R In Love	The Black Album
Bob George	The Black Album
Supercalifragisexy	The Black Album

Year	Songs by & credited to Prince	Credited to pseudonym	Co-writer	Written for/ recorded by	Album – title	Single	Notes
1994	2 Nigs United 4 West Compton				The Black Album		
	Rock Hard In A Funky Place				The Black Album		
	Pussy Control			[symbol]	The Gold Experience		
	Endorphinmachine			[symbol]	The Gold Experience		
	Shhh			[symbol]	The Gold Experience		
	We March			[symbol]	The Gold Experience		
	The Most Beautiful Girl In The World			[symbol]	The Gold Experience		
	Dolphin			[symbol]	The Gold Experience		
	Now			[symbol]	The Gold Experience		
	319			[symbol]	The Gold Experience		
	Shy			[symbol]	The Gold Experience		
	Billy Jack Bitch			[symbol]	The Gold Experience		
	Eye Hate U			[symbol]	The Gold Experience		
	Gold			[symbol]	The Gold Experience		
	Hollywood			George Clinton	[Various Artists] 1-800-NEW-FUNK		
	Love Sign			Nona Gaye	[Various Artists] 1-800-NEW-FUNK		
	Color			The Steeles	[Various Artists] 1-800-NEW-FUNK		
	Standing At The Altar			Margie Cox	[Various Artists] 1-800-NEW-FUNK		
	A Woman's Gotta Have It			Nona Gaye	[Various Artists] 1-800-NEW-FUNK		
	Minneapolis Reprise			Mpls	[Various Artists] 1-800-NEW-FUNK		
	Get Wild**	NPG		NPG	(Various Artists) Pret-A-Porter		Soundtrack
	Superhero			NPG/The Steeles		Single	
1995	Rock & Roll Is Alive (& It Lives In Minneapolis)			[symbol]		Single	
	Purple Medley			[symbol]		Single	
	Get Wild	NPG		NPG	Exodus		
	DJ Gets Jumped	NPG		NPG	Exodus		

New Power Soul	NPG		NPG	Exodus
DJ Seduces Sonny	NPG		NPG	Exodus
Count The Days	NPG		NPG	Exodus
The Good Life	NPG		NPG	Exodus
Cherry Cherry	NPG		NPG	Exodus
Return Of The Bump Squad	NPG		NPG	Exodus
Mashed Potato Girl Intro	NPG		NPG	Exodus
Big Fun	NPG		NPG	Exodus
New Power Day	NPG		NPG	Exodus
Hallucination Rain	NPG		NPG	Exodus
NPG Bum Rush The Ship	NPG		NPG	Exodus
The Exodus Has Begun	NPG		NPG	Exodus
I Want You			Rosie Gaines	Closer than Close
My Tender Heart			Rosie Gaines	My Tender Heart
Children Of The Sun	♀	Mayte	Mayte	Children of the Sun
In Your Gracious Name	♀		Mayte	Children of the Sun
If I Love U 2Night	♀		Mayte	Children of the Sun
The Rhythm Of Your Heart	♀		Mayte	Children of the Sun
Ain't No Place Like U	♀		Mayte	Children of the Sun
Love's No Fun	♀		Mayte	Children of the Sun
Baby Don't Care	♀		Mayte	Children of the Sun
However Much U Want	♀		♀ / Mayte	Children of the Sun
Mo, Better	♀	AH, EMH*	Mayte	Children of the Sun
Most Beautiful Boy In The World	Paisley Park			

TOUR: THE GOLD EXPERIENCE TOUR, EUROPE, JAPAN

1996

Chaos And Disorder	♀		♀	Chaos and Disorder
I Like It Here	♀		♀	Chaos and Disorder
Dinner With Delores	♀		♀	Chaos and Disorder
The Same December	♀		♀	Chaos and Disorder
Right The Wrong	♀		♀	Chaos and Disorder

Year	Songs by & credited to Prince	Credited to pseudonym	Co-writer	Written for / recorded by	Album – title	Single	Notes
1996	Zannalee	♀		♀	Chaos and Disorder		
	I Rock Therefore I Am	♀		♀	Chaos and Disorder		
	Into The Light	♀		♀	Chaos and Disorder		
	I Will	♀		♀	Chaos and Disorder		
	Dig U Better Dead	♀		♀	Chaos and Disorder		
	Had U	♀		♀	Chaos and Disorder		
	Jam Of The Year	♀		♀	Emancipation		
	Right Back Here In My Arms	♀		♀	Emancipation		
	Somebody's Somebody	♀	BLE,HW*	♀	Emancipation		
	Get Yo Groove On	♀		♀	Emancipation		
	Courtin' Time	♀		♀	Emancipation		
	We Gets Up	♀		♀	Emancipation		
	White Mansion	♀		♀	Emancipation		
	Damned If Eye Do	♀		♀	Emancipation		
	Mr. Happy	♀		♀	Emancipation		
	In This Bed Eye Scream	♀		♀	Emancipation		
	Sex In The Summer	♀		♀	Emancipation		
	One Kiss At A Time	♀		♀	Emancipation		
	Soul Sanctuary	♀	Sandra St Victor	♀	Emancipation		
	Emale	♀		♀	Emancipation		
	Curious Child	♀		♀	Emancipation		
	Dreamin' About U	♀		♀	Emancipation		
	Joint 2 Joint	♀		♀	Emancipation		
	The Holy River	♀		♀	Emancipation		
	Let's Have A Baby	♀		♀	Emancipation		
	Saviour	♀		♀	Emancipation		
	The Plan	♀		♀	Emancipation		
	Friend, Lover, Sister, Mother, Wife	♀		♀	Emancipation		

Song		Artist	Album
Slave	O(+>		Emancipation
New World	O(+>		Emancipation
The Human Body	O(+>		Emancipation
Face Down	O(+>		Emancipation
Style	O(+>		Emancipation
Sleep Around	O(+>		Emancipation
Da, Da, Da	O(+>		Emancipation
My Computer	O(+>		Emancipation
The Love We Make	O(+>		Emancipation
Emancipation	O(+>		Emancipation
She Spoke 2 Me		Prince/NPG	Girl 6
Don't Talk To Strangers		Prince	Girl 6
Girl 6	NPG	NPG	Girl 6
Pain	O(+>	Chaka Khan	Living Single

1997

Soundtrack

*

LC,WM,MF,JLN	Lisa Coleman, Wendy Melvoin, Matt Fink, John L. Nelson
MD,JJ	Morris Day, Jesse Johnson
DC,JLN	David Coleman, John L. Nelson
LC,WM,MF,BM,BZ	Lisa Coleman, Wendy Melvoin, Matt Fink, Brown Mark, Bobby Z
JLN	John L. Nelson
EL,LS,SE	Eric Leeds, Levi Seacer, Sheila E
LC,WM	Lisa Coleman, Wendy Melvoin
EL,MF	Eric Leeds, Matt Fink
DZ,LS,EF	David Z, Levi Seacer, Elisa Fiorillo
MD,LS	Morris Day, Levi Seacer
MD,JJ,TL	Morris Day, Jesse Johnson, Terry Lewis
LS,TM	Levi Seacer, Tony Moseley [aka Tony M.]
TM,KJ	Tony Moseley, Kirk Johnson
LS,M,FB	Levi Seacer, Martika, Frankie Blue
LS,JC	Levi Seacer, Ingrid Chavez
RG,FJ	Rosie Gaines, Francis Jules

LF,JM   Lowell Fulsom, Jimmy McCrackin
LS,ML   Levi Seacer, Monie Love
AH,EMH   Andrew Hopkins, E.M.Hunter
BLE,HW   Brenda Lee Eager, Hilliard Wilson

**

Songs written by Prince/pseudonym, recorded by other artists and later recorded by Prince/pseudonym and/or associates.

SONGS NOT WRITTEN BY BUT RECORDED BY ♀ FOR HIMSELF OR OTHERS

Year	Title	Writer	Recorded By	Album Title
1995	House Of Brick 'Brick House'	The Commodores	Mayte	Children Of The Sun
1996	Betcha By Golly, Wow!	TRB,LC*	♀	Emancipation
	Eye Can't Make U Love Me	JAS,MBR*	♀	Emancipation
	La, La, La Means Eye Love U	TRB,WH*	♀	Emancipation
	One Of Us	Eric M.Brazilian	♀	Emancipation

*

TRB/LC   Thomas Randolph Bell, Linda Creed
JAS,MBR   James Allen Shamblin II, Michael Barry Reid
TRB,WH   Thomas Randolph Bell, William Hart

The above discography is not a complete listing of every single record written and/or by recorded by Prince/The Artist. Singles taken from albums and remixes are generally omitted. It is hoped that the above gives an indication of the vast number of songs The Artist (under his original name of Prince or one of his pseudonyms) has written on his own or, where indicated with others, available on general release; along with other major undertakings in any given year. In addition to the above listing, Prince aka TAFKAP, ♀, NPG, or Paisley Park was involved in the production of albums by other artists as well as producing many promotional videos to accompany his own single releases and independent "Undertaker" video, which was available through regular commercial outlets. More recently, The Artist has made CDs available exclusively through his own retail outlet. By The Artist's own reckoning, he has approximately 1,000 songs written but not yet released.

SONGS WRITTEN AND RECORDED BY ♀ --AVAILABLE ONLY BE MAIL ORDER FROM [SYM]'S OWN 1-800-NEW-FUNK OUTLET

Prior to ♀'s parting of the ways woth Warner Bros., ♀ established his own retail outlet. While cortractually barred from recording elsewhere by Warner Bros., under the terms of his recording contract, releases available form this outlet were by people other than ♀. Despite this, it was widely believed that ♀ had considerable involvement in those releases. Since ♀'s departure from Warner Bros. in 1995, a considerable number of ♀'s releases have been available from this outlet.

Year	Songs by & credited to ♀	Credited to others ♀ believed involved	Recorded by	Album – title single	Notes
1994		Gold Nigga (Pt. 1)	NPG	Gold Nigga	
		Guess Who's Knockin'	NPG	Gold Nigga	
		Oilcan	NPG	Gold Nigga	
		Deuce & a Quarter	NPG	Gold Nigga	
		Black MF in the House	NPG	Gold Nigga	
		Gold Nigga (Pt. 2)	NPG	Gold Nigga	
		Goldie's Paradise	NPG	Gold Nigga	
		2gether	NPG	Gold Nigga	
		Call the Law	NPG	Gold Nigga	
		Johnny	NPG	Gold Nigga	
		Call the Law (Pt. 3)	NPG	Gold Nigga	
1995		The Plan	NPG Orchestra	Kamasutra	
		Kamasutra	NPG Orchestra	Kamasutra	
		At Last (The Lost Is Found)	NPG Orchestra	Kamasutra	
		The Ever Changing Light	NPG Orchestra	Kamasutra	
		Cutz	NPG Orchestra	Kamasutra	
		Serotonin	NPG ORchestra	Kamasutra	
		Promise/Broken	NPG Orchestra	Kamasutra	
		Barcelona	NPG Orchestra	Kamasutra	
		Kamasutra/Overture /8	NPG Orchestra	Kamasutra	

Year	Songs by & credited to ♀	Credited to others / ♀ believed involved	Recorded by	Album – title single	Notes
1997		Coincidence or Fate	NPG Orchestra		
		Kamasutra/Eternal Embrace	NPG Orchestra		
	Face Down	♀		Jam of the Year (Live)	Audio tape only
	The Truth	♀	Kamasutra	The Truth	CD single
	Don't Play Me	♀	Kamasutra	The Truth	CD Single
1998	The Truth	♀	The Truth		Billed as Acoustic
	Don't Play Me	♀	The Truth		
	Circle of Amour	♀	The Truth		
	3rd Eye	♀	The Truth		
	Dionne	♀	The Truth		
	Man in a Uniform	♀	The Truth		
	Animal Kingdom	♀	The Truth		
	The Other Side of the Pillow	♀	The Truth		
	Fascination	♀	The Truth		
	One of Your Tears	♀	The Truth		
	Comback	♀	The Truth		
	Welcome 2 the Dawn (Acoustic ver.)	♀	The Truth		

A triple-CD set entitled Crystal Ball is also known to be in the pipeline and for which orders have been taken since 1996. However, the set has not yet been released and official sources have so far only listed 13 of the said 30 tracks which will appear on this set. Below is a list of possible/prbable inclusions. Official ones are marked with an asterisk.

Disk 1
Crystal Ball
Dream Factory
Acknowledge Me
Ripgodazippa
Love Sign (Shock G Silky Smooth Remix) *
Hide the Bone*
2Morrow*
So Dark
Movie Star*
Tell Me How U Wanna Be Done

Disk 2
Interactive
Da Bang*
Calhoun Square*
What's My Name*
An Honest Man
Sexual Suicide*
Crucial*
Cloreen Baconskin (With Morris Day – a Time outtake from 1983)*
Good Love (From Bright Lights, Big City soundtrack)
Strays of the World

Disk 3
Days of Wild (Live)*
Last Heart
Poom Poom*
She Gave Her Angels
18 and Over*
The Ride (Live)
Get Loose
P. Control (Remix version)
Make Yo Mama Happy
Goodbye

SONGS WRITTEN AND RECORDED BY PRINCE AND COVERED BY OTHER ARTISTS

Artist	Song
Acid Factor	When Doves Cry
Age of Chance	Kiss
The All Stars	The Prince Mix
The Art of Noise With Tom Jones	Kiss
Sandra Bernhard	Little Red Corvette
Blood Uncles	Let's Go Crazy
Bette Bright & the Illuminations	When You Were Mine
Mariah Carey & Dru Hill	The Beautiful Ones
Randy Crawford	Purple Rain
D'Angelo	She's Always in My Hair
Diesel Kings	Purple Rain
	The Belle of St. Mark
	Shortberry Shortcake
	Noon Rendezvous
Dorothy	Still Waiting
Dune	Nothing Compares 2 U
T. C. Ellis	Bambi (rap)
EPO	When 2 R in Love
Penny Flanagan	When You Were Mine
Freedom	
Do It All Night	
Brian Gallagher	The Most Beautiful Girl in the World
Gear Daddies	Little Red Corvette
Ginuwine	When Doves Cry
Goo Goo Dolls	I Could Never Take the Place of Your Man
The Gutterbrothers	Kiss
Herbie Hancock	Thieves in the Temple
Hindu Love Gods	Raspberry Beret
The Hollies	Purple Rain (live)

Debra Hud	Gotta Broken Heart Again
Kazda	Sign o' the times
T. J. Kirk	Rock Hard in a Funky Place
LaMazz	Nasty Girl
La Toya Jackson	Private Joy
	1999
Millie Jackson	I Wanna Be Your Lover
Rebbie Jackson	I Feel for You
Chaka Khan	I Feel for You
Cyndi Lauper	When You Were Mine
Living Colour	17 Days
Kell McCulloch	The Arms of Orion
	Girls and Boys
	I Feel for You
	I Wish U Heaven
	Kiss
	Little Red Corvette
	Nothing Compares 2 U
	Paisley Park
	Purple Rain
	Raspberry Beret
	Sign o' the Times
	Take Me With U
	Thieves in the Temple
	Trust
	When Doves Cry
	Pop Life
Stephanie Mills	How Come You Don't Call Me Anymore
Meli'sa Morgan	Do Me Baby
MXM	Nothing Compares 2 U
Native	Sometimes It Snows in April

Artist	Song
Nuttin' Nyce	Nasty Girl
Sinead O'Connor	Nothing Compares 2 U
Ricky Peterson	Purple Rain
Pansy Division	Jack U Off
Pointer Sisters	I Feel for You
P. J. Proby	Sign o' the Times
Joe Roberts	Adore
Mitch Ryder	When You Were Mine
S.B.B.L.	Purple Mix
Simple Minds	Sign o' the Times
Sound Sensation	1999
	Girls & Boys
	Kiss
	Little Red Corvette
	Mountains
Susan Streitweiser	When Doves Cry
Quindon Tarver	When Doves Cry
TLC	If I Was Your Girlfriend
Tina Turner	Let's Pretend We're Married
Crystal Waters	Uptown
Ween	Shockadelica (incl. in L.M.L.Y.P.)
Rober Wyatt	The Cross

Bibliography

Anderson, Christopher, *Michael Jackson: Unauthorized* (London: Penguin, 1994)

Bogle, Donald, *Toms, Coons, Mulattoes, Mammies & Bucks: An Interpretive History of Blacks in American Films* (New York: Continuum, 1991)

Bream, Jon, *Prince: Inside the Purple Reign* (New York: Collier Macmillan, 1984)

Brown, Geoff, *The Complete Guide to the Music of Prince* (London: Omnibus, 1995)

Dannen, Frederic, *Hit Men: Power Brokers and Fast Money Inside the Music Business* (London: Random House, 1990)

Davis, Miles, with Quincy Troupe, *Miles: The Autobiography* (London: Picador, 1990)

Dyson, Michael Eric, *Between God and Gangsta Rap: Bearing Witness to Black Culture* (New York: OUP, 1996)

——, *Reflecting Black: African-American Cultural Criticism* (Minneapolis, MN: University of Minnesota Press, 1993)

George, Nelson, *Buppies, B-Boys, Baps & Bohos: Notes on Post-soul Black Culture* (New York: HarperCollins, 1992)

——, *The Death of Rhythm & Blues* (London: Omnibus, 1988)

Hill, Dave, *Prince: A Pop Life* (London: Faber & Faber, 1989)

Hinton, Brian, *Joni Mitchell: Both Sides Now* (London: Sanctuary, 1996)

Holmquist, June D. (ed.), *They Chose Minnesota: A Survey of the State's Ethnic Groups* (St Paul, MN: Minnesota Historical Society Press, 1981)

hooks, bell, *Black Looks: Race and Representation* (Boston, MA: South End Press, 1992)

——, *Yearning: Race, Gender and Cultural Politics* (Boston, MA: South End Press, 1990)

Hoskyns, Barney, *Prince: Imp of the Perverse* (London: Virgin, 1988)

——, *Waiting for the Sun: The Story of the Los Angeles Music Scene* (London: Viking, 1996)

Jones, Lisa, *Bulletproof Diva: Tales of Race, Sex and Hair* (London: Penguin, 1994)

Kureishi, Hanif, and Savage, Jon (eds), *The Faber Book of Pop* (London: Faber & Faber, 1996)

McGrath, Tom, *The Making of a Revolution: MTV* (Philadelphia, PA: Running Press, 1996)

Nilsen, Per, *Prince: A Documentary* (London: Omnibus, 1993)

O'Brien, Lucy, *She Bop: The Definitive History of Women in Rock, Pop and Soul* (London: Penguin, 1995)

Passman, Donald S., *All You Need to Know About the Music Business* (London: Penguin, 1995)

Shaar Murray, Charles, *Crosstown Traffic: Jimi Hendrix and Post-war Pop* (London: Faber & Faber, 1989)

Tate, Greg, *Flyboy in the Buttermilk: Essays on Contemporary America* (New York: Simon & Schuster, 1992)

Vincent, Rickey, *Funk: The Music, the People, and the Rhythm of the One* (New York: St Martin's Press, 1996)

Index

Index